SEX *and the* EIGHTEENTH-CENTURY MAN

Sex *and the* Eighteenth-Century Man

➤➤➤ *Massachusetts and the History of Sexuality in America*

THOMAS A. FOSTER

Beacon Press, Boston

Beacon Press
25 Beacon Street
Boston, Massachusetts 02108-2892
www.beacon.org

Beacon Press books
are published under the auspices of
the Unitarian Universalist Association of Congregations.

10 09 08 07   8 7 6 5 4 3 2 1

This book is printed on acid-free paper that meets the uncoated paper
ANSI/NISO specifications for permanence as revised in 1992.

Text design by Yvonne Tsang
at Wilsted & Taylor Publishing Services

Library of Congress Cataloging-in-Publication Data

Foster, Thomas A.
Sex and the eighteenth-century man : Massachusetts and the history of
    sexuality in America / Thomas A. Foster.
        p. cm.
Includes index.
    ISBN 978-0-8070-5039-2 (pbk. : alk. paper)   1. Men—Sexual behavior—
    United States—History—18th century. 2. Men—United States—History—
    18th century. 3. Men—United States—Social conditions—18th century.
    I. Title.

HQ28.F68 2006
306.7081'097309034—dc22   2006012858

For Marlon

↦ *Contents*

Contents

➻ *Introduction*

Sex and Men

Popular images of white manhood in colonial America include that of hearty settlers, shirtsleeves rolled up, farming or laboring; of minutemen and soldiers readying muskets for battle; of elite gentlemen with powdered wigs and quill pens; or perhaps the Founding Fathers. None of these images immediately draws to mind sexual behaviors or sexuality. But in colonial America, sex was an integral part of manhood.

Most Americans don't think of sex as part of this picture because sex is generally believed properly to belong to the realm of private behavior and to be part of personal identity. Thumb through any college-level U.S. history textbook or browse the history shelves at your local megachain bookstore, and you will find general histories of colonial America so tied to the public, especially to politics, war, and state formation, that sex is seen as out of place.

But as many historians have now shown, in colonial America sexual activity was very much a public concern. In fact, it was the business of the state. It was regulated, controlled, discussed, and crafted as part of an effort to create social stability and define racial, class, and gender social boundaries. Additionally, early modern culture did not cordon off the sexual as a private realm of individual behavior and identity. The classic Puritan sermon, the jeremiad warning that the sexual sins of individuals signified social corruption and collective spiritual peril, is but one example of the way that the social and sexual remained intertwined in early America. Sex was not only symbolic of an interior moral state but emblematic of the moral condition of society.[1]

Many also don't think of sex as part of the picture of white manhood in colonial America because normative men are associated with that which is public and important, with their sexual selves held in check. The portrayal of such men remains generally unconcerned and unassociated with sex and sexuality. But while normative masculinity asserts itself as not associated with sex and sexuality, it is, of course, partly defined by appropriate sexual desires and behaviors. And even though sex is most often used to define and denigrate so-called deviant male types—men of color, homosexuals, and those for whom sexual urges are said to be uncontrollable—those images are not simply about defining minority deviant subjects. They operate primarily to define normative manliness.[2]

Recognizing the relationship of sex and sexuality (the desires, behaviors, and identities associated with eroticism) with manliness (the embodiment of qualities considered befitting a man) brings us one step closer to understanding not only manhood in early America but the continued problems associated with constructions of manhood today. The emphasis on masculine strength and dominance, many claim, leads to an inability to cope with emotions and intimacy in sexual relationships, misguiding many men to wall themselves off and to seek masculine achievement through reckless sexual conquests. In this line of thinking, then, the continued association of femininity with emotional sensitivity and of masculinity with sexual gratification creates a host of contemporary social problems ranging from fatherless families to the spread of sexually transmitted diseases, and HIV and AIDS to sexual harassment, sexual assault, and rape. The paradox of manhood is thus how to embody idealized force without overstepping ever-shifting social bounds. This perilous situation has led many to surmise that masculinity is in crisis because of a set of new social constraints forged in the women's rights movement, which challenges male supremacy and addresses social gender inequalities.

Difficulties with the idea and embodiment of manhood, however, are not new. Whatever changes men's roles in society have undergone in recent years, the problem of demonstrating masculine sexual strength and power without violating boundaries is an old one. Even the founding generations confronted a troubled relationship of sex and manliness.

In early America, Anglo-American manhood was tied closely to ownership of property and to marriage. This social position brought with it authority over household dependents, including women, children, slaves, and servants and entitlement to "fraternal respect" and "civic standing." This book demonstrates that male social roles, including master and servant, suitor, husband, and father, all had sexual aspects. I focus on how sex figured in the two most important areas of an eighteenth-century man's life: his calling, or career, and his household. Although I focus on these two most important areas, it will become clear that discourses of male sexuality were unbounded, taking place in virtually all areas of early modern life, linking so-called private sexual behaviors to more public cultural, political, economic, and commercial concerns.[3]

This book starts by examining eighteenth-century marital sexuality and its bearing on norms of manliness. It also identifies talk about sex and the role it played in forging relations among men, especially in creating bonds crucial for securing connections that were critical for commercial and economic networks. I also pay close attention to portrayals of the sexuality of marginalized men, including Africans and Indians, transients, and other cultural outsiders; to criminal sexuality, especially rape and sodomy; and to the cultural emergence of nascent sexual types—the bachelor, the effeminate, primping fop, and the sodomite. Representations of cultural outsiders, sexual crimes, and deviant sexual types yoked sexuality and manliness to larger concerns about orderly social relations among men and about commerce and morals; newspaper coverage about rape, for example, developed and popularized the image of the black rapist while using that image to solidify racial bonds based on an understanding of normative white male sexuality. These representations were especially important as foils that implicitly defined, by way of contrast, normative manliness and its relation to sexuality.

Our contemporary ideas about manly sexual behaviors and desires are in part developed in the public sphere, in the amalgamation of discourses unevenly combining religious beliefs and more secular messages. This mixture creates both dominant models and deviant or alternative models of sexual masculinities; titillating stories about sexual conquest, for example, foreground a moral lesson about the centrality of self-control for male sexuality for proper manliness but also give celebratory voice to the minority figure of the rake or libertine. Such a public arena first appears in the eighteenth century and in the realm of secular print. In Boston, which had both a vibrant and a dedicated Christian Congregational culture and a secular and commercial print culture, a public sphere through newspapers in particular began to form nearly a generation before the next largest cities of Philadelphia and later New York. Focusing on how sex figured in the lives of our Founding Fathers and their ancestors in arguably the most formative century of this nation's history broadens our understanding of their cultural world. We cannot understand manhood in America today or in the past without coming to terms with the often troubled sexual aspects of masculinity.[4]

Eighteenth-Century Sexuality

When studying sex and manliness in eighteenth-century Massachusetts to show the ways that a particular place and time configured manliness, I made a startling discovery. Long before turn-of-the-twentieth-century psychologists began framing some individuals as sexual deviants with particular personalities, case histories, and interior selves, many early Americans made similar connections between personhood and sex interests and behaviors. It is true that they did not employ the same language and did not consistently view some as "gay" and others as "straight." But they certainly viewed sexual desires and interests as potentially part of an individual's makeup.

This is a surprising discovery because current understandings of the history of sexuality have emphasized a model of "acts" rather than "identities" to describe the way early Americans thought about sexual behavior and identity. In this model one's sexual acts did not reflect a larger sexual orientation or identity. Rather, some sexual behavior was defined as transgressive because it disrupted social authority relations, especially among men. More generally, any individual was potentially capable of sinful sexual acts, such as fornication and sodomy. Seventeenth-century Harvard instructor Michael Wigglesworth, for example, wrote about his lust for male pupils as part of a terrifying package of sinfulness that plagued him. Like drunkenness or other immoral excesses, sexual behaviors were viewed as behaviors, rather than part of a broader personality or deeper psychological essence. Sex was not *who* a person was; it was merely *what* he or she did.[5]

This book, however, alters this narrow view of sex in early America. Instead, sexuality in eighteenth-century Massachusetts appears to be an inconsistent and shifting mixture of acts *and* identities. It is true that for much of the preindustrial era, the dominance of biblical conceptualizations of sexuality contributed to the broader cultural notion that certain sexual behaviors (sodomy, for example) were universal rather than indicative of a sexual minority. Moreover, this model fostered a belief in reform and redemption rather than acceptance or rejection of a minority subject.

Other evidence, however, suggests that at times eighteenth-century connections between sexual acts and inner disposition look more like modern orientations. Eighteenth-century understandings of the connections between moral selves and exterior comportment had a deep impact on the way that early modern Americans thought about sex. Sexuality in eighteenth-century Massachusetts could be revealed in a man's external persona or outward appearance, his social comportment, including dress, speech, and manners, or his sexual behaviors. All were understood to indicate interior moral states and character. Understandings of the normative body made the same link: physique, fitness, and health could indicate interiority, including character and morality. The implication is clear: contrary to a strict model of acts, an eighteenth-century self contained an interiority.[6]

In this book I conclude that the general use of the acts-versus-identities narrative describes only the shift that occurred in certain circles. That narrative compares official colonial languages of church and court that emphasized sexual acts and behaviors that needed to be corrected with the medical and psychological languages of the late nineteenth century, which viewed sexual behaviors as indicators of interior states and even personality and character. In many ways the model that this book challenges compared colonial apples with modern oranges.

In part this comparison is a direct result of sources consulted by historians. The most prevalent sources, colonial sermons and draconian court pronouncements, were compared to the burst of sexological and psychological writings of the early twentieth century. However, when we trace the discourses of church and court, for example, we find more continuity from the colonial era to today than dramatic change. By looking at newspapers, personal papers, and the testimony of those in courts, rather than simply the legal statements of colonial governments, a broader understanding of sexuality in early America becomes possible.

Using acts versus identities as a paradigm for conceptualizing the difference between preindustrial and modern understandings of sexual behavior and identity not only short-circuits investigations in sex and sexuality in early America but also encourages the disregard of complexities today. Although the paradigm accurately signals the rise of psychological and sexological discussions of sexual orientations, the stark comparative framework encourages the kind of oversimplification that leads many to assume sex could only be, and was always thought of as, an act in colonial America and *is* only and always thought of as part of an identity or corresponding sexual orientation today.

In both secular and religious discourses today many still do not adopt contemporary models of sexual orientation. Many religious discourses in modern America continue to view same-sex sexual behaviors as momentary and not as indicators of unique personhood. The rhetoric of many who reject homosexuality, for example, draws on an understanding of sex that denies orientations and focuses instead on sexual acts as sinful or immoral behaviors to be stopped. Similarly, today many individuals also personally feel that their sexual behaviors are simply acts, unrelated to their sexual identity or broader personhood. For these men, their sexual behaviors are simply "acts" unrelated to identity or their sexual orientation. Men who identify themselves as heterosexual but who have sex with other men for either pay or pleasure, for example, confound those who assume sexual orientations to be rigid and definable. Thus, the paradigm also feeds a false sense of understanding about neatly contained modern categories of sexual orientation and encourages people to ignore the endurance of both acts and identities models today.

Why Massachusetts?

From the vantage point of the early years of the United States, Boston appears unflatteringly to be a stagnant port city, its population static and its economy anemic. But before Boston was eclipsed by New York and Philadelphia, it was not only the central hub for Massachusetts and the rest of New England, but for much of the first half of the eighteenth century the largest port city in the British mainland colonies. In the 1730s its population of roughly seventeen thousand inhabitants, almost entirely Anglo-Saxon and Protestant, was nearly double that of either New York or Philadelphia. Boston was home to a substantial merchant class whose wealth was derived from shipping and trade, from war, and from slavery. The Bay Colony was also linked to the British Empire through the world of print, especially newspapers, which reported news and reprinted articles from abroad, and through imported fiction and other books.

As a hub of British commercial imperial activity and colonial print culture, eighteenth-century Boston's sexual culture was a mix of local and metropolitan ideas about normative sexuality. As a provincial city still heavily influenced by Puritan religious culture, Boston was, however, ambivalent about its cultural ties to the British Empire. Boston's print culture sometimes portrayed London as a desirable model of eighteenth-century urban and refined sociability. Narratives of sexual immorality in London and Europe, appearing in newspapers, sermons, and other literature, also warned Bostonians, however, of the corruption and vice that accompanied commerce and urban development. These depictions characterized Boston's sexual culture as, by contrast, more chaste, yet vulnerable to the same corrupting forces.

Despite the cultural importance of an enduring Puritan influence, Boston's status as a major provincial port meant that diverse cultural and social vantage points and interests intersected in discourses of sexuality and manhood. Publications and sermons produced by learned ministers and public officials articulated official views, and court testimony and depositions give us access to lay perspectives as well as legal norms. Both official and lay perspectives intermingle in newspaper accounts of court cases. A comparison of different records reveals a range of cultural models of manliness and normative male sexuality that circulated between the overlapping arenas of pulpit, court, and print. Although legal statutes that pertained to sexual crimes retained a draconian Puritan tenor, popular sentiment was often not harshly punitive. Lay reactions to long-term, same-sex sexual interests and to consensual interracial sexual relationships ranged from a derisive dismissal to a fragile tolerance, and the individuals in these relationships were clearly prepared to risk both popular derision and official condemnation.

Massachusetts was not home to a visible subculture of foppish men; nor was it the location for a large number of prosecutions for rape or sodomy. It wasn't even a place with an especially diverse ethnic and racial population. Still, in the early eighteenth century "fops" and "sodomites" were culturally significant figures or types—so much so that we can speak of a discourse of effeminacy and a religiously based discourse of sodomy in Massachusetts. Similarly, though prosecutions for rape and other violent sexual crimes were low, narratives of sexual assault had cultural resonance and were at times linked to a discourse of racialized sexuality. Thus, it did not require a visible local subculture of effeminate men or sodomites or a high incidence of rape or interracial sex to make such subcultures and behaviors the object of cultural concern.

Early eighteenth-century culture in Massachusetts was marked by an amalgam of older Puritan notions regarding how best to build and maintain a godly society and newer eighteenth-century discourses about commerce and manners. As Richard Gildrie has argued, new standards of "American Puritanism" emerged in the convergence of orthodox Puritan and secular concerns. As a result, a significant Puritan influence endured in New England culture through the Great Awakening in the 1740s. This combination of secular and religious discourses linked local anxieties about consumption, urban development, and commerce to sexual comportment. Newspaper commentaries, for example, drew upon (and reinvigorated) culturally powerful, religiously based new concerns about distinctions between true refinement and dissolute or effeminate attachment to luxury and fashion. Here religious and secular preoccupations became fused in narratives of same-sex sexuality, rape, effeminate appearance, the meaning and purpose of marital sexuality, and racialized sexuality.[7]

Sources

On September 25, 1690, *Publick Occurrences* was published in Boston, but it was immediately suppressed. America's first newspaper had lasted just one issue. Only four years into the eighteenth century, the *Boston News Letter* made its debut. It was the first continuously published American newspaper, appearing some fifteen years earlier than the first newspaper in Philadelphia and more than twenty years before the first issue of the *New York Gazette*. By 1719 Boston was home to another newspaper that would survive most of the colonial era, the *Boston Gazette*. By 1735 two other papers, the *Boston Evening Post* and the *Boston Post Boy*, would compete for readership. In addition to these four main papers, four shorter-lived papers would appear as well. Thus, between 1721 and 1741 Boston had no fewer than five newspapers in any given year—producing, as Charles Clark points out, a combined output totaling one copy of a newspaper for every four Bostonians, or one copy for every sixty-seven residents of Massachusetts. Boston papers, like other early American newspapers, were generally two- to four-page weeklies. They contained a variety of news and information, much of it selected and reprinted from European presses; other news came from local sources. By midcentury a newspaper's circulation was six hundred copies per week, on average. By the Revolutionary era an explosion in print brought newspapers to smaller towns and communities throughout Massachusetts. And as scholars have pointed out, actual readership in the relatively literate New England colonies went far beyond the number of issues printed or sold: coffeehouses and taverns were popular places for townspeople to gather, exchange information, read aloud, and share newspapers.[8]

As I have suggested, Massachusetts newspapers popularized religious views, but they also joined them with secular, commercial, and social concerns. Local news of court proceedings, of items for sale, and of banking and shipping made newspapers an important site for the cultural production of linkages between sexual, commercial, and political concerns. By placing notices of rape cases, foreign sodomy trials, and commentary on courtship and marriage alongside notices of political events and shipping schedules, printers incorporated sexuality into discussions of public concern. By reprinting news from Europe and elsewhere, newspapers also tied the Bay

Colony to the British Empire. Newspapers connected both the very local and the very broadest of imperial perspectives. In so doing, these publications both tied residents to the British Empire and allowed them to explore the vexed question of their social and cultural distinctiveness.

Massachusetts' presses printed more sermons than any other colony in the eighteenth century, and the Bay Colony published more sermons than any other print genre. These sermons are a terrific source for the examination of official religious discourses. The Puritans' descendants, like their ancestors, viewed sexual desires as natural urges to be channeled into marriage and regulated within its confines; the mastery of one's sexuality led not only to the stable marriages upon which the Christian social order rested but also to Christian offspring, who ensured the continuation of that order. Officials thus condemned extramarital sexual behavior, yet appreciated sexual pleasure not only for the purposes of procreation but also because it enhanced emotional bonds between husbands and wives. Sermons also reveal perceived connections between sexual morality and threats to cultural and social order. A man's sexual behavior jeopardized not only his own moral standing but, equally important, the Puritans' standing as a covenanted community. By examining locally written, locally reprinted, and even imported sermons, I can analyze the Christian views of male sexual comportment and masculinity that held sway in the Bay Colony.[9]

Although eighteenth-century courts gradually decreased their policing of moral behavior, they still remained important arenas for the articulation of community definitions of sexuality and its relation to social order. It is true that by the middle of the eighteenth century, courts differed significantly from their seventeenth-century counterparts in the attention they paid to English forms of law. Seventeenth-century courts relied heavily on substantive notions of justice designed to preserve a Puritan moral and social order, whereas eighteenth-century courts increasingly followed English precedent and were more concerned with adhering to procedural rules. Nonetheless, Massachusetts courts throughout the eighteenth century continued to hear cases about sexual crimes: capital crimes such as sodomy, rape, and incest were tried by the Superior Court of Judicature, and lesser crimes, such as sexual assault and fornication, were tried at the county level in the Court of General Sessions. The extant testimony from depositions, court record books, and petitions from court cases involving these sexual crimes provide an excellent source of information on the conjunction of official and popular attitudes about male sexuality and its bearing on eighteenth-century masculinity.[10]

A wide range of imported literature, also very valuable for the study of sexual culture, most of it coming from London, made its way into Massachusetts. Although Boston retained a provincial wariness of imported novels, other imported books and serials such as *The Tatler*, *The Spectator*, and *The Guardian* were very popular. (These continued to be imported and read throughout the eighteenth century.) The impact of these imports, with their emphasis on manners and sociability, can be seen in a number of provincial publications. Local newspapers such as the *New England Weekly Journal* and the *New England Courant* at times echoed the style and content of *The Spectator* and *The Tatler*—at least in comparison with the more conventional and official style of the *Boston Evening Post*, the *Boston Gazette*, the *Boston News Letter*, and, later, the *Independent Chronicle*. The earlier *Weekly Journal* and the *Courant* are both examples of what Charles Clark calls the "literary newspaper." These papers more often included longer essays—usually on manners and social intercourse—than the main papers, which tended to confine themselves to briefer items and to editorialize less. Bostonians' interest in imported books and serials, like the reprinted news items in Boston papers, illustrates the melding of local and broader metropolitan cultural norms and preoccupations.[11]

In eighteenth-century Massachusetts, Anglo-American manhood was largely equated with becoming an independent householder; it was tied closely to marriage and conferred manly prerogatives, including patriarchal authority over women, children, slaves, and servants. Part 1 examines the sexual component of this social position. Chapter 1 argues that sex was indeed a crucial part of securing and maintaining that social position and examines changing understandings of sexual intimacy within marriage. Such discussions were fueled by a tension between the belief that sexual intercourse in marriage was primarily about procreation and an increasing emphasis on sexual pleasure as a way of nurturing and expressing love within marriage. Finally, this chapter examines the years following the American Revolution, when newspapers and other print genre contained an outpouring of discussions aimed at glorifying marriage and returning men to home and hearth. By the end of the eighteenth century, the biblical edict to go forth and multiply had changed from a mission with implications for securing an outpost of the British Empire to one of generating a nation of virtuous American men.

Chapter 2 examines the ways in which a man could fail sexually in his most important social role, that of husband and head of household. Examining divorce, infidelity, adultery, and incest, it argues that the manly prerogatives of husband and head of household depended significantly on his ability to adhere to norms about male marital sexual performance as well as on his mastery over his wife's (and other dependents') sexual behaviors. A wide variety of sources singled out men who failed to meet expectations regarding male sexual behavior as well as male mastery over dependents. By the end of the eighteenth century the implications for disrupted households had shifted; a man's failing had gone from being one that threatened godly social order to one that inhibited the development of an Anglo-American republic.

Part 2 examines sex, manliness, and the broader community. Chapter 3 explores how discourses of seduction and rape reflected notions of appropriate and deviant masculine behavior as it pertains to control over sexual and emotional desires. These discourses also reveal paradoxes in gendered norms of sexual comportment. In the culture of eighteenth-century Massachusetts, women were seen both as innocent victims and as lewd and seductive. Dominant, aggressive male sexuality was idealized, yet men were also supposed to exhibit self-mastery and restraint. Men could be seducers and even rapists, yet commentators also frequently pointed to the vulnerability of men in romance. During the Revolutionary era, depictions of rapes committed by British and Hessian troops underscored cultural connections between American republican virtue and manly self-control. By the end of the eighteenth century, increased individual freedoms, especially among young people, however, generated greater concern over seduction and abandonment.

Although marriage and family were central for formulating manly norms and ideals, in eighteenth-century Massachusetts a variety of actions, including sailing, soldiering, and succeeding within commercial networks, largely excluded women and relied upon masculine ideals that developed in a self-consciously all-male world. Chapter 4 examines sex and the social order of male respectability. It probes the social and cultural function of sexual reputation and shared sexual values in the formation of male relationships based on trust and sexual self-control. Mutually shared understandings of normative manly sexuality could forge ties that were crucial for developing fraternal respect and civic standing. But sex was also a threat to masculine social order. Throughout the eighteenth century, court records and printed discussions presented a variety of sexual transgressions involving women, children, and servants as wrongs committed by one man against another.

The final part focuses on specific illustrations of figures that crystallize connections between sexual acts and interior states of character and manliness. Chapter 5 examines bachelors as male figures who frustrated manly duties and also implicitly embodied deviant sexuality. Bachelors not only eschewed the marriage bed and thus normative heterosexuality but also denied themselves the manly status that came with siring Christian heirs for personal posterity as well as for society. Portrayals of effeminate bachelors such as the fop linked critiques of exterior qualities of dress, physique, and manners to deviant sexual practices such men were assumed to commit, including sodomy and masturbation. These portrayals, which assumed that interior desires and moral states could be revealed by bodily and social comportment, were also linked to social and cultural concerns about the corrupting effects of metropolitan and commercial culture. Here, as elsewhere, eighteenth-century culture vividly connected manly public personas to sexual selves.

Cross-cultural sexual relations, the subject of chapter 6, offer a particularly good site for examining understandings of racialized sexuality and manliness. Attitudes toward sexual relations between blacks, Indians, and whites demonstrate a fragile popular tolerance for interracial unions that is tempered by evidence from slander charges and other court records indicating that whites associated interracial sexual unions with dishonor. Newspaper portrayals and court accounts of sexual assaults committed by non-English peoples offer a stronger whiff of eighteenth-century racism. With their sustained focus on the threat to communal stability that the unbridled sexuality of blacks and Indians posed, these depictions competed with the somewhat more optimistic rhetoric of Christian assimilationism. This sexuality was said to corrupt Christian morality, disrupt masculine household order, and even threaten, through miscegenation, Englishness itself. Depictions that focused on black male hypersexuality not only illustrated the norm of manly self-control but also described minority and majority populations along the lines of race, status, and religion.

The final chapter articulates the evolution of eighteenth-century understandings of same-sex sexuality. It examines court records, print literature (including newspapers and imported fiction), and letters and diaries to plumb the connections between same-sex sex and masculine subjectivity. In the culture of eighteenth-century Massachusetts, sodomy was not yet consistently viewed as a marker of character structure and inner disposition. Although the modern heterosexual-homosexual bifurcation had not yet fully developed, this was not a period without an understanding of interior sexual selves.

I ⇥ *Household*

CHAPTER I

"He Is Not a Man, That Hath Not a Woman"

MEDWAY, MASSACHUSETTS, JUNE 1772. Physician Aaron Wight opened his *Massachusetts Almanac*, dipped his pen in ink, and slowly began to draw the tip of the pen across the page. He coaxed the black ink to make two long lines, then shorter ones across the top, angling them in to complete the image of a coffin. Once outlined, he filled in the ominous shape until it was black as night. He had buried his wife of four and a half years that day and, as he occasionally did, illustrated the journal entry with an appropriate sketch. The finality of her passing was punctuated by the image of the black coffin. She had died at four the previous afternoon, most likely from complications of the birth of their son, John, that morning.[1]

Now, thirty years old and with a newborn son, Wight was a widower. But like most men of his time, he would not be alone for long. On January 8, just three days after his infant son died, he noted in the *Ames Almanac* his first visit to one Anne Marshall. Perhaps it was love at first sight, for after only three other meetings with Anne, Wight traveled to Framingham to meet with her father. And after seeing Anne another five times in February, on the 26th of that month, as was the custom in eighteenth-century Massachusetts, the couple publicly announced their intention to wed. Wight may not have recorded the publishing of their banns in his journal, but he did make note that month of having brought her to his own house and of visiting again with her father. In April they traveled to Boston together. In May he noted another visit at his own house.

But Anne Marshall would not become the next Mrs. Wight. By summer, things must have soured between the two. On July 6 and 7, with a bold double line, he underlined and sectioned off the words "Then Took a Final Fair [*sic*] Well Anne Marshall." The following month he noted visiting her father and retrieving some of his clothing. In November he illustrated a final meeting with her father with a picture of a watch. Perhaps she had broken off the engagement and the watch had been given to him to smooth over hurt feelings. Dr. Wight was once again single, but not for long.

Anne Marshall had lived in Medfield, and it was probably on one of his trips there that Aaron Wight met another of Medfield's eligible women, Pol Haven. By early 1774, in his copy of *Stearn's Almanac,* he began to record this new courtship. On February 14 he noted, "talkt with poly Haven first all things well." Just one week later, he noted the first time they "staid" together. (In eighteenth-century Massachusetts it was not unusual for those courting to spend the night together.) By March 4 he recorded an important date: "Went to see pol Haven 3 time, make or brake." The date was undoubtedly a success, as an entry one week later revealed a new level of intimacy: "went to see pol Haven went in at the Back Dore." As the relationship blossomed, Wight continued to note meetings. By April 4 he adorned his journal with a picture of a woman in a large dress, presumably Pol. In April he saw Pol a few times each week. He brought her to see his house. He carried her back to Medfield.

Marriage was clearly on his mind, and he noted the marriages of friends and family during these months of courtship. On March 31 he drew a picture of a newly married husband and wife to mark the marriage of his brother-in-law. On April 30 he presented Pol with a present from his heart and noted it in his journal, "silver buckels." They continued to see each other through the summer months, Wight recording no fewer than ten occasions in June and July. With some sense of pride, he drew a picture of his new chaise and on the 28th, just one day later, noted, "see pol Haven had a ride in Chays with her." Not only was Wight a wealthy physician who could afford such a new carriage, but he was in love. The ride marked a measure of success and satisfaction.

For the next several months he continued to note their meetings. Public records reveal that they published their banns on October 29. On November 15 he remarked, "concluded to marry Thursday." Just two days later, on a page extensively adorned, unlike any other in his *Ames Almanac,* he recorded "married to pol Haven." He must have been glad to marry again. He noted the coming of winter on November 21: "First Snow then see pol Haven." The two traveled to Boston on November 29 and stayed there for several nights. On December 8 he wrote: "got my wife home." Only a year earlier he had just ended his relationship with Anne Marshall, and just two years earlier he had buried his first wife. But some seventy-five Pol Haven diary entries later, Dr. Wight, who would serve as a hospital surgeon during the American Revolution and would live to be seventy-one, was once again married.

Dr. Wight was unusual in that he illustrated his diary with images, but he was typical in his regard for marriage and courtship. For men as well as for women, marriage was a key part of adulthood. Marriage brought emotional and financial stability, security and happiness. Once married, many men who kept diaries noted their wedding anniversaries with regard. Boston merchant Benjamin Bangs wrote in 1765, "This Day is 15 years we have been Married. O that we Rightly Consider & Render Thanks To a Mercifull God for His Wonderfull Mercy To us in sparing our Lies & ye Lives of All the Eight Children He Has given us." For men, marriage was a crucial part of achieving (and maintaining) full manhood. Throughout the eighteenth century, the emphasis on marriage did not waver.[2]

Despite a large literature on companionate marriage ideals, comparatively few historians of Anglo-America systematically explore the sexual or erotic dimension of gender roles in eighteenth-century marriage. The bulk of the scholarship on the social history of marriage, especially among middling propertied families, focuses instead on the social and economic functions of households, on the social roles of husband and wife, and on the authority relations between them. Even those who concern themselves with the changing terms of emotional relations between husband and wife, with a few exceptions, don't explain in detail the contribution of sexuality to emerging companionate ideals.[3]

Sexual intimacy was an important part of early American marriage. Colonial courts allowed divorces and separations due to sexual misconduct or sexual inability. But what was the function of sexuality in a marriage, and to what extent was it the husband's responsibility? Throughout the eighteenth century, marriage marked a man's transition to adulthood. Men were expected to marry, produce offspring, enjoy the companionship of a chosen wife, and head an orderly household. In keeping with the hierarchical relations between heads of household and their dependents, husbands bore the brunt of responsibility for harmonious marital relations, including sexual relations.

Reproduction was but one feature of a multifaceted understanding of the ends of marital sex. First, a man's capacity to father children was a key feature of his adult identity not only because it secured his social status as family head, but because it was central to his specifically sexual identity: it was a measure of masculine sexual prowess. Second, sexual desire, according to the teachings of the day, was energy to be regulated, and marriage provided a sanctioned arena for the expression of carnal urges. One important feature of adult manhood was the capacity to moderate sexual wants —both one's own and those of one's wife—and direct them toward their proper ends. Those ends included procreation and the containment of potentially socially disruptive lust. But more than that, for many commentators, sexual intimacy between husband and wife was clearly understood to complement and enhance emotional bonds in an era that increasingly valued companionate marriage.

During the Revolution, social disruptions and a soldier's life away from home and hearth created conditions conducive to increased frequency of out-of-wedlock sexual relationships. In the postwar era, newspaper commentators, evidently perceiving themselves to be in competition with the glorious thrills of illicit sex, portrayed marriage as a continued source of romantic and intimate pleasure for men in particular. Numerous accounts, purportedly authored by men, were intended to convince others of the personal value of the marital union—and in so doing underscored the important benefit of stable marriages for the fledgling nation.

Daniel Defoe's book on love, sex, and marriage, *Conjugal Lewdness; or, Matrimonial Whoredom,* for sale in the Bay Colony by 1735, captures the essence of what most residents of eighteenth-century Massachusetts understood to be the role of marital sexuality. Sex was always bound up with several compatible goals. Defoe outlines these as *"desire of Children," "to avoid Fornication,"* and *"to lighten and ease the cares and sadnesses of Houshold-affair"* or *"to endear each other."* This view had changed little since the seventeenth century and was expressed in both imported and domestic literature.[4]

Discourses of marital sex defined the male sexual role as one of procreative fatherhood and at the same time linked fatherhood to sexual virility. The procreative ideal also incorporated the view that marriage was ordained as the proper outlet for the natural sexual urges of both men and women. One feature of a man's marital duty was his responsibility for regulating and satisfying both his own and his wife's desires. Many authorities stressed that marital sex was a physical expression of love and affection. As Defoe would write, it was meant to "endear each other."

Well into the eighteenth century, dominant marriage ideals stressed that marital love emerged over time, largely following, rather than preceding, the wedding night. But slowly during the course of the century, romantic ideals stressing eroticized mutual attraction during courtship and as a basis for marriage choice began to make significant headway against the more measured ideal of mutual affection.

The culturally ubiquitous norm of male self-mastery as a prerequisite for exercising authority over dependents was infused with discussions of male marital sexual responsibility. Whether the emphasis was on procreation, control of what was viewed as natural sexual desires, or the strengthening of the bond between husband and wife, adequate sexual performance was a key component of masculinity. That performance was understood to include the maintenance of a mutually satisfying sexual relationship between husband and wife.

In the eighteenth century, normative sexuality was an important part of nurturing stable households—the building blocks of a godly society. The popular London wedding sermon *Marriage an Honourable Estate,* reprinted and sold in Boston in 1752, for example, stated that "marriage is the resource of all principalities, states, and kingdoms in the world." The popular 1746 text *Reflections on Courtship and Marriage* expressed similar sentiments about the importance of marriage for both individuals and for communities. "The *Conjugal Tie*" was the "sacred Cement of all Societies," according to the author.[5]

By the end of the eighteenth century, sexuality still held the promise of generating and stabilizing households, but now this had national implications. Republican and early national discourses romanticized both yeoman family farms and commercially successful families. However, mutually satisfying and relationship-enhancing marital relations remained significant for securing household order.

"Desire of Children": The Virile Man

As freedom in courtship and marriage choice increased in the eighteenth century, commentaries on the legitimate ends of sexual relations within marriage multiplied. Some authors dug in their heels and insisted that the paramount purpose of marital sex was procreative. One such publication, *Eunuchism Display'd,* which was published in London in 1718 and was still being sold in Massachusetts by booksellers such as Thomas Cox in Boston well into the 1730s, took this position. This treatise on eunuchs ostensibly was about determining the suitability of eunuchs for marriage, but it also explored the purpose of marital sexuality. The essay had three parts. The first defined varieties of eunuchs, from famed singers to men born with genital deformities. The second and third parts examined the "Nature and End of Marriage," using civil and ecclesiastical law to outline arguments against the marriage of eunuchs.[6]

In outlining traditional prohibitions against eunuchs' marrying, the treatise relied on the central importance of procreative sex in marriage. In this regard, "an Eunuch *can no wise answer that End*." Eunuchs' inability to reproduce, according to the author, was the reason that *"Civil Law," "The Roman Catholick Church," "Lutherans,"* and *"None of the Reform'd Churches whatsoever, allow the Marriage of* Eunuchs." Drawing in particular on the religious injunction to *"Encrease and Multiply,"* the anonymous author remarks, "He does not say, *Divert yourselves, give a Loose to your Brutish Passions; do what your sensual Appetite and mere Nature prompt you to, merely to please and satisfy your Inclinations,* but *Encrease and Multiply*." Thus, the exasperated author insists on the importance of men and women controlling their *"Passions"* in accordance with Christian teachings. *"Nature"* may prompt sexual *"Inclinations,"* but they are to be controlled if one is to follow the teachings of the church. A eunuch, a man without the "Faculty of Power of Generation" through "Nature" or "who is any wise deprived of the Parts proper to Generation," ought not to marry. In the final section, the author outlines arguments in favor of eunuchs' marrying in order to rebut them. (The main rationale was that some eunuchs were "capable to satisfy the Desires of Women.") Granting that certain eunuchs may indeed be capable of sexual intercourse, the author argues that they "can only satisfy the Desires of the Flesh Sensuality, Impurity, and Debauchery." Thus they perverted marital sexuality by dissociating sexual pleasure from procreation.[7]

Given the eighteenth-century emphasis on reproduction, it is not surprising that obituaries often extolled the accomplishments of the reproductive man and associated a large progeny with virility. One Boston diarist wrote on the death of a Mr. Ebenezer Draper of Dedham. His entire obituary, recorded in the diary, read: "Died at Dedham Mr Ebenezer Draper aged 85 from him have Descended 17 Children 51 grand children and 52 great grand Children in all 120." Newspapers, too, often carried obituary notices that lauded the man who had gone forth and multiplied. Consider the following—no doubt apocryphal—news from London carried by both the *Boston Weekly News Letter* and the *Boston Evening Post* in 1752 reporting on the death of Dublin resident Daniel M'Carthy "in the 112th Year of his Age." It read: "He buried four Wives, his fifth Wife, now a Widow, he married when he was Eighty-four, and she but Fourteen, by whom he had about Twenty Children, she bearing a Child every Year; he was a very healthy Man, no Cold did ever affect him." In summing up his life, the papers pointed out that one of M'Carthy's major accomplishments was that he sired a child every year from age 84 until 104.[8]

Papers such as the *Boston Gazette* also linked masculine virility in the sense of reproductive power to a uniquely healthy environment in the British mainland colonies.

> To give an Instance of the Health, Constitution and Fruitfulness of our *North America* born People: There is one Daniel Robins, aged about 66 Years, born in North America . . . is so Strong & healthy, that he hath lately travelled oftentimes 40 Miles a Day, rather than ride an easy Horse. He is the Father of Thirteen Children, Eleven of which are married, and by them he hath had Sixty Two Grand-Children, born in less than Eighteen Years Time, which with his other Children, makes Seventy five Persons. . . . Thus it appears, that said *Daniel Robins* hath successfully kept and fulfilled that great and necessary Commandment of *Multiply, be Fruitfull and Replenish the Earth.* In this Wilderness Country, and by what hath been already said of him, he hath kept every other Commandment as truly and as well as he hath done that.

Robins was an exemplar of North American manhood. His life stood as a testament to the values of fortitude and productivity. Remarking that he had "kept every other" Christian directive, the essay linked his prolific virility to a general strength of character and morality. Similarly, Samuel Mills, a yeoman of Long Island "who was born in America," was described in his obituary as having "left behind him Nine Children, eighty Grand Children, and Fifty-four Great Grand Children." Mills's entire obituary was dedicated to extolling his value as a man who produced children, grandchildren, and great-grandchildren. Such individuals were singled out as models of masculine control and productivity; they had mastered what lesser men squandered, their God-given sexual energy, and used it for the good of the community. In the colonial era, this meant harnessing their masculine sexuality and using it as a means to build up and enlarge a Christian community in the New World.[9]

The tall-tale quality of some of these obituaries and anecdotes and their humorous emphasis on tireless sexual productivity also suggest the importance accorded to sexual prowess; it, too, was an important dimension of normative manhood. The following tongue-in-cheek tale about a "young Man" who had sired "no less than eight Boys, all Twins, born of four Women within a Fortnight's Time," ties together progeny and prowess with a particular jocular clarity. It concludes by remarking on this man's prodigious contribution to the colony: *"A fine Hand this, to assist in peopling some of our new Townships, which by desolate and unimprov'd for want of Inhabitants; and without some such Assistance may continue so for some scores of Years."*[10]

After the Revolutionary War, similar tongue-in-cheek notices took on new significance. One such notice described a man in North Carolina who at age sixty-five fathered three children from his wife and also from each of her two sisters. Another notice from Salem whimsically described a local gentleman who courted a woman for five evenings, and five days after their marriage, she gave birth to five daughters. By the end of the Revolutionary era, virile men held the promise of siring an entire nation.[11]

Signifying a broad cultural embrace of the importance of marriage for manliness, throughout the eighteenth century, sermons as well as newspapers and domestic and imported literature contained an emphasis on the masculine ideal of the virile husband. Ensuring the creation of descendants was a main goal of marital sexuality and central to the definition of manliness. At the same time, numerous progeny indicated masculine virtue and sexual prowess in particular.

Marital Sexuality and the Regulation of Desire

Sex within marriage was supposed to produce Christian heirs. Marital sex was also said to prevent the socially disruptive and morally corrupting consequences of the unregulated expression of sexual desires. Even the most old-fashioned commentators generally recognized the importance of controlling sexual activity by yoking it to one legitimate location—the marital bed. (Within marriage, sexual desire, like any other passion, was to be enjoyed only in moderation.) And despite the belief that both men and women needed sexual outlets, as patriarch and head of the household the husband was largely responsible for establishing and maintaining normative sexual relations within marriage.

Men were encouraged to take control of their own urges. In an essay titled "On Entrance into LIFE, and the Conduct of early MANHOOD," reprinted in the *American Herald* in 1786, moderation and self-control were emphasized: "You have violent passions implanted in you by nature for the accomplishment of her purposes. But conclude not, as many have done to their ruin, that because they are violent, they are irresistable. The same nature which gave you passions, gave you also reason and a love of order." This was in part due to popular notions that men were more capable of rational thinking—and thus of the regulation of their physical desires—than women. Marriage was a legitimate means to hedge in sexual desire and an arena for the expression of it.[12]

As marriage was the site for sexual expression, adultery was a frustration of that outlet. Consider the following characterization of adultery from a Boston sermon in 1716. Adultery was "*Sinning against the means*. Because *Marriage* is one means prescribed for the *avoiding* of Fornication or Uncleanness." Likewise, according to the sermon, "A *Married State* is prescrib'd as *one means,* to avoid this wickedness." Such comments on the usefulness of marriage for channeling sexual energies were also found in the popular sermon *The Wedding Ring*: "Marriage is like Water to quench the Sparks of Lusts-Fire, I Cor. 7.2. *Nevertheless to avoid Fornication let every Man have his own Wife.*" Although such sentiments could apply to both sexes, men were singled out more often than women. The institution of marriage was a sanctioned means to satisfy the carnal urges of young men. Those men who chose a single life, the sermon explained, "fry in the Grease of their own Sensuality."[13]

Even when sex was explicitly linked to reproduction, eighteenth-century discourses about procreative sexuality reflected an appreciation of its potential to provide physical pleasure. Thus, the popular wedding sermon *Marriage an Honourable Estate* described marriage as a place "where the natural desires of the two sexes are securely enjoy'd, and their progeny made certain and peculiar by the inclosure of marriage."[14]

Reproductive manuals, which combined popular sentiment and folklore (and, I should note, often diverged from the teachings of the church), also expressed the notion that procreative sex was inherently pleasurable. *The Problems of Aristotle* acknowledged the positive aspects of marital sex, stating that "carnal copulation" could "ease and lighten the body, clear the mind, comfort the Head, and the sence, and take away many griefs and melancholy." The text even emphasized the pleasure of the act while denigrating it. Question: "Why is there such delight in the act of Venery?" Answer: "Because this act is a base and contemptible thing in it self, naught and unclean so far, that all Creatures would naturally abhor it, were there no pleasure in it."[15]

That sex within marriage was intended to produce children did not rule out for all commentators the legitimacy of engaging in sexual intimacy purely for pleasure. In a departure from official doctrine, as espoused by the church, texts even broached nonprocreative sexual practices, such as oral sex, by couching them in terms of ideas about conception. In answer to the question of whether "Carnal Copulation be done by the Mouth," the author drew on the example of pigeons and explained that they "do play by the Beak, yet they do not couple together this way, nor conceive." The text did not stop there, however. The passage continued: "And therefore *Aristotle* sheweth it thus, whatsoever goeth in at the mouth, is consumed by digestion; but if the seed should go in at the mouth, then that should also be consumed by digestion." The text could be construed as a sex manual that titillated its readers: it was the source of controversy in at least one parish. Such books were seen as informative but were also condemned for stirring up tastes for activities that many ministers believed were better left unmentioned.[16]

As with any sensual desire, orderly sexual relations required moderation, a key aspect of eighteenth-century masculinity. In 1788 the *American Herald* published an essay entitled "Choice of a Husband by a Gentlewoman of Prudence," in which manly moderation was spelled out in detail. According to the author, a man should be "master of his passions." The author melded the qualities of masculine moderation to the picture of the moderate husband. Writers on both sides of the Atlantic touted moderation in marital sexuality, warning of the moral, physical, and even emotional damage that would follow from unrestrained sexuality. For example, Defoe's *Conjugal Lewdness; or, Matrimonial Whoredom* explained that sexuality was to be enjoyed "with a temperate Affection, without violent transporting Desires, or too sensual Applications." Similarly, medical information reprinted in the *Boston Evening Post* in 1770 included the following: "The semen discharged too lavishly occasions a weariness, indisposition to motion, convulsions, leanness, dryness, heats and pains in the membranes of the brain, with a dulness of the senses, especially of the sight, a *tabes dorsalis*, foolishness, and disorders of the like kind."[17]

"To Endear Each Other"

Marrying simply to secure a legitimate venue for sexual gratification was warned against. The *Boston Evening Post* reprinted from "Pope's *Miscellanies*" a column entitled "Thoughts on Various Subjects," which cautioned against overemphasizing the importance of the message that marriage was "to avoid fornication." The suggestion that if a man married primarily because he could not live chastely—rather than for friendship and companionship—his relationship would be as burdensome as a "perpetual Blister" struck at least one man as important enough to be mentioned in his diary.

Similarly, a maxim printed by the *Post* in 1759 quipped, "he who marrieth where he doth not love, will be sure to love where he doth not marry."[18]

In the eighteenth century, newspaper commentators and authors of published essays, sermons, and poems all expressed the importance of melding procreative and companionate ideals. As companionate ideals were increasingly emphasized, the procreative emphasis was joined to a general discourse on sex as a means of expressing emotional intimacy and compatibility. Companionate and procreative sex should not be viewed as competitive models, although certain authors may have emphasized one end over the other. As companionship became increasingly important, the two ends of marital sexuality were conjoined, and procreative ends grew ever more complicated, incorporating ideals of pleasure, fertility, and emotional connectedness.

Sexual desire and physical intimacy were meant to bring married partners emotionally closer. They were a carnal expression of an emotional and psychological state. In 1769, hoping to impart what he knew best about the selection of a marriage partner, a lonely John Cleaveland, only a year after his wife died of breast cancer, wrote to his daughter, Mary. She had written asking for "Thoughts and desiring" his fatherly "advice relating to a Matter of great Importance in this Life." In his letter he wrote: "I say I would have you chuse for yourself." The prospective husband should be a man who "appears upon all accounts to be the most agreable and suitable to stand in that Relation to you. this [*sic*] is chusing: and not to accept of any one that does not appear most agreable both to you Judgment and Fancy." "It is my prayer that you may have a most lovely, agreable, and suitable Person for your Companion in Life." For Cleaveland, "fancy" was not a new criterion. He explained that he and Mary's mother, his deceased wife, chose each other this way, and he mentioned hoping to find another spouse who can also be a "friend." William Greenleaf similarly advised a friend in Lancaster to choose a spouse who could best bring her happiness. He wrote to Katherine Quincy, "Katy I wish your welfare as much as I could an own Sister's, if I had one. They tell me Dr. Atherton is seriously disposed to devote himself to your service for Life and wishes to make you happy; if you think you can be happy with Him, don't refuse Him the opportunity." Happiness was a key to success in marriage. Greenleaf emphasized happiness and compatibility and stressed that the decision was hers to make.[19]

Throughout the eighteenth century, newspaper discussions of companionship in marriage stressed compatibility and intellect over beauty or wealth as criteria for selecting a spouse. In 1733, for example, the *New En-*

gland Weekly Journal ran an essay on "happiness" in "love and marriage" and framed it as an achievement made possible by choosing the right mate. "Marriage," it read, "enlarges the Scene of our Happiness and Miseries. A Marriage of Love is *pleasant*; a Marriage of Interest, *easy*; and a Marriage where both meet, *happy*. A happy Marriage has in it all the Pleasures of friendship, all the Enjoyments of Sense and Reason, and indeed, all the Sweets of this Life." Sermons such as *The Wedding Ring* brought these ideas of compatibility together in a suggestively phrased simile: "Husbands and Wives are like Locks and Keys." Such phrases stressed compatibility and intimacy between husband and wife using a double entendre that hinted at a specifically sexual intimacy.[20]

An essay appearing in the October 1789 edition of the *Gentleman and Lady's Town and Country Magazine* similarly extolled the excitement of physical contact in the context of virtuous love. In an essay about a woman who wins over a confirmed bachelor, the man, so captivated by his future wife's beauty, is described as falling instantly in love and seeing the true value in companionate love: "He looked back in horror at his former debaucheries, and was convinced that there was no real felicity but when a mutual passion prevailed." Connecting physical intimacy with emotional sentiment, the essay described how the man reacted upon seeing his future wife fishing on the banks of a river. Finding her irresistible, "grasping her round the waist, he stole a kiss which was more expressive than all he could have said for years." Similarly, when the *Hampshire Gazette* carried a poem entitled "A New-England Ball," it made clear the association between dancing, flirtation ("sparking"), and physical intimacy. The poem ended by saying that in the final hour of a dance if "she's in Good trim—that hour is spend in squ—zing."[21]

Seaman Ashley Bowen of Marblehead linked physical intimacy with his attraction to his fiancée. Prior to their ever having met, Bowen recorded in his journal the details of a dream he had in which he met his wife-to-be. In his dream, she had a particular mole on her face, and he was struck by her physically as well as emotionally. Some time after this dream, upon meeting the woman he would later marry, he wrote: "So, they all quitted the room and I had a fair opportunity to examine her real moles and marks with real sweet kisses of real substance of lips and breast and all the qualifications a young woman could be endowed with to make a man happy." For Bowen his sense of being "happy" came from her "lips" and "breasts" and a range of other "qualifications." For young men like Bowen, sexual desire could appear paramount, but, in general, attraction was both physical and psychological.[22]

Sexual love was important enough that an anonymous poem included with an English wedding sermon reprinted in Boston used the story of Adam and Eve to symbolize an ideal match. It waxed romantic without any reference to the value of producing heirs.

> A Mate was giv'n, divinely fair,
> To fill his wishful Arms;
> Supriz'd he gaz'd, and soon drew near,
> Attracted by her Charms
> Her conversation more endears,
> As Side by Side they rove;
> Her Innocence, and winning Airs,
> Inflame his Heart with Love.

In these stanzas the poem stressed companionship and physical intimacy. Appearing at the end of the popular wedding sermon, the poem pointed to the importance of romantic and erotic sentiment in marriage.[23]

Some periodicals poked fun at the sexual component of marriage relations. Consider a 1768 tale from the *Boston Chronicle* that underscored the husband's sexual contribution to marriage. The story was about a war waged by the Greeks upon the Duke of Benevento. One Theobald, Marquis of Spoleto, as an ally of the duke's, came to his assistance and upon taking some Greek men prisoner, ordered them to be castrated and returned with the promise of many more such men in the future. A woman whose husband had been taken prisoner came to the camp crying and was granted the opportunity to speak with Theobald. When he asked her why she grieved, he was told, "my Lord, says she, I wonder that such a valiant hero as you should trifle away your time in warring with women." Puzzled by the statement, Theobald pressed her for an explanation. "My Lord," she answered, how can you "deprive our husbands of what gives us health, pleasure, and children? When you make eunuchs of them, it is mutilating us, not them." And so the woman used humor to secure her husband's safety. For as the author explained, "The whole army was so pleased with this woman's ingenuous declaration, that they restored her husband to her, and all they had taken from her." As the woman departed, Theobald asked her what she would accept as punishment for her husband if he was ever caught in battle again. "He has eyes, said she, a nose, hands, and feet: these are his own, which you may take from him if he deserves it; but leave him, if you please, what belongs to ME."[24]

Eighteenth-century commentary linked the traditional ends of marriage—procreation and the avoidance of fornication—with companionate ideals. William Gouge viewed "due benevolence" as a duty within marriage, in part because sexual relations were not only for "increasing the world with a legitimate brood" but also "for linking the affections of the married couple more firmly together." In a similar vein, Nicholas Culpeper's *Directory for Midwives* pointed out that even the reproductive ends of marriage could be frustrated by a lack of compatibility. Barrenness in women could be caused by "want of love between man and wife," the text explained, thus linking procreative aims with companionate ideals.[25]

Notices of age-inappropriate marriage matches appeared frequently in eighteenth-century pamphlets, sermons, and newspapers. Such matches allowed writers to comment, often satirically, on legitimate and illegitimate motives for marriage. Commentators typically used marriages between the young and the old to condemn matches based on lust or mercenary motives, also often using the comic figures of copulating elderly to make their point. Overall, the accounts indicate a cultural fascination with the appropriate ends of marital sexuality and a condemnation of marriages that could not foster both companionate and procreative ends. Notices of May-December marriages and between elderly couples indicate that by the second quarter of the eighteenth century, procreative and eroticized companionate ideals had been increasingly intertwined.

Marriages entered into for mercenary motives came under fire for the way they perverted the idealized sexual intimacy of husband and wife. One author, for example, condemned mercenary marriages principally because they violated the companionate norms that he touted.

> What abominable *Prostitutions* of Persons and Minds are daily to be seen in many of our Marriages! How little a Share has *real Friendship* and *Esteem* in most of them! How many *play the Harlot,* for a good Settlement, under the *legal Title* of a Wife! And how many the *Stallion,* to repair a broken Fortune, or to gain one. Are these *Muckworms* to expect any *social Happiness* with each other?

Here the anonymous author implies a distinction between the legitimacy of sex in a companionate marriage and the reprehensible sexuality of those who marry in the pursuit of financial gain. He condemns "Harlots" and "Stallions" and points to the legitimate goal of marriage: "*social Happiness* with each other."[26]

The popular sermon *A Wedding Ring* reminds us that eighteenth-century Anglo-American culture embraced the idea that harmony was the foundation for a good marriage: "Husband and Wife should be like the Image in a Looking-Glass" or "like an Eccho that returneth the Voice it receiveth." Marriages between older men and younger women violated norms of companionship based on compatibility (but not, it is worth noting, the goal of procreation) and were thus ridiculed. Thus, a 1752 marriage notice in the *Boston Evening Post* between a ninety-year-old man and a twelve-year-old girl described the bride, using heavy-handed sarcasm, as having "all the Accomplishments that can be expected from one of her Age, to render the married State happy." The editor, in his bracketed comments, similarly sniffed: *"A very suitable Match! An old Boy, and young Girl!"*[27]

The dominant criticism of marriage between men and women of disparate ages was that they were not based on bonds of friendship. Thus *"An old Man is not an Help-Meet for a young Woman."* Conversely, *"A young Man is not a Meet-Help for an old Woman. Raw Flesh is but an ill Planter for rotten Bones."* In the absence of such compatibility, they were merely satisfying their sexual urges.[28]

Notices about marriages between old women and younger men, which often highlighted mercenary motives, also made frequent reference to sexual relations, ridiculing unions that were suspected of being driven by lust. One such tale described the marriage of a seventy-year-old woman to a "young Lad of 14 Years of Age." Another story was about a young man who had apparently promised to marry a woman "of above Fourscore." She claimed to have been intimate with the nineteen-year-old and, after making a scene in church, complained to the parson that the young man had used her for sexual gratification.[29]

Notices in which both partners were very old frequently pointed to the perversion of marital ideals through amusing tales that depicted aged bodies in bed. One humorous essay on preventing "unhappy Marriages" read, "When two old Creatures, that can hardly hear one another f—t, but hauk and cough Night and Day, and can propose not the least Comfort to themselves in the Thing, yet will marry together to be moor miserable, let them be deemed *non compos*." With his euphemistic references to failed sex (the two could not "Comfort" themselves in the "Thing"), the author mocked their marriage as foolishness: they could neither produce children nor share physical intimacy.[30]

During the social disruptions of the American Revolution, the ability of people to meld the sexual purposes of companionship and procreation was hindered. The Revolution afforded men and women greater freedom in the selection of romantic partners, but not the social stability necessary for nurturing companionate relationships. Soldiers, who broadened their experiences in the context of wartime, also engaged in more out-of-wedlock sex.

Continental soldier Benjamin Gilbert, in his letters and diary, often commented on his frequent opportunities for intimate encounters. Shortly before the Battle of Yorktown, Gilbert, writing to another lieutenant on war conditions and the location of the enemy, commented on the warmth and hospitality of single women in the area. "The Ladies are exceeding Amouris but not So Beautifull as at the Northward, tho there is some rare Beauties amongst them. Amourise Intrigues and Gallantry are every where approved of in this State, and amongst the Vulgar any man . . . may have his fill." Gilbert apparently was one who expected to have his fill during the war. Writing the following year to another friend, he complained, "Nothing is wanting on my part as a soldier to make me happy, but C=t [cunt] Cash and New Cloths." Gilbert ceased complaining the following year when he reported to the commander of his company of light infantry that he and his men had "established" a place to enjoy the company of prostitutes and sexually available women. As historian John Shy points out, Gilbert "recorded no less than fifteen visits" to this house he called "Wyoma."[31]

Thomas Paine linked sexual depravity and immorality to the national cause by singling out Loyalists in America. In 1777 the *Independent Chronicle* published a lengthy essay entitled "The American Crisis," "by the author of *Common Sense*." In the essay, Paine, in frustration, explained, "Some secret defect or other is interwoven in the character of all those, be they men or women, who can look with patience on the brutality, luxury and debauchery of the British court, and the violations of their army here." He continued, "A woman's virtue must sit very lightly on her who can even hint a favourable sentiment in their behalf. It is remarkable that the whole race of prostitutes in New York were Tories; and the schemes for supporting the Tory cause, in this city, of which several are now in jail, and one hanged, were concerted and carried on in common baudy-houses, assisted by those who kept them." To bolster the patriotic cause of the Revolution, Paine linked sexual immorality with a general state of corruption in his portrayal of the British and their American supporters. That the British were using American women as prostitutes enhanced the image of American vulnerability and British exploitation and abuse, in gendered terms. In other newspaper accounts, British officers were depicted as cavorting with prostitutes. In one such story a British officer was shot dead when he refused to stop for sentries who wished to block the women from entering the camp.[32]

In contrast, the idealized American soldier held to the companionate ideal. Many men who left home and local social networks for faraway towns and camps reflected on loved ones back home. Major Henry Blake, for example, in his diary of 1776 wrote down music to songs that indicated this sentiment. Songs like "Farewell Sweet Hearts & Wives" expressed the realization that war was not only a political event but a disruption to home and hearth, an event that separated husbands and wives, and men from their partners. A similar song printed in the *Boston Gazette*, allegedly written by a soldier while "Prisoner with the Enemy," contained lines that harped upon the staying power of focusing on romantic love with a woman. It contained the lines "Sweethearts and wives will bless our lives, / Sublimest joys convey, / With mingled charms in their dear arms, / How bright the glorious day." Unlike depictions of British men, who perverted sexual intimacy by turning American women into prostitutes, American soldiers, in the ideal, used their determination to secure home and hearth to endure the hardships of war.[33]

After the Revolutionary War ended, an outpouring of print commentary emphasized marriage and family over the solitary and sexually loose life to which most men had been exposed during the war. Consider a poem that appeared in the *Continental Journal* on July 14, 1785, that included these lines:

> When on thy bosom I recline,
> Enraptur'd still to call thee mine,
> To call thee mine for life!
> I glory in those sacred ties,
> Which modern fools and wits despise,
> Of Husband and of Wife.
> One Mutual flame inspires our bliss,
> The tender look the melting kiss,
> Ev'n years have not destroy'd.

Allegedly authored "By a Husband," the stanzas included lines that emphasized physical expressions of affection as well as enduring attraction and long-lived companionship.[34]

In the postwar era newspapers carried an overabundance of similarly romantic writings that emphasized for men the rewards of marriage, family, and home. Articles explained the virtues of marriages that were based on mutual friendship and affection. Consider, for example—in "Maxims on Love"—the sentiment that "A Marriage entered into without mutual tenderness, is one kind of rape." That same article concluded with the advice: "*In marriage, prefer the* person *before* wealth, virtue *before* beauty, *and the*

mind *before the* body—*Then you have a* WIFE, a FRIEND, and a COM-
PANION."³⁵

Essays with titles like "In Praise of Marriage" took pains to prop up an
institution that was in no real danger of fading away. But such energy and
enthusiasm for marriage can be understood in the postwar context of Revolutionary America. Marriage at this time was still a key role for men and
was explicitly linked to strength of character. As one essay concluded, "In
short, no man can be a fine *Gentleman* that is not a man of *Honor,* and no
man of honor makes a *bad Husband*."³⁶

Commentators enthusiastically portrayed marriage as a source of deep
friendship, companionship, and love. The marital union was a place where
"Love, friendship, honour, truth, & pure delight, Harmonious[ly] mingle."
Such essays not only touted marriage as the correct path for young men's
lives but attempted to sell men on the idea by espousing an ideal of friendship in a "happy marriage."³⁷

These essays depicted the happy marriage as one where "the honey
moon increases to years of bliss," and they assured readers that a successful
marriage could make "life a continual courtship." Essays published from
Salem to Plymouth touted the notion that marriage would bring men happiness and "permanent pleasures." Nearly all of these articles, in addition to
playing up the happiness, eroticism, and stability to be found in marriage,
underlined these aspects with an emphasis on lasting and renewed emotions
within marriage. In the words of one such typical article, marriage was a
"Perpetual fountain of domestic joy!"³⁸

The marriage frenzy had direct consequences for the birth of the new
nation. In 1789 the *Berkshire Chronicle* carried a notice of a marriage and explicitly commented on the trend toward marriage. "The rage for marrying
seems to be prevalent in this place. Few of our youth pass the age of twenty-
one years, before they tie the connubial knot." The notice continued by
linking the move to marry with the success of the new nation. "And our
wise legislators, we apprehend, will be under no necessity of prescribing a
law similar to the Roman, to encourage the propagation of the human
species." Thus the newspaper referenced the model of the Republic of
Rome to tie such marriages to the state of the fledgling American republic.
But it underscored that America was in no need of legal interference for carrying out what was considered to be the natural desire to regenerate.³⁹

For some enslaved men of African descent the principles of the American
Revolution added fresh reasoning to the argument that all men were enti-

tled to the right to choose their own romantic and sexual partners. In 1774, when several men petitioned the Massachusetts government for their freedom, they included in their list of grievances against slavery the fact that it harmed the family and specifically black men's masculine prerogatives. As historian John Wood Sweet points out, "they asked, 'How can a husband leave master and work and cleave to his wife. How can the wife submit themselves to their husband in all things. How can the child obey thear parents in all things.'" Slavery, they argued, prevented them from establishing and enjoying the patriarchal family unit. Slavery denied black men and women the marital ideal. "'The endearing ties of husband and wife we are strangers to,'" explained the petitioners. Moreover, their inability to control their own marriages created further problems: "'For we are no longer man and wife then our masters or mestresses things proper marred or onmarred.'"[40]

Many whites viewed this perspective with concern. Writing to his son in 1783, Loyalist William Taylor described what he perceived to be the problematic state constitution and its negative influence on "Negros" in the area. He wrote to explain that he was "deprived" of his slave's labor. Luke, he explained, had "taken the Liberty as severall Negros have (of late) to look upon themselves as free." The reasoning, he explained, was from "our bad constitution in declaring all to be Free not excepting the Blacks." Taylor viewed this as "unjust," as it would "deprive the owner of their property." Taylor complained that the Constitution did not make provisions for their "future mentainance & the Owners are still liable by Law...to mentain them if they are in want."[41]

According to Taylor, Luke's unhappiness stemmed from being denied permission to marry the woman of his choosing. Two years earlier Luke had asked him for his "consent" and assured Taylor that he did not intend to leave his household. What Luke wanted was to be married so he could "live Honest." But Taylor denied permission once learning that Luke's mate had "four or five Children & her Mistress made her mostly mentain them herself." Luke, apparently never fully recovering from the emasculating disappointment, became increasingly unhappy, and a few months before Taylor penned the letter, he left to live in Boston. Resenting what he perceived as Luke's lack of gratitude, and failing to grasp the republican principles of manly independence, Taylor ended his letter: "I abhor Lukes imposition on the Family when I treated him in all respects as well as any white Man & he did no more Duty than he see fit." For Luke being a free man importantly included the manly right to choose his own wife. The rhetoric of the American Revolution, which emphasized the liberty and freedom of all men regardless of birth or station, inspired those who felt their independence to be hindered to stand defiantly and assert their desires with hope for a newfound legitimacy.

The emphasis on monogamous marriage changed little in the eighteenth century. The greater significance, of course, shifted as the postwar early republican context breathed new life into older models of sexual manliness. Men in the early eighteenth century could have seen their sexual self-control as contributing not only to their own happiness and the success of the marriage but to the creation of a stable and godly colony in the New World. By the end of the century, their descendants could view their self-control as one signal quality of citizenship in a new nation. The core quality may have remained the same but was reworked and reinvigorated with remarkable new meaning. But, as we will see in the following chapter, while sex held the power to secure the manly prerogative of becoming a successful father, husband, head of household, and masculine citizen, it also had the potential to unsettle and disrupt.

CHAPTER 2 ◄–◄–

Sex and the Shattering of
Household Order

A LTHOUGH HEAD OF HIS HOUSEHOLD, a man did not have the cultural
authority to engage in any and all forms of sexual activity that
pleased him. Men who failed to master their sexual passions could create
disorder within their own households. They could even destroy the cohesion of their households, and their position as head, through the sexual
assault of dependents, including servants, wives, and children. Men could
disrupt, and even end, their household status by having sex with someone
other than their wife, by committing adultery.

Divorces could be sought on the grounds of adultery, consanguinity,
desertion, bigamy, and sexual incapacity. Although it is true that throughout the eighteenth century a "husband's characteristic obligation was provision of support [and] the wife's, obedient service," a closer look at what
constituted "support" reveals that sexual and financial obligations were often intertwined.[1]

Elsewhere, using seventeenth-century records from couples divorcing
on the grounds of male sexual incapacity, I have described men who fell
short of the model of masculine virility as "Deficient Husbands." Although
residents of Massachusetts would not have recognized the term, court
records reveal that individuals petitioning for divorce did use terms like
"unnatural Husband" or described a man as "unfit" for the position of husband. While some husbands lacked virility and fell short of idealized masculine sexual strength and power, others were overbearing and abusive,
embodying too much power and strength. In either case, moderation had
been violated. Finally, household disruption was caused by marital infidelity. In some cases, male infidelities led to the dissolution of a marriage
and the dislodging of the head of the household and marital union. Viola-

tions of the marriage bond reflected directly on the husband not only when he was the unfaithful individual but also when his wife strayed. In all cases, men were responsible for ensuring proper sexual expression in their households. Sex could (and did) disrupt homes and dismantle power relations and positions of authority.[2]

Deficient Husbands

Impotence or sexual incapacity, given the emphasis on satisfactory sexual relations as a "duty" of the "office of husband," jeopardized manhood. "Impotence" meant the "erosion of manliness" by signaling general, as well as sexual, inability, "weakness, deficiency, or powerlessness."[3]

At least in the ideal, men shouldered the responsibility for satisfactory sexual relations between husband and wife. Records from divorcing couples reveal that when a woman tried to mobilize a case against her husband, the arsenal of charges included sexual incapacity, as well as lack of financial support—and the two were often inextricably fused together. The manly ideal of virility emphasized strength and mastery in sexual matters between husband and wife. Although individuals continued to assess men by their sexual incapacity, we should not assume that the courts played a large role in enforcing any standards. Although the ideal did not change, proportionately the numbers of men divorced for sexual inability dropped in the eighteenth century from the Puritan era. In the seventeenth century one in six divorcing couples included the charge of male sexual incapacity. In the eighteenth century only a handful of cases appeared in the courts. Increased incidence of premarital sexual relations in the eighteenth century probably led to a greater awareness of sexual compatibility for marrying couples.[4]

Eighteenth-century Massachusetts print culture was rife with examples of failed manhood. The virile man's opposite is ridiculed in the following example from the *Boston Gazette* in 1749: "Yesterday was married Mr. Thomas Patten of this Town, a Widower of 83 Years of Age, to Mrs. Sarah Clarke of Tewksbury, a spry Widow of about 49 Years of Age: 'Tis possible this Couple may have Offspring; but the good old Gentleman is not able to turn himself in his Bed without seizing a Leather Strap fixed in a Jice over his Bed." Here the feeble man stood as a comic foil for an idealized masculine sexual capability. Reliant upon an elaborate apparatus, which included leather straps and joists, Patten lacks sexualized masculine independence and strength.[5]

Motifs of male dominance and command in intimate relations reflected men's broader social authority over dependents. These motifs are clear in the eighteenth-century colloquial language of sex—in slang words for male genitalia such as "prick" or the common slur for sexually aggressive men, "whoremaster." Men were also said to "knock" and "breach" women, both very common words for sex. The sex and reproduction manuals of the period also underscore male mastery and power: in such texts male genitalia "stand" and "perform" the work of reproduction. Finally, consider a poem in *Aristotle's Compleat Masterpiece* about marital sexual relations that begins: "Now my fair Bride, now will I storm the Mint; / Of Love and Joy, and rifle all that's in't." Thus the text associated male sexual performance with warlike and violent connotations ("storm" and "rifle").[6]

Evidence from divorce records and other papers reveals a masculine pride at being able to give pleasure to women. Here the measure of sexual prowess was not simply based on the number of conquests or the ability to take and use a woman at will. Here the power was based on pleasing a woman physically. Consider, for example, that when one Mary Stokell testified about neighbor Abel Sawyer's infidelity, she mentioned having heard Mary Lancaster with him. She stated: "While he was upon her he asked her if it felt good." Her testimony also suggested that the size of a man's sex organ may have been eroticized: "After Sawyer was gone sd Lancaster said he was a glorious hang." In another divorce case, one John Donnell testified that while at the house of Caleb Mory, he heard a man ask his partner, "does it feel good?" This seems to suggest that some men emphasized their perceived ability to please their lovers.[7]

Deficient husbands could be blamed for unsatisfied wives. Testimony in the divorce case of Elizabeth and Joseph Bredeen of Marblehead underscores that a man's failure to meet his sexual responsibility could jeopardize the welfare of his wife. Elizabeth's petition in 1744 stated that she lived in a "very infirm low state of health, actually [?] brought upon her as she is advis'd by ye peculiar circumstances of ye sd Joseph's bodily parts." Joseph, she wrote, was "naturally and incurably so defective in his body, that he is utterly incapable of Procreation." Her statement linked her health problems to her husband's sexual defects, which she regarded as sufficient grounds for divorce.[8]

In the absence of any outward signs of defect in either partner, medical texts highlighted husbandly responsibility for procreative sexual relations by recognizing that blame for a woman's inability to have children might rest with the husband. According to *The Problems of Aristotle*, even a woman's barrenness might be blamed on the husband. The author writes that women's failure to "conceive" "proceeds sometimes of the man, that is, when he is of a cold nature . . . his seed is unfit for generation." It also found that infertility could occur when the husband's "seed is somewhat waterish and therefore doth not stay in the Womb." Thus, in the absence of clear physical explanations, the failure to conceive was often assumed to be a result of abnormal male reproductive organs. This emphasis underscores the masculine duty of procreation.[9]

Women were held less responsible for infertility, given the allied appreciation of sexual relations as a means of strengthening the bond between husband and wife. Indeed *Aristotle's Compleat Masterpiece* argued that men were generally without an excuse for infidelity, given the rarity of instances in which women were incapable of intercourse. Such a view underscored the eighteenth-century notion that marriage was a chief means of regulating and modulating sexual activity. Stressing the importance of sexual relations within marriage, the author quipped that with barren women "her Husband may make use of her, unless she be impenetrable." Here the author uncouples the expression of sexual desire from procreative goals. For him and for others, the "impenetrable" woman frustrated the ends of marriage not because she was infertile but because she denied her husband his legitimate sexual outlet.[10]

Physical reasons for insufficient marital sexual relations, whether the fault of the man or of the woman, frustrated the husband's ability to be head of household both in terms of siring children and in terms of overseeing proper intimacy. This view was also expressed by individuals in Massachusetts. For example, consider a divorce case brought by Jesse Turner against his wife, Grace, because she was "incapable of carnal copulation." Because sexual incapacity was grounds for annulment, the court decreed the divorce in June 1740. Turner, in his testimony, however, did not especially emphasize that her "defect of nature" frustrated the end of procreation. Rather he stressed that her inability to have intercourse prevented their intimacy. He claimed the divorce by reason of the "right of human nature," which incorporated a multidimensional understanding of the purpose of marital sex: she was *both* "impotent & incapable of being his wife." For Turner sexual pleasure, as well as reproduction, was a legitimate foundation of marriage in its own right—and he framed actualizing this pleasure within his marriage as his right.[11]

The Turner case was of local note, and gossip that swirled around the case evidently focused on the genitalia of both parties and linked their condition to their respective genders. Benjamin Walker, Junior, wrote about the case in his diary that month. As Walker had heard the story, the divorce petition was the result of Jesse Turner's "desire" for normative relations with his wife. Walker had heard that the case was a "he-said, she-said" situation, with Jesse "saying shes no woman" and his wife saying that he was "more than a man in bigness." Finally, Walker wrote that he had heard the outcome of the midwife's search and was aware that the midwives and court declared that Mrs. Turner was impenetrable, "having a Callious growing in the Vagina." The court apparently did not take into account what seems to have been a temporary condition. In a surprising postscript to this story, Jesse fathered no fewer than five children with his new wife, Lydia. Grace gave birth to four children, after marrying Joseph Church.[12]

Men who fell short of popular standards of sexual ability also failed to meet broader masculine ideals. When Joel Richardson, a yeoman from Woburn, petitioned the governor for divorce from his wife of twelve years on the grounds that she treated him cruelly, had tried to poison him, and had committed adultery, the testimony revealed the surprising twist that Richardson himself was sexually incapable. Presumably, given that Joel had publicly declared their two children to be his own and that, as several people testified, he was kind to the boys and kind to his wife, Susannah did not file for divorce on the grounds of his sexual incapacity. Although he escaped that particular humiliation, testimony suggested that she had tried to end the marriage by murdering her husband. Regardless of his charges against his wife, Joel's sexual ability became an issue for the case. According to testimony, Susannah, on at least one occasion, had admitted that Joel "had no business with the children for they was none of his." Three doctors were summoned to the court, examined Joel Richardson, and confirmed what a long line of neighbors and kin would come to testify. Aaron Putnam, practitioner of "Physik and Surgery," testified that he examined Joel two different times within about a week and declared: "as to his Parts of Generation & find him according to my best judgment non compos corpes utterly incapible of procreation."[13]

Underscoring eighteenth-century associations of masculinity with sexual performance, testimony from community members revealed that Joel's wife, Susannah, connected his sexual inability with his status as a man. One Benjamin Wright, for example, testified that he had heard Susannah say "Joel was not a man and god knew it and god that made him knew it." Others told the court that they had also heard Susannah speak disparagingly of her husband. Timothy Wright stated that he had heard Susannah say that Joel had "not enough to make a mark in a dish of Meal; or in the lightest Snow that ever fell," apparently testimony to his inability to produce semen. Unhappy in her marriage, Susannah used Joel's sexual incapacity to publicly insult and humiliate him. Unfortunately, surviving records do not tell us how the case was resolved.[14]

The divorce case of Simeon and Judith Walker will further illustrate the importance placed on satisfactory sexual relations between husband and wife. As the above case suggests, husbands who were considered impotent or anatomically lacking could be subjects of gossip. Men's sexual inadequacy could serve not only as a cause for marital disruption but also as a topic for communal derision.

In 1773, after eighteen years of marriage, Judith Walker petitioned the governor and his council for a divorce from her husband, Simeon, whom she described as "a person wholly unfit to be a husband." In addition to stating that he provided for her inadequately (a virtual prerequisite for filing for divorce), she charged that he was "unfit" "by reason of a natural defect, impotency & frigidity," and therefore "Simeon never was nor ever can be capable of performing the peculiar part of that relation." For Judith, Simeon had failed on two counts, financial and intimate. Thus, "because of the total neglect," "together with his incapacity of duly sustaining the relation of an husband," Judith requested a dissolution of their marriage. Simeon not only failed in his capabilities through "natural defect" and "impotency," but also lacked normative desire as evidenced by her statement that he suffered from "frigidity."[15]

Simeon responded to the accusations by testifying that not only had he provided adequately for his wife but he had "in all things done & performed towards her the Duties and Offices of the Marriage Relation & in particular has been during all the Term aforsd and now is a Person competent fit & capable to perform the Peculiar Part of that Relation, and has not been deficient in the Performance thereof... has not nor does he now labour under any natural Defect Impotency or Frigidity which might render him incapable thereof." He also refuted Judith's charge that he had abandoned her, adding that in 1768, unhappy with her neighbors, she asked him to buy a farm at Cohass and "make provisions for her comfortable support there." Head of two households at that point, Simeon traveled between the two places, Cohass and Shutesbery, and according to his defensive testimony, "continued to perform towards her all the Duties & Offices of an Husband." He added the specific detail that since his return home the January before their court involvement, he had "often times during the said Term performed with her the peculiar Part of the Marriage Relation."

But after defending himself on both charges, financial and sexual, Simeon raised a complicating issue. "It is well known," he contended, "that her first Pretence in seeking a Divorce was a pretended Report that she had heard that a Bastard Child at Cohass had been laid to the Charge of the said Simeon." Thus, he further countered the claim that he was sexually incapacitated, and attempted to discredit his wife, by stating that she had claimed to hear gossip that he had fathered a child with another woman. For his part, Simeon told the court that he wanted her to drop the petition and continue as his wife.

For most community members, the financial and sexual obligations of a husband were closely associated. One of at least fifteen people to testify, Levi Walker, Simeon's brother from neighboring New Salem, stated that Simeon was always away in Cohass and left his wife totally undersupported. Emphasizing neglect, Levi added that whenever Simeon was in Shutesbery he "treated his wife with much neglect," adding "this has been the common repute in the neighbourhood." Others, like Samuel Shaw, also were aware that she did not receive much financial support. Shaw had purchased a farm from them and was well aware of the financial arrangements. He testified that Simeon had instructed him not to give any of the payments to his wife. Moreover he linked the lack of financial support with a general failure of intimacy: "It was commonly reported that the said Simeon inclined to avoid the company of his said wife when he was at said Shutesbury." Others countered this depiction of Simeon as a bad provider. One Elisabeth Cady stated that Simeon often visited Judith and that she was always well taken care of.

The court heard many individuals with testimony regarding the specific charge of Simeon's sexual inability. His brother, Levi, had direct evidence on the question of Simeon's anatomy. He stated that "the genital parts of the said Simeon were never larger than such as are common to Children of two or three years old." One Thomas Temple of Shutesbury confirmed Levi's testimony, telling the court that "by Examination and feeling with his Hand he knows that Simeon Walker...has a Deficiency in those parts proper to the male Sex...not larger than those of a Boy of two years old." Some offered evidence of gossip that shored up the charge that Simeon was indeed underdeveloped. One Dinah Pratt testified to having heard Judith defend her husband's reputation as a sexually inadequate man. Pratt stated: "Judith, upon my telling her that Tom Temple had told that her Husband was not a man, said her Husband was as much a man as poor Tom Temple, she believed, & added she didn't know but he was as much a man as any many and was as much of a man as she desired and further saith not." Others confirmed Simeon's charge that Judith had indeed had a pregnancy out of wedlock. But the mounting evidence that she had miscarried was ambiguous evidence at best on the matter of Simeon's condition.

Simeon's condition, whatever it was, appeared to be a familiar topic of discussion among family and neighbors. Some offered evidence that the community suspected her husband was impotent and that any pregnancy she had was not his doing. Elisabeth Cady told of an altercation she had with Judith when Simeon was working at her house and Judith came to visit him. Referring to Judith's pregnancy, Elisabeth, insinuating that the child was not his, told her: "if it's true what some Folks say you need not come to see him." This charge of infidelity resulted in a physical confrontation and Judith's ostensible defense of her husband. According to Elisabeth: "she then came to me & gave me a push & said I'll have you to know he's as good a husband as yours or any body's & added that she had miscarried two or three times." Judith's passionate defense of her husband undoubtedly was meant to bolster her own reputation as a virtuous wife. Others confirmed that Judith had a reputation for bristling at communal derision of her husband's sexual failing. Silent Wild testified that it was "frequently said by people of Shutesbury in a Way of Humour that the said Simeon Walker was deficient in those Part peculiar to the male Sex." Wild further stated that he "has observed frequently that the mentioning of it to his wife would raise her resentments," adding for emphasis, "nothing would so soon fire them."

Although the court apparently did not see sufficient reason to grant the divorce, the testimony in the case brought to light the widespread talk about the marital problems of Judith and Simeon—and the strong association of manliness and male sexual ability. The court apparently believed that there was sufficient possibility that he had gotten her pregnant and found it inconclusive that he did not provide well for her.

Dangerous Patriarchs

Unlike those husbands who lacked sufficient power and authority in matters sexual, some violated the masculine ideal of moderation and self-control by sexually assaulting their dependents. Increasingly through the eighteenth century, heads of household, like rulers in the body politic, were to govern with reason and compassion. For the most part, heads of household had a level of authority and independence that allowed them sexual access with impunity to dependents, including wives, servants and slaves, and even children. However, when instances of abuse or incest became known, community norms and systems of evaluation could be activated. Such condemnation would have signaled to other men, even those engaging in such behavior without public scrutiny, that masculine ideals did not condone the unbridled sexual assault of household dependents.[16]

Throughout the eighteenth century, concern about sexual relations with servants drove narratives that emphasized the importance of maintaining household order. As always, such tales need not be local to carry the moral lesson intended for the local readership. In 1730 the *Boston Gazette* included the following "news from Paris," which would have neatly illustrated the price of sex with servants:

> They write from Coutance, the only Son of a rich Farmer in that Neighbourhood, having used some secret Gallantries with a young Servant in the House, by visiting her in her Chamber in the Night time, had once unhappily by drinking more than ordinarily, mistook her Door, and enter'd the Room of his Father, who believing him to be a Thief that was come to assassinate him, took up a Fusil, and shot the young Man dead upon the Spot; but when the poor Farmer came to discover what an Accident had happen'd, he went raving Mad.

Here a young man with a bright future ruined it by his inability to control his passions. Drink and sex led to his downfall. Additionally, his actions brought destruction not only to his own life but to his family, as well. The lesson was clear: the author combined the image of a man incapable of controlling his drinking as well as his lusts with the image of a man who would lose his mind and destroy those around him. The "rich Farmer" at the start of the tale became a "poor Farmer" through his son's lack of sexual self-restraint.[17]

In Massachusetts, when marital discord arose, sexual relationships with servants could bolster a charge of bad behavior on the husband's part. When Mary Fairservice petitioned for divorce, which she received in 1770, she claimed that her husband was abusive, financially irresponsible, and unfaithful. For his part he claimed that she had slandered him, first moving out and then asking to move back when she found life with her mother and sister more abusive. He defended himself to the court claiming that he "treated her with all the indulgence and affection that a Husband . . . ought to" but that she was unkind, jealous, and had maligned him by charging that he had "criminal conversation with a Negro Woman Slave in the family." The accusation, he contended, was not one to be taken lightly. According to John Fairservice, the allegation was brought "in so public a Manner as to cause almost an intire loss of your Respondents Trade of Business." Thus, the accusation that he managed his household affairs poorly, failed to control his sexual appetites, and had engaged in an interracial extramarital affair signaled to the community that his woeful inadequacies at home indicated his inability in his world of "Business."[18]

The complaint that the appearance of being a man who engaged in sexual relationships with servants and other dependents affected his business reputation was a valid one. In general, historians have overlooked the importance of hewing closely to masculine ideals of sexual comportment for success in business and trade. To be sure, most men could, and surely did, keep such affairs discreet or were able to secure silence from their partners. It is clear, however, that in an era that relied on reputation for business and commercial dealings, the total man was assessed. A man who failed to govern his passions or control his household would not have been evaluated as the best man with which to conduct business. This did not mean that sexual infidelities were impossible; it meant that a man who could not engage in such behavior without keeping it private or within the walls of his own house could not be trusted in other areas.

Given their position as arbiters of moral comportment, ministers suffered doubly from the smear of sexual impropriety within their own households. They also jeopardized their professional positions. Reverend David Hall of Sutton wrote in his diary the disgust and shame he felt on hearing of his mentor's sexual indiscretion with a servant. In June 1750 Hall wrote about his recent journey to Boston. "I heard three good sermons in Boston but one thing attended Maloncally Enough. The Parson Expected to have preached the Converntion sermon was past by, Mr. William Williams by name, of ill fame of his being unchaste or at least rude in behaviour towards his maid." Williams's sexual relationship with his maid cost him his position. According to Hall, "The Church of which he is Pastor are like to break with him upon." For Hall, the story of a minister who violated his dependent and disrupted his own household for sexual gain was a typical tale that instilled feelings of sadness. "A Maloncolly thing: an old Minister & of good repute. The Lord Sanctify the Providence. The Lord make on wiser & to cease from man." For Hall, the story was particularly disturbing, as Williams had "Preacht" his "ordination Sermon." In the end, Hall shrugged his shoulders but also was clear enough in his own moral judgment of the action to prefer death over the shame and humiliation of losing one's calling to sexual impropriety. "Well, let him that think he Stands take head lest he fall. Rather Let me die O Lord if Ever follow in such a way of wickedness." While his position as a minister may have led to hyperbole, the intensity of the emotion underscored the general feeling for most men, minister or merchant, that the public emasculation of appearing unable to control one's household and one's self within that household could be unbearable.[19]

The following two abuse cases indicate that people expected the husband's sexual behavior to conform to the norms of moderation. In 1781 Elizabeth Bernis, only a year and a half after marrying Samuel Bernis, a husbandman from Lexington, was granted a divorce on the grounds of cruelty. In addition to detailing for the court the starvation and physical abuse that she suffered, she described a sexual assault that occurred while she was recuperating from one of his beatings. "He stript the Bed Cloaths off her, & used her in so barbarous a manner, that she miscarried." In addition to the abuse, she charged Samuel with having given her venereal disease from his infidelity. Similarly, in 1771 one Jonathan Knight viewed Samuel Bernis's conduct as a reason for Abigail Bradstreet's not wanting to live with her husband, Joseph. A group of neighbors who listened to Abigail explain that her husband lived beyond his means testified accordingly. After signing his name, Knight added the following: "Said Abigail further said . . . as a reason why she declined living with her husband, that her husband would do it for her (meaning, as I understood her, that he would have carnal knowledge of her body) which, as she was with Child, put her to great pain, & almost killed her the next day." Such testimony yoked unacceptable behavior in both financial and sexual areas. That the testimony was underlined emphasizes the especially egregious nature of the sexual assault. The husband in this case violated his position as husband and disregarded the safety of his unborn child.[20]

Similarly, Bostonian Tabetha Hearsey complained in her divorce petition that Israel, her husband of more than twelve years, had subjected her to physical and sexual abuse. Tabetha complained that her husband had overstepped the bounds of legitimately exercised patriarchal authority by transgressing norms of sexual intimacy. Israel, she claimed, failed to control his "wicked and unnatural lust." Furthermore, he tried to enforce his authority by "inflicting the most grievous pains" because of her "refusal to comply" with his attempts to use her for "things too shocking to utter." She also complained that he had tried to get other men to seduce her so that he could accuse her of adultery and obtain a divorce.[21]

Despite their strictures about sexual moderation and fear of sexual excess, New Englanders were reluctant to accuse patriarchs of raping members of their own households. The Superior Court never tried men for raping their own servants even though the sexual exploitation of servants by masters presumably was widespread.[22]

Newspaper commentators were more likely than not to use the occasional item about the sexually "abus'd wife" to poke fun at disordered households. A reprinted news item from South Kingston, appearing in the *New England Weekly Journal* in 1739, depicted a woman who had complained to the justice of the peace of her town in the middle of the night that her husband had "abus'd her." The justice, "being in Bed and very sleepy," looked at her "sternly" and "told the poor Woman that if she insisted upon a Prosecution, the Law must certainly be executed, and her Husband would unavoidably be castrated." Acting as if he were prepared to take action ("seeming to be then forward to prosecute the Affair"), the justice "told her, he would provide a Doctor and the Business be done with the utmost Safety." Confronted with this scenario, the woman naturally "beg'd Pardon, went off, and left the Justice to take out his Nap." This item portrayed sexual assault within marriage as properly a private matter—and women who thought otherwise, as foolish.[23]

The only exceptions to a patriarch's general immunity from prosecution for assault on his own dependents were the handful of cases of incest tried before the Superior Court. The Superior Court prosecuted at least four men for incest, in 1729, 1752, 1754, and 1782. The moral clarity of incest laws reflected in part early Puritan legal codes and biblical condemnations. Incest was a gendered crime: only men were accused of it, and there are no records of charges involving male children. Those males who might have been sexually abused would have suffered in silence. In an era of deference and hierarchy, boys, young men, male apprentices, servants, and slaves could have been subjected to manipulation and coercion by men or women.

In the eighteenth century a father's sexual interest in his children or relatives violated biblical teachings and Massachusetts law and perverted patriarchal ideals of self-control and family order. In 1752 the Superior Court of Judicature found Jonathan Fairbanks of Douglas guilty of incest with his stepdaughter, Sarah Armstrong. According to the court testimony, the incest had occurred over a span of five years. The court's verdict was that the father and his stepdaughter "wickedly voluntarily Incestuously & Carnally did know each other." Although the court's mention of voluntary sex implied that the stepdaughter had consented and was not coerced, she was not sentenced. This suggests that the courts recognized the father as the primary culprit, responsible for undermining the orderly household hierarchies that his role as household head put him under a special obligation to preserve. That she was not punished indicates that the court considered her a dependent, reliant upon Jonathan Fairbanks's good will and victimized when he failed in his responsibilities toward those over whom he had guardianship.[24]

The courts ordered those men who were convicted of incest to wear a letter stitched to their clothing for the rest of their lives. The label was a form of public humiliation that served to protect the community but also to remind both the criminal and his neighbors of the heinous nature of his moral deviance and its threat to social order. Jonathan Fairbanks was punished precisely in this way when he was ordered to be whipped twenty times, to stand at the gallows for one hour, and to wear an *I* for the rest of his life. His punishment in 1752 was also reported on October 9 in the *Boston Evening Post,* as were other, similar punishments. The newspaper notices detailing such crimes and their punishments served to magnify across a wider community of readers both the convict's public humiliation and its moral lesson.[25]

Fathers and patriarchs who abused their positions of authority were undoubtedly more numerous than records suggest. In the case of the Temples, detailed information on one family's situation came to light only years later and appears to have been triggered by marital infidelity. Sarah Temple, married for twenty-five years, petitioned the court seeking a divorce from Stephen on the grounds that eleven years previously he did "incestuously violate the chastity of his own daughter" and fathered a child with another woman. Stephen, a housewright from Upton, in hopes of redemption, made the following startling confession:

> [I] behaved in such a manner towards my daughter Susannah Temple that I acknowledge I have violated the marridg [*sic*] covenant and have behaved my self unbecomingly towards my wife many times. I do humbly promise to for the future to cary my self well towards my wife and daughter Susannah and the rest of the family. I do hereby give my wife full liberty if ever I be have [*sic*] myself unbecomingly towards her or Susannah or any of the rest to carry a complaint to any Justice of the Peace and have me Punishd according to Law.[26]

At the time of the court hearing, Stephen's stepdaughter was married and living in Worcester. She testified for the court what had happened when she was thirteen. One day, "Having had a long fit of sickness," she was on the bed with her younger sister. Her "father got on to the bed ... and said he wanted to kiss me." Evidently employing his authority as father and masking his sexual interest in a thin veneer of paternal interest, he, according to his stepdaughter, "said he wanted to know whether my brest [*sic*] was grown." Susannah testified about other instances of abuse, many of which revealed a similar pattern of disguised sexual interest. One "Sabbath Day," when she was alone with him, "he got on to the bed to me," she told the court, and "he then asked me whether I knew how young women are every month, and said I must pull up my petticoats."

Further testimony revealed his method of manipulation as head of household. His stepdaughter stated: "I told him it was wicked," but she complied because she "was afraid of him and thought I must obey him." "I did as he said I must." His position of authority controlled his stepdaughter even after the abuse had progressed to intercourse: "he got on to me and pushed into me so hard that he hurt me very much, and left his seed upon me." Appealing to his position as father and guide, the stepdaughter testified that at another time she "told him that he had often told me that I must not do any thing that was wicked. I told him it was a Sin." But undeterred, he told her "it would not be a Sin in me, if I was against it. And that the Sin was in him." Moreover, he appealed to her sense of shame, stating that "it would never be known," and he pressured her to keep it secret by bargaining with her own body: "He then said if I would not let it be known he would not meddle with me for two months." Here the stepfather violated his position of authority by using it to pursue an incestuous sexual relationship. Documentary evidence of the manipulation and method would never have been recorded had Stephen's wife not used the testimony when she filed for divorce eleven years later. For the courts, his violation of his duty as head of household, husband, and father made him ineligible for that position.

After the Revolutionary War, disordered households in Europe, including those sullied by incest, symbolized European immorality and American virtue implicitly by way of contrast. One such tale of a man who murdered his daughter and afterward "sat six hours on the body of the deceased" before unsuccessfully attempting suicide by slicing his own throat, underscored the depravity of such men. His crimes of incest, murder, and attempted suicide were punctuated at the closing of the article by the remark that the daughter had "several children by her unnatural father, and by whom she has been nine times pregnant."[27]

Male Infidelity

When men engaged in extramarital sexual relations, they risked their status as husbands and heads of household. According to historian Nancy Cott, of the 229 petitions filed by individuals seeking divorce in Massachusetts between 1692 and 1786, roughly two-thirds include wives charging husbands with adultery, indicating that even with a strict understanding of the husband as provider, sexual infidelity was relevant. And as companionate marriage developed, male infidelity became even more significant throughout the century. In the colonial era no woman made adultery the sole reason for petitioning for divorce, but beginning in the Revolutionary era many did so. Throughout the eighteenth century, for female petitioners charges of sexual infidelity were nearly always part of additional charges of financial neglect, abuse, lost love, or mismanaged households.[28]

Although legally the definition of *adultery* hinged on the status of the woman (it was adultery only if the woman was married), it was a tremendous source of concern and talk in eighteenth-century America. For lay individuals and commentators alike, male infidelity got tongues wagging, and many thought it noteworthy to record instances of cheating husbands in their journals and diaries. Benjamin Bangs observed the marital discord that arose from a husband's unfaithfulness when he visited a couple. According to his diary, on a sunny October day with a cold frosty night, Bangs traveled from Wells to Stowe, Maine, visiting York and Kittery before taking a ferry to spend the night in Portsmouth. There he saw what he called a "warning to all married people," "for the man and wife do not lodge together. She says he keeps a whore and at her expence."[29]

The topic of unfaithful husbands produced sensational newspaper notices that commented on male failures at household mastery. Boston newspapers carried a range of information, from drier news on shipping and politics to more sensational accounts designed to sell papers. In this regard they collected what printers considered to be of particular interest to readers. Newspapers carried such stories and worse, far and wide. In 1752 the *Boston Evening Post* printed an account of a woman in London who killed her husband for his suspected infidelity.

> She had long suspected him of Infidelity to her Bed, and that Night it seems she had received some fresh Proofs of it; she was either too weak or too cowardly to make an open Attack upon him, but smothered her Resentment till he was asleep. She carried to Bed with her a sharp Knife, and while he was unsuspecting of Danger, in the most cruel Manner cut off his Genitals. He awaked in Agony, but as Assistance could not be speedily procured, he bled to Death.

Presumably, the victim's wife chose to remove his "Genitals" thinking it would be a suitable revenge for what she suffered. Consider, also, the following 1732 report in the *Boston News Letter* about a woman in Ireland who married her father's servant "for Love," but eventually killed him in "a fit of Jealousy" after discovering he had been unfaithful. The story detailed the murderous scene: "She inticed him to Bed somewhat earlier than ordinary, and when asleep, with a large sharpenn'd Knife, provided for that purpose, she dismembered him, and then left him in that miserable Condition." The man died, and the woman was committed to prison "in the utmost Despair." The notices carried a symbolic second meaning, however: individuals who committed infidelity lost their manhood.[30]

Marital problems were no small affair. In an era before no-fault divorce and at a time when marriage was seen as key for a stable society, marital discord was on par with any other serious social issue of the day. In 1751 John Cleaveland's mother, Abigail, for example, when writing on the suicide of a woman in town who had cut her own throat with a razor, morally equated the social evils of the day. A "dreadful time," she wrote, with "murder and adultery, swearing, lying, stealing, scoffing, and self murder."[31]

In 1759 the future president John Adams weighed in on the sexual grounds for divorce, writing in his commonplace book that such expectations were healthy. Echoing the legal statute at the time, Adams wrote: "Divorce. Is it for the Benefit of Society, for the Convenience and Happiness of human Life, to allow of Divorces, in any Cases. I think it is. I think that either Adultery or Impotence are sufficient Reasons of Divorce." Divorce, according to Adams, should not be granted in cases of what he called "Dissonance." Such differences should be thoroughly examined during courtship and not serve as cause for divorce. After all, wrote Adams, "By Conversation with a Lady, and Tryals of her Temper, and by Inquiry of her Acquaintance, a Man may know, whether her Temper will suit him or not. But he can never know whether she will be fruitful or barren, continent or incontinent." Thus, given strictures against premarital sex, sexual problems such as impotence could serve as just cause for divorce. So, too, could adultery. But following this logic, men who claimed to seek sexual and romantic relationships outside their marriages because of incompatibility would be drawing attention to their own failure to select a proper spouse.[32]

Although, in general, early courts placed great value in gossip and hearsay, in cases where a woman could prove she contracted venereal disease from her unfaithful husband, the charge of adultery became more substantiated. The husband's physical ailment was often easy to prove, as men tended to leave a long trail of witnesses. Men who contracted venereal disease nearly always enlisted the help of male friends and doctors, who, in divorce cases, were later called into court. For example, when Rose Corles petitioned the court for a divorce from her husband of eight years, Timothy, a yeoman from Bromfield, she charged that he had engaged in sexual relations with one Deborah Barker, also of Bromfield. Testimony from several men confirmed Rose's claims that Timothy had indeed contracted venereal disease. One Robert Moutton testified that several years earlier Timothy had told him and his landlord that he had the "french disease" and sought advice. After being told which doctor to consult, the men were quick to ask from whom he had contracted the disease. Having "meddled with nobody else," Timothy was certain it was Deborah Barker. Dudley Wade, the physician who later examined him, testified: "upon examination I found he had got it. I told him I made it my rule to make my patients tell who they took it of, he replied & said one Deborah Barker with whom he had kept company some time. I put him upon a course of medicine which in a little time cured him." For the courts, the testimony concerning Corles's venereal disease sufficiently bolstered the testimony of others who had only seen the couple lodging in the same room, or emerging from the same room one morning. In the absence of any eyewitnesses to sexual intimacy between Barker and Corles, testimony from men about Timothy Corles's treatable case of venereal disease sealed his fate and ended his marriage.[33]

Venereal disease stood as a somatic mark of a man's profligate character. It combined the physical with the spiritual. Venereal disease signified not only a physical illness but a man's illness of character—his lack of manly vigor and fortitude. In 1783, when Mary Holman petitioned for divorce, she charged that her husband, a Worcester trader, had "indulged himself in Adultery and in Cohabitation with common prostitutes. That in pursuance of lewd practices as aforesaid the said Stephen hath contracted such diseases as are shameful and fatal to the Human Race." On her behalf, a letter was submitted to the governor and council from the pastors of the Chelsea Congregation in Sutton, justices of the peace for the same town, and selectmen of Sutton. All attested that she was a woman of "sober life & conversation" and had "obtained the Reputation of being a woman of Real Worth." They therefore hoped that the court would give her "full Credit" for her claims. And they added, "on the other hand we must say, that we have the highest Reason to believe she is married to a man of a very profligate Character." Echoing their attack on his character, another man testified that he knew Stephen and that he had said that "he was sensable he had deceaved many woman in order to get his will of them."[34]

In an era of rudimentary treatments, the physical damage that those unfaithful husbands who contracted venereal disease suffered could signify their deviance from masculine ideals of physical vigor and manly self-control. Status did not always protect men. Gentleman John Pell from Great Barrington, for example, lost his wife of ten years when she petitioned the courts for a divorce, complaining that he had failed to properly support her and had instead lived a life of "extravagance and debauchery." Pell's lifestyle had "wasted his Estate," "ruined his constitution and character," and had resulted in his giving his wife "the venereal disorder" that he had contracted through "illicit commerce with a common prostitute." For his wife, Abigail, it was a total package of disreputable manhood. He was a ruined husband and the courts agreed.[35]

For John Pell, his actions, also both financial and sexual, combined to dismantle his social position as husband and head of household. According to testimony in his divorce case, Pell had once been imprisoned for counterfeiting money and while in custody had asked a friend for money to buy "roots and herbs" to treat his venereal disease. The friend instead secured a doctor, who proceeded to "make an amputation, and to take of the mortifyed parts." Pell's friend, who witnessed the operation and several subsequent others, was convinced that Pell had "suffered much loss in those opperations which nature has not nor ever will restore." Pell, who transgressed the social and legal bounds of commercial dealings, violated marital fidelity, and could not maintain himself, in the end found his manhood both physically and symbolically reduced.[36]

We should not forget that in this time and place the vast majority of men who transgressed marital and household boundaries were never caught, and not all those who were chastised left a historical record. That women were able to secure divorces in cases that constituted a general husbandly failure—those that combined the lack of material as well as emotional comforts with poor character, sexual or otherwise—indicates that even in the late eighteenth century deviating from proper masculine sexual behavior could wreck one's marriage and household.

Of course, many men who found themselves in difficult situations (of their own making) simply absconded, never to face the courts. Sarah Kingsley finally petitioned for divorce eleven years after her husband left her and their two-year marriage, apparently so that he could marry a woman in Connecticut. Some who spoke with his second wife testified that Enoch Kingsley had not stayed in Connecticut much longer than the time it takes to have a couple of kids, leaving his second wife and moving on to Virginia, never to be heard from again. Such men placed extraordinary financial burdens on their families. Sarah Kingsley complained that she had her own "proper Estate attach'd & taken by the creditors of the sd Enoch & is still exposed to have all her Effects seized and taken from her by the sd Enoch's other creditors to the great distress of herself and the children."[37]

As we have seen in several cases of incest, some men willfully flaunted the marital covenant, showing little or no regard for the penalties. Thus, while social pressures to remain faithful to one's wife may have been strong, many men openly showed no regard for such conventions, drawing instead on a masculine counternorm that embraced individuality and risk-taking. Consider the following story of a man clearly not intimidated by public knowledge of his adulterous behavior. Neighbors who testified in the divorce case of Martha and Adam Air described walking past a house and upon hearing a noise, looking in the open window just in time to see Adam "in the act of copulation" with a local woman. Deciding to confront the adulterer, the neighbors entered the house and "stood behind them as they lay on the floor." This apparently did not faze the couple, and one neighbor, Abigail, after "observing them some time," confronted Adam, asking if he "was not ashamed" of his actions "when he had a Wife at home." Adam, in response, "got up and answered, one woman was as good to him as another." Thus, he indicated that he had no regard for the sacred bond of husband and wife. Moreover, "he then put up his nakedness before our faces and went away." For Adam the threat of being discovered and maligned only emboldened his transgressive nature. By standing naked in front of his accusers and asserting his manhood, he expressed the popular view that manly actions, as individual actions, took cultural precedence over official religious, moral, and legal teachings.[38]

Husbands who cheated not only disrupted the business of household order and risked their social position, but also exacted an emotional toll on wives and family. Women, slightly more often than men, employed the language of lost "happiness" in cases of adultery and, in suing for divorce, placed the blame for this loss of "affection" on the husband. When she petitioned for divorce in 1747, Eleanor Gray, for example, stressed the sadness she felt upon losing her husband and singled out love lost as a factor in pursuing divorce. She accused her husband of admitting to having a child with another woman, but what upset her most was that "the hatred wherewith he now hates me is greater than the love wherewith he loved me." As in most cases involving the birth of a child as clear evidence of the adultery, the court granted her a divorce. Other cases also indicate the importance of happiness and love. In 1758 Jacob Brown's wife similarly complained that she "Lived Extremely unhappy in the Marriage State." Likewise, Kezia Downing filed for divorce in 1765 after her husband, Doctor Nathaniel Downing, gained control over her estate and then began pursuing other women, charging that "His affections toward me grew Cold and [he] Treated me In a Most unnatural Manner." Underscoring the normative evaluation of a husband as one who loves and cares for his wife, she referred to her cheating, "Cold" spouse as her "unnatural Husband" and requested a divorce.[39]

Similarly, in 1736 Sarah Blodget petitioned for a divorce from her husband of sixteen years and used language that depicted him as having failed at husbandly sexual companionship. Blodget complained that after marrying him in 1720, she lived with him "unhappily" for the following nine years, during which time he "never treated her as a Wife." She even left for a year in order to regain her health. Upon her return, however, the situation was no better, he "declaring (as he had often done before) that he had no Love or Affection for her neither would he have any thing to do with her." In short, she valued marital "Affection" and associated it with sexual intimacy. Indeed, she went on to say that her husband "has no Conjugal Affections for her & has several times told her he had made himself an Eunuch & how true it is your Petitioner knows not." She sought a divorce so that she "may no longer Continue under the Yoke of a Cruel husband, who takes no care to provide for her and has no real Love or Conjugal Affection for her." Significantly, Blodget framed her husband's sexual neglect not as an inability to procreate but rather as a loss of "real Love or Conjugal Affection."[40]

The Revolutionary War created ample opportunity for men to form temporary relationships while away from their families. Chloe Welch, who in 1770, before the outbreak of war, married Luke, a laborer from Bromfield, found that her husband's life away from home enabled him to create new relationships. Luke, when in the Continental Army, had "taken a woman" with whom he lived and called his wife. According to divorce papers, the two "lived together in Camp, as man and wife, from which conduct there are the strongest reasons to presume that he has at several times been guilty of Adultery with said woman."[41]

Contrary to popular conceptions of war as a male sphere and home and hearth as a woman's, the American Revolution was a fully integrated war. Not only did women participate in the war by domestic actions and the occasional martial act, but they were commonplace in the camps, providing a wide range of support services for the military. Several men testified to having seen Luke Welch with a woman in his tent. All the men who testified to seeing them together, including one man who said he had "often seen him in bed with her," explained that Luke called the woman his wife.[42]

In the post–Revolutionary War era, printed tales of European men (especially those of royal birth) who flaunted their marriage vows and created disordered households cast a light away from any locally occurring cases and focused on stories from abroad. Such anecdotes in this new republican context positioned Europe as lacking in virtue. A reprinted notice of an address given by John Jay, chief justice of the state of New York, began by defining the patriot's cause as a "break from...those clouds of anarchy, confusion and licentiousness, which the arbitrary and violent domination of the King of Great Britain had spread, in greater or lesser degrees, throughout this and the other American States." In such stories the focus on aristocratic and royal immorality similarly underscored, by way of contrast, the virtues of republican manhood. One such story about the "Duke D'Ossonne" described his unhappy relationship with his wife and his interest in an actress, which produced jealousy in the duchess. One day, having found "rich" material that he had purchased for his romantic interest, the duchess "had it made into a gown." Upon showing it to the duke and asking if "he did not think it was a charming gown," he quipped, "Yes...it is a fine piece of stuff, but ill used." To this the duchess replied: *"Every body says exactly the same of me."* Such tales often pointed to the failure of European men to master their sexual urges. Another such notice appearing in 1785 purported to be a "Political Creed" from the *London Packet,* in which British subjects vowed to be, among other things, "licentious," engaging in "promiscuous fornication" and "ribaldry." In 1788 the *Boston Gazette* printed an essay titled "King Charles II's Amours," which included his being "violently addicted to women; and only valued them for the sensual pleasures they could yield." This referred to his frequenting prostitutes and holding "nocturnal debauches."[43]

Throughout the eighteenth century, monogamous marriage was considered central to social stability. In the colonial context, this meant that households were "little commonwealths," and their order ensured the order of the commonwealth at large. In the new nation, household stability undergirded republican order and ensured that a fledgling nation would not degenerate into factions and bloodletting but would remain governable and patriarchal. Throughout the eighteenth century, these ideals of family and society were linked to Christianity and to ethnicity. A white Protestant colony was the goal. Creating virtuous male heads of household was the means. In time, so, too, was a white Protestant nation the goal of the founding generation.[44]

One of the ways in which orderliness and stability were linked to race was through the depiction of racial and ethnic "others" as embodiments of unmasculine chaos. Although the Bible contains numerous instances of men with several wives, which can be construed as support for polygamy, early Americans followed the traditional interpretation of biblical support for monogamy. A variety of print sources depicted Native Americans as uncivilized because of their deviance from monogamous marriage practices. In 1705 Cotton Mather published a sermon that singled out a number of laws that Native Americans broke, including having "Two Husbands, or Two Wives" and adultery ("any Man be found a Bed with another Mans Wife"). As the reference to "Two Husbands, or Two Wives" suggests, many English writers associated Indians with the practice of polygamy. Polygamy, and its association with sexual promiscuity, signified that Indians were uncivil; it symbolized savage and pagan states. Similarly, Mary Rowlandson, in a vehemently anti-Indian account of her captivity, highlighted her Indian master's polygamous marriage as a way of underscoring his status as a "savage." Rowlandson drew attention to her captor's polygamous marriage to further her depiction of Native Americans as uncivilized. ("My master had three squaws, living sometimes with one and sometimes with another one.") For settlers and missionaries, monogamous marriage was an important foundation of Christian social order. Indian polygamy signified their uncivil state.[45]

Conversely, the adoption of monogamy by Indians signified assimilation to Christian and civil mores. A letter from James Oglethorpe on the Christian potential of Indians in Georgia, reprinted in the *New England Weekly Journal*, stated that local Indians "do not approve of *Plurality of Wives*" and used this as evidence that they "understand" and "assent" to the "*Moral* Part of Christianity."[46]

This racialization of monogamy would hold true throughout the eighteenth century and would serve to define the non-Anglo-American world. Stories and notices of the non-English world, including Turks, Muslims, Asians, and Indians, focused on their deviation from Christian monogamy. During the Revolutionary era, for example, one Jeremy Belknap owned a copy of *Bickerstaff's Boston Almanac*, which published a story about the inhabitants of Tahiti, an island in the South Sea. It included a description of their sexual customs: "Among such a people as this we ought not to expect that chastity should be held in very high esteem." Many of the residents, according to the author, "have formed themselves into a society, distinguished by the name of Arreoy, in which every woman is common to every man, thus securing perpetual variety as often as their inclination prompts them to seek it." "If any of the women happen to be with child, the poor infant is smothered the moment it is born, that it may not be an incumbrance [*sic*] to the father, nor interrupt the mother in the pleasures of her diabolical prostitution." Thus the decoupling of sex from monogamous marriage and the production of offspring was linked to the ethnic and religious background of the "Arreoy."[47]

Cuckolded Husbands

Men whose wives engaged in sexual and romantic relationships, in violation of the marriage contract, were emasculated in still other ways. Cheating wives were, of course, in their own right to blame for their infidelity, but implicitly, as a dependent of the husband's, the infidelity reflected on the husband as well. Even a man who could position himself as an innocent victim of wifely indiscretion had his authority as husband and head of household held in critical evaluation. Men, as guardians, protectors, and heads of the marital relationship, were expected to develop and guide successful and secure bonds between husband and wife. In the absence of a companionate marriage, husbands were, at a minimum, expected to maintain the respect of wives and of men in the community. A violation of a man's marriage was not only, then, the fault of his wife or her lover. Blame for her actions also lay on his shoulders.

The vast majority of male petitioners seeking divorces charged adultery, but slightly fewer women did so. This is undoubtedly because the courts responded more warmly to charges of adultery lodged by men than to those lodged by women. Of male petitioners, fully half succeeded in making adultery the sole reason for their divorce.[48]

Given their social and cultural authority, men were viewed as the proper initiators of sex. Massachusetts law, for example, defined adultery as occurring when "any man be found in Bed with another mans wife." The act, therefore, made the man who committed adultery the active party and the cuckolded husband the unmanly victim. Language used in divorce records exemplifies this emphasis on men as instigators. Consider, for example, the case of Hagar, a black servant whose husband, Boston, accused her of adultery. The two were married in 1731, but ten years later they appeared in court: Boston was seeking a divorce. He claimed that she, "*being Instigated* [my emphasis] by a White Man," was guilty of adultery. Likewise, Joseph Brown claimed that things were fine with his wife, whom he had married in 1726, until Thomas Clarke "Seduced her and gained her Affections from him" in 1733. Other cases use similar language, language that indicates that the crime against the husband was committed less by his wife than by another man.[49]

Given the racialization of monogamy, men filed charges when slander-
ous talk involved the sexual misconduct of their wives with men of color.
Thus, David and Abigail Marble, a white couple, filed charges against
widow Elizabeth Dwelly, accusing her of stating that "David Marbles wife
...was a poor Negro whore and danced with Joshua Jemmy...a Moletto
man." The tale of interracial sex earned Abigail the epithet "poor Negro
whore"—a potent slur that attached both racial and status insults to the depiction of her sexual immorality. This story impugned not only Abigail's
morality but also offended David's honor and authority as head of household. Unrepudiated, it indicated his loss of mastery and was doubly shameful because the cuckolding was at the hands of a nonwhite.[50]

Given the Protestant hegemony in Massachusetts, Shakers, a small minority in late eighteenth-century Massachusetts, could fall under disrepute
similar to that which was generally reserved for nonwhites. A 1781 article in
the *Independent Chronicle* focused on a woman who had committed adultery
and used the tale to cast derision on all Shakers. "From several parts of the
country, we are informed of the extraordinary behaviour of a number of
people, who appear to be actuated by a kind of religious frenzy," began the
article. "They are commonly called SHAKERS," explained the author before continuing with a particular emphasis on their sexual immorality. "We
are told that at the Superior Court holden at Northampton last week, two
persons of this sect were indicted for Adultery, to which they both plead
guilty." "They are to sit on the gallows, receive a number of stripes each,
and to wear the letter A on their outer-garments." Having carefully re-
hearsed the details of the conviction, the newspaper notice continued with
specific details that focused on their particular transgressions from Christian teachings. "It is said the woman, conceiving her husband to be an UN-
HOLY man, thought she ought not to cohabit with him, or suffer him to
partake of those conjugal pleasures which were his right only to enjoy; but
threw herself into the arms and embraces of one of the Brotherhood, who
was, as she supposed, more righteous, and 'tis said is pregnant by him. It
is hoped these disturbers of the peace will all be properly taken care of."
Thus, this newspaper notice not only reported on the court actions but included the somewhat unusual full explanation of what had caused the
woman to commit adultery, her unusual opinion of what was "holy," and
what constituted the sexual and romantic obligations of husband and wife.
The author of this newspaper notice linked the image of the disordered
household, whereby a male head had been violated not only by his wife but
by her sexual partner, to all Shakers by focusing on their disturbance to

communal norms, calling them "disturbers of the peace" and by calling for "all" to be summarily dealt with.[51]

When adultery committed by women was connected to other issues, it served to reinforce a larger message about the depravity of the individuals of that household and, implicitly, the husband's failure to secure order. Interracial adultery, in particular, signaled disorder. A notice from New London in 1771 described disastrous cases. One case was of Zebulon Potter, "a Molatto" who was convicted of "Adultery with a White Woman, and was sentenced to be whipt 20 Lashes, to be branded with the Letter A on his Forehead." "The Woman, a few Months since, in Consequence of the Amour, was delivered of a Mohogany Coloured Child." The woman awaited trial in jail, and "Her Husband has procured a Bill of Divorce."[52]

During the Revolutionary War, lengthy periods in which husbands were away from home and wives were uncertain about their whereabouts apparently created doubt in some wives' minds about their obligation to their wedding vows. Squire Baker, like many men who left their wives for an extended period, portrayed himself to the courts as the victim of a wife who had been unfaithful to him while he carried out his patriotic duty. A laborer from Marblehead, Baker had enlisted in the service of the United States under the command of General Glover and remained absent for the duration of the war, "having never until the present time had any communication with his said wife." Having no word from her husband for four years, Dorcas gave birth to a child and then, one year later, eloped and abandoned the house. According to his testimony, Squire (like some other men of his day), "returning from long & painful services in the Cause of his Country, finds his domestic happiness thus destroyed & his affairs ruined." That his wife had violated their marital contract while he was fulfilling his manly obligation to protect and defend his country further underscored his victimization and left no doubt that the disorder was not entirely his fault.[53]

Given the cultural interest in companionate unions, adultery was not, however, simply about one man disrupting another man's mastery over his dependents; nor was it simply about "threatening the legitimacy of his children." A story appearing in the *Boston Evening Post* about a man's travels and multiple marriages included the following account of betrayed love: "we lived together in a Cottage with great Quiet, Industry, and Content; till my Landlord, who was a Man of Quality, debauched my Wife, which had almost broke my Heart. This Sting and Disgrace having thrown me into a violent Melancholy, I was in a declining Condition." The focus here was not only on humiliation at the hands of another man, but even more so on his misery at his wife's betrayal of their emotional bond. Thus, the debauchery of his wife "broke" his "Heart." To traditional bases for adultery prosecutions—protecting patriarchal bloodlines and avenging the insult to male patriarchal authority—and to the theme of social humiliation, we can add the emotional injury of a broken heart. Divorce cases such as these suggest that adultery was in part a betrayal of the ideal of husband and wife as love partners. As we have already seen, Joseph Brown claimed that he and his wife, whom he had married in 1726, were happy until 1733, when Thomas Clarke "Seduced her and gained her Affections from him." In his petition, he complained that his wife's "love and affections have been long since withdrawn from the Petitioner and fixed on the Said Clarke."[54]

When printer and merchant Isaiah Thomas petitioned for divorce from his wife of seven years, he emphasized the loss of love and happiness between the two, given her affair. According to his bill of divorcement, "his said Wife was not only destitute of that affection and regard for him which is necessary to render a State of Matrimony easy & happy but that she had not even that Confidence in him without which by a mind not strictly virtuous the Marriage Covenant could not be preserved inviolate." Mary Thomas and her lover, Major Thompson, made no effort to conceal their relationship. The divorce records indicate that she insisted on taking a trip with Thompson against Isaiah's wishes, and on their trip they were seen in compromising positions by no fewer than five people—in as many locations. Thomas was granted his divorce.[55]

Whether committed by the husband or the wife, infidelity ultimately signaled the failure of the husband to create and maintain an orderly, stable, and monogamous household. When husbands sought sexual relationships outside their marriages, they exhibited a lack of manly self-control. When wives engaged in extramarital relations, their betrayal challenged a man's position as head of household and showed him humiliated by her disrespect. His reputation would also have been challenged by the man with whom his wife had had the affair. In divorce testimony, both men and women not only complained of the disruption to household order that adultery caused but also used the language of lost love to express the emotional toll that was exacted.

Early Americans who focused on the important role that sex played in establishing household order recognized that sex could also threaten stability. Throughout the eighteenth century, men who destabilized their households through sexual transgressions injured their social standing but also, symbolically, the larger social order, which was built upon a collection of orderly families. Part II closely examines social order and community and the importance of sex for men and manhood in the general context of community relations.

II ⤙ *Community*

CHAPTER 3

Rape and Seduction

Masculinity, Misogyny, and Male Sexuality

M OST MEN READING THE *Boston Chronicle* would have smiled at the notice printed in the paper on Monday, December 21, 1767. Under the heading "Important and Humorous Intelligence Just Imported" was a notice from London that typifies the culture's fascination with sex and power. In black and white the author of the notice quipped: "A foreigner is taken up for ravishing a lady of distinction with his fiddle-stick. His trial comes on next concert night." The story captured the schizophrenic nature of discussions about sex between men and women. Its humor relied on ambiguity. In eighteenth-century Massachusetts, the language of rape and ravishment was fraught with ambiguity and double meaning. To be "ravished" was to be criminally raped. Courts and commentators alike used "ravishment" and "rape" interchangeably. At the same time, sexual passion that was intensely pleasurable was said to be a form of ravishment: to be ravished was to enjoy pleasures at a heightened level. The term also had spiritual connotations. Christian worship drew on a sense of an eroticized spiritual bond with Christ, and pious Christians frequently employed the term "ravishment" to describe the intense experience of oneness with Christ. Thus, in the language of the time, the idealized sexual male would ravish his wife and enjoy being ravished by Christ. The "ravishing" in this story, then, could be read as rape, and the trial as a court action. Or the "ravishing" may have been an intensely pleasurable moment, and the trial, a test of the foreigner's prowess, his ability to please her again at their next tryst. For the author, it didn't much matter how the reader interpreted the story. Sex was funny at the same time that it was threatening. In either scenario, the fiddler's masculinity was on display.[1]

———

In eighteenth-century Massachusetts, men who raped women appeared before the courts infrequently. Rape and sexual assault, however, came to the attention of men and women in a variety of settings. Men could be associated with rape and sexual assault not only as seducers and sexual aggressors but also as community members, as husbands and kin of victims, and as jurors and witnesses in cases about sex crimes. As readers, they also came across rape and seduction narratives in various print media, and as editors and commentators, they wrote and reprinted such narratives themselves. Women, too, were not only victims but also witnesses of sexual crimes and readers of rape and seduction narratives. In these various contexts, men and women articulated standards of normative sexual desire, delineated gender ideals, and probed the limits of legitimate male authority.

Most court cases involved defendants who lived in the same town as their victims, and the primary concern of the courts, the parties to these cases, and those who testified in them was the disruptive impact of violent and coercive sexual behavior on communities, household order, and the authority of male household heads. As gendered sex crimes, rape and sexual assault also branded their male perpetrators as "barbarous" brutes and offended social hierarchies among men. Newspaper accounts of rape cases amplified these concerns over the disruption of male social hierarchies and masculine order by accenting crimes involving lower-status men and non-whites, strangers, and extreme violence. Narratives of rape and seduction in court cases, newspapers, and imported English literature also reveal apparent paradoxes of sex and gender. In eighteenth-century Massachusetts, people viewed women as both submissive and sexually threatening and men as dominant yet vulnerable. These seemingly contradictory views informed conceptualizations of seduction and rape and reveal tensions over masculine and feminine sexual comportment.[2]

Coerced Sex and Masculine Social Order

Rape was a gendered sexual offense. The 1699 statute defined "Ravishment or Rape" as sexual intercourse committed by a man on a woman "against her will," or sexual intercourse committed by a man against a girl under the age of ten. The act read:

> If any man shall Ravish any Woman committing Carnal Copulation with her by Force against her will. Or if any man shall unlawfully and carnally know and abuse any Woman Child under the age of Ten Years,

every person and persons offending in either of the cases before mentioned, being thereof convicted, shall be accounted Felons, and shall be adjudged to suffer the pains of Death as in cases of Felony.

Thus, rape was defined in gendered terms, not simply as forced sex; there was no provision for same-sex rape; nor was there a provision for the rape of men. Advice literature also defined rape as an act against a woman's will. "Rape or Ravishment," wrote Gouge in his *Young Man's Guide*, "is a violent deflouring [of] a Woman who never consented thereunto."[3]

Between 1698 and 1797 forty-three indictments of rape or attempted rape were heard by the Superior Court of Judicature (renamed the Supreme Judicial Court in 1780). Twenty-four of the accused men were found guilty of attempted rape (one man was tried in two different cases), five were found guilty of rape itself, thirteen were acquitted, and one resulted in no presentment. That twenty-four men were convicted of the lesser, noncapital crime of attempted rape suggests both the barriers to proving that a rape had occurred and the reluctance of all-male juries to impose the death penalty. At the same time, they did not want the defendants to go unpunished: men convicted of attempted rape were punished with fines and whipping.[4]

Given that rape was a capital crime, conviction required two witnesses to the fact of penetration, an almost insurmountable evidentiary barrier. Moreover, if the victim was not a minor, independent proof of "Force" was usually required to back up the victim's claim that she had not consented; her word was almost never enough. To compound the barriers to conviction, force was defined as physical brutality, not emotional or structural power.

Rape was a crime between men as well as a crime against a woman. Symbolically it was less an affront to womanhood than an assault on male household authority: a court case involving a rape charge was an insult to the father or husband of the victim. His authority as head of household was undermined regardless of the outcome: an acquittal would point to his failure to regulate his wife's or daughter's sexuality; a conviction would signify another man's affront to his household authority.

Given this broad understanding of rape as a crime between men, newspaper depictions ridiculed women who attempted to restore social order in the wake of rape. In 1758, for example, the *Boston Evening Post* published the following story from The Hague:

On Wednesday noon a married man, who has a wife and five small children, stood on the pillory at the end of Dyot-street, Broad St. Giles's, for assaulting a girl about ten years of age, with an intent to ravish her.

Several hundreds of the female sex in that part of the town, who are of the Amazonian kind, assembled near the the [sic] pillory, and, notwithstanding all the peace of officers could do to prevent it, they treated the poor wretch so inhumanly, by cutting and mangling him, that it is said he is since dead of the wounds; but some of those gentry are like to pay dear for their sport, several of them having been since taken into custody.

Here the newspaper depicts the man as nearly martyred, despite his evident guilt for the attempted rape of a child. Rather than describing him as a social outcast, the newspaper emphasized his respectability, pointing out that he was a "married man who has a wife and five small children," and thus made him into a surprisingly sympathetic figure. Indeed, the paper bracketed his guilt to focus on his female attackers, who overstepped traditional gender bounds by avenging the rape.[5]

In Massachusetts when some men sued to protect the reputation of their wives, their own reputation was at stake too. In many ways the conflict lay between to the two men involved. In an example of a husband suing to punish his wife's attacker, it is clear that the husband feels personally wronged by the attack. Thus, although men often approached the courts on behalf of female dependents, in these cases husbands approached for their own purposes too. In June 1763, at a Superior Court of Judicature session held at York, Maine, Peter Staple, a gentleman from Kittery, sued Thomas Hammet, a Berwick yeoman, appealing the judgment of the court session the previous October. At that session a jury had convicted him on a plea of trespass where the charge was that on August 20, 1761, he, "with force and Arms[,] made an Assault on Abigail the wife of the plaint: and her ravished, lay with and carnally knew, and from the house of the plaint: took with him whereby the plaint lost and was depriv'd of the company and comfort of his Wife." Staple complained that from the date of that first attack, "the said Thomas did often take with him" his wife, "whereby the plaint lost the comfort and company of his said Wife and her affections were thereby alienated from him." An inferior court ruled that Thomas should recover 1,000 pounds in damages, but after being heard by a jury, the award was reduced to the still substantial amount of 450 pounds. The damages were awarded despite testimony that the relationship was consensual.[6]

When men accused of rape were well known to their victims and their neighbors and were securely attached to their community as householders, the focus was on the crime's disruption of male social order. Take a 1698 case involving the rape of Mary Hawthorne, a married woman. A deposition from Bethia Halloway, "of full age," stated that the accused, Moses Hudson, a husbandman from Lynn, was "oftin" at the house of Nathaniel, also husbandman, and Mary Hawthorne. She said that ten days after the alleged attack, Mary confronted Moses in her own house: "Mary Hawthorne Said to Moses Hudson now you wretch so what you have brought on your Selfe and Said Hudson Replyed & Said I did not think you would have told your husband & Mary Hawthorne answred you know that I told you I would if Ever I lived to See my husband." After the rape, Mary apparently immediately went to her husband, and during the assault itself, Mary invoked her husband as her protector, not the local authorities. Nathaniel was the party that Moses would have to face first.[7]

Moses Hudson, for his part, also viewed his offense as one primarily against Mary's husband. Witness Bethia Halloway described a discussion between Hudson and Mary's husband, Nathaniel, some days after the attack in which Hudson asked Nathaniel to forgo pressing charges. According to Halloway, Mary's husband lashed out at Hudson, calling him a "vile man for abusing his wife." Hudson replied that "he could not blame him for being angry with him for what he had done," but pleaded, "if you make complaint against me I shall loose my life." Hudson continued, saying to Nathaniel that if he "would not complaine of him," Hudson would "make it up & he would never do so againe so long as he lived." He also said by way of explanation and excuse that he "had no Ill thoughts" toward Mary, but when "he Saw her" "god had left him." Thus, Moses approached the husband knowing that he had wronged him. Suggesting that he was helpless and in a condition of original sin, he implied that he did not deliberately insult Nathaniel. He certainly considered his future to be in the hands of Nathaniel, rather than Mary, and he put himself in the position of a supplicant. Nathaniel was having none of it, and the couple filed charges, seeking legal retribution for the attack. Hudson was acquitted, however, perhaps, as Barbara Lindemann suggests, because his social standing was equal to that of Mary and Nathaniel.[8]

In another case involving neighbors and social equals, the court was similarly unable to reach a guilty verdict. The accused, Thomas Proctor, a mason from Woburn, and his alleged victim, Abigail Kindall, the wife of mason Nathaniel Kindall, apparently knew each other well enough to have spent time alone in the house while Abigail's husband was away. Emphasizing her vulnerability, the charge was that Proctor had come to the Kindalls' house while "no body... [was] with her but four Small Children." In his defense Proctor admitted that he had been at the Kindalls' house "Many times" and that he "might be there in April about the time Spoken of in the

Evening for any thing he Know: for he had occation to Pass by Sd house Every Day to & from his Work." He flatly denied, however, being there after the family "was in bed" or that he had raped Abigail. His social standing and the fact that Abigail concurred that he had sat and smoked at the house that evening might have raised sufficient doubt in jurors' minds about her nonconsent, leading to his acquittal.[9]

Whereas familiarity between married women and their alleged attackers led to acquittals, single women fared better with accusations of attempted rape. Thus in 1754, when housewright James Lindsay defended himself against the charge that he had attempted to rape a local yeoman's adult daughter, he complained that the charge had been "concealed for more than a Year" and that she did not accuse him of rape "untill after the Said Mary by her Own Conviction was begotten with Child" by him. Thus his defense, in part, relied on the fact that Mary had consented to have sex with him in the months following the alleged attack. The jury, however, found him guilty, and the court ordered him to either pay a fine or be whipped.[10]

The majority of cases brought before the Superior Court involved defendants of low social standing. In such cases, rape disrupted the community of respectable men—the affront was to their dignity as a community of patriarchs who should be able to protect their women against harm by servants, transients, and laborers. Rape committed by such men was an attack on the authority of patriarchs as a whole. The case of James Gatton, a laborer from Boston, accused in November of an assault on Sarah Blewill in June 1738, a female child "under ye age of ten," reveals that friends and neighbors acted swiftly to protect children from sexual and physical abuse. In 1738, when William Brown and his brother heard a "child make a noise & Cry out," they investigated and found James Gatton on top of Sarah. When they confronted him, he got up, "Buttoning up his Breeches," and flatly told them he had done "nothing." Having stopped the assault, the two brothers "Secured" Gatton and went to the girl's house to tell her mother what had happened. The Browns did not themselves approach the authorities, viewing it instead as a wrong committed against the Blewills' household. They left it up to them to decide how to pursue justice. Once brought to trial, Gatton was found guilty and whipped.[11]

In the early eighteenth century a disproportionate number of rape cases heard by the Superior Court involved defendants who were black or Indian servants and slaves. Although Indians were not especially closely associated with violent sexuality in the racial discourses of the early eighteenth century, when they were hauled off to court on such charges, racial stereotypes did—according to the few cases available to us—apparently weaken their position as defendants. In 1703 the York County Court of General Sessions tried John Amee, an Indian, for committing "rudeness" and "unchristianlike" behavior against Sarah Tinny, a twenty-three-year-old white woman. One Elizabeth Tyler testified that she was at the house on the day of the attack and overheard Sarah call her attacker an "Indian Dog." Moreover, Tyler stated that when she heard John Amee threaten to "nok" Sarah, she retorted by asking whether he planned to "nok her with a hatchet or hammer." (According to Tyler's testimony, Amee replied that "he would nok her with his Prick.") Thus, Sarah lobbed a racial slur at the man she was defending herself from. Here testimony about Amee's sexual assault played up his ethnicity—the sexual assault was likened to an Indian hatchet attack —the type of imagery that Boston newspapers used regularly.[12]

Rape was especially disruptive when the attacker and victim were strangers and when the attack was very violent. In 1746 a jury found laborer John Bryant guilty of the attempted rape of "Single woman" Rebecca Jackson. Bryant was charged with "Stoping his Handkerchief in her Mouth, locking her into the Chamber of one John Palmen in Middleborough," and "then and there drawing his Cutlash and . . . then and there got upon her and Got out his private parts and would have forceably have had the Carnal knowledge of her body had he not been prevented." Bryant's violence was compounded by what the court considered abduction. In this case, the jury did convict, sentencing Bryant to be whipped twenty-five stripes.[13]

Concern over such cases reveals the perceived disruption of community order by social and cultural outsiders. One such case, resulting in the death penalty, involved one London, a black servant of Boston merchant Peter Lucee, who was convicted of raping Sarah Clarke, a sixteen-year-old girl whom he met while delivering goods. Passing through Roxbury on his way to Dedham, London was asked by a Roxbury resident to give Sarah a ride to Needham. At some point en route, he "carryed her out of the Road into the Woods" and eventually, wielding a "Penknife to affright her," raped her. Boston newspapers, attesting to the public outcry at his crime, carried several notices of his trial and execution. Having escaped by setting fire to the jail (only to be reapprehended), London had a doubly newsworthy execution; indeed two different papers carried news of it on the same day. It was also noted by Benjamin Walker, Junior. Rapes committed by cultural outsiders and transients not only posed a danger to women but signaled the disruptive effects of geographic mobility and of lower-status men when not under the surveillance of patriarchs.[14]

Whereas court cases often involved only a handful of witnesses, newspaper notices and commentaries, through their wide circulation, amplified concerns over the threat that rape posed to masculine social order and to hierarchies of men. Furthermore, newspapers also reprinted reports from other colonies and from abroad— regular reports of sexual crimes originating in London, for example. Since for New Englanders London already signified the increased mobility and urban vice associated with imperial commerce and culture, these reports of sexual depravity abroad underscored especially well the need for vigilance. New England patriarchs had to redouble their efforts to maintain order in the face of economic and urban development.

Newspapers were not especially interested in rapes committed by neighbors. They were, however, much more likely to focus on rapes committed by strangers and/or ethnic outsiders than on rapes committed by householders and neighbors. Newspaper accounts reflected the local understanding that sexual assaults by one man on another man's household dependent disrupted domestic order and social relations among men. Thus, many newspaper notices mentioned cases in which restitution had to be directed at the male guardian whose honor had been affected. Consider, for example, the following 1773 news item in the *Essex Gazette*: "We hear from Winthrop, on Kennebec River, that a Rape was lately committed there by a married Man, on the Body of a Girl of 13 Years of Age.—We further hear that the Affair was compromised by the Offender's paying, to the Father of the Girl, the *immense* Sum of Two Hundred Pounds." Rapes were often presented as violations of a man's honor. One story from Philadelphia about a farmer "coming to market in a wagon" with his wife and daughter highlighted that "two fellows" stopped them. "One of whom putting a pistol to the farmer's breast, obliged him to be a quiet witness of the most brutal violation of his wife by the other villain."[15]

Usually these depictions involved violent assaults. One brief notice appearing in the *Boston Evening Post* in 1736 is typical of the shorter accounts: "Last Week a seafaring Man was whipped Ten Stripes at the publick Whipping Post in this Town, for beating and abusing a Woman in a very barbarous manner at Malden, because she refused his unlawful Embraces." Given the violent nature of the attack, this was an unambiguous case of male culpability and female innocence. The rapist's identity as "a seafaring Man" stressed his transience, and the article also emphasized the woman's resistance to his violent attack. We should note that the term "barbarous" was often used to describe violent attackers and their acts. Such men were uncivil outsiders.[16]

When reprinting news items or apocryphal stories of rape from abroad, newspapers also sensationalized their accounts by focusing on the accompanying violence and bodily injury. Consider, for example, a letter from Chester, England, printed in the *Boston Evening Post* in November 1750: "Daniel King, a Quaker, was convicted of assaulting a Girl of four Years of Age, with an Intent to ravish her. It appear'd upon the Evidence, that he had torn open the poor Creature with his Fingers, and most vilely used her." Here the notice drew attention to the violence and brutality of the assault.[17]

In 1733 the *Boston Gazette,* in the same issue, ran two stories from London on an especially brutal sexual assault. The first emphasized the violence of the crime.

A few Days since in the Evening, a young Woman going between Greenwich and Charlton in Kent, was set upon by three Men, who carried her out of the Road and committed a Rape on her Body, and otherwise abused and beat her in such a barbarous manner, that she became almost senseless; they afterwards threw her into a Pond, with an Intent to drown her; she was soon after found & dragg'd out half dead. Two of the Men have been since taken up and secured in the round-house at Greenwich, in order to be examined, as soon as the Woman, who is very ill of blows & bruises she received is able to appear against 'em.

The rape was a violent sexual crime against social order; the accent was on its physical brutality. The narrative of the young woman traveling alone at night highlighted the dangers that geographic mobility and independence posed to youth. As a notice from London, it also may have evoked the corruption associated with commercial and urban development. Like the "seafaring man," these strangers were "barbarous," capable of murder as well as rape. Notice also that the modifier "barbarous" applied to the beating, not the rape itself. The emphasis was on the violence rather than the sexual nature of the crime.[18]

Receiving more information from another source, the printer included on the same page a much longer account of the crime. It began:

The following is a more particular Account of the barbarous Usage the poor Woman met with on the Road to Charlton, than is mentioned in the News Papers, viz. The Woman passing thro But. Lane in this Town, and asking a Man, who overtook her, the Way to Charlton, had for Answer that he was going thither, and would shew her the Way; and soon

> after joining two of his Companions, they all went together, and carried her into a Gardener's Garden, upon this the Woman said that this could not be the right Way; where-upon they threw her down, and used her in a most indecent Manner.

This part of the second account focuses on the deceitful behavior of these strangers. From there the account takes a shocking turn, emphasizing the sexual violence and perversity of the crime.

> The poor Creature, after many Struggles getting up again, and begging for Mercy, they knock'd her down with a Club, and then, with their Hands, they tore her Privy Parts in a terrible Manner, which done they stuff'd her with Horse Dung, and afterwards threw her into a Pond near the Place, where she lay senseless till pull'd out by a Butcher who came that Way.

Underscoring the brutality of the attack, the grisly details stand out with almost pornographic clarity. Here the emphasis was on the degradation of the raped woman's body as well as the insensible brutality of the men who ignored her pleas for mercy.

As the appearance of the local butcher suggests, the article then focused on the townspeople, praising them for providing the victim a place to recuperate from the attack. The emphasis was now on the importance of restoring social order. While the woman was recuperating at a "Workhouse" in town, the "parish called a Vestry, and unanimously agreed to prosecute the Offender or Offenders when taken, at their own Expence." The article concluded: "'Tis hoped the Example of this Parish will be followed by others, wherever such Barbarities shall happen." The author did not explicitly voice the usual lamentation about society gone awry and the moral dangers of urban life. The phrase "wherever such Barbarities shall happen" implies, though, that such violent events, though deplorable, were a predictable feature of contemporary life.[19]

Of course, this newspaper's notice, like others, was long on lurid details and short on the crime's moral lesson. In a courtroom, a careful recitation of details was a necessary element for showing proof of coercion and nonconsent in a rape trial, but the violence and the sensational details in these newspaper accounts support Cornelia Dayton's observation that printers in eighteenth-century New England increasingly included items of "the maiming or dismembering of women's bodies" in order to provide more (misogynist) entertainment for their "urban, commercial, elite readers."

Here the restoration of communal order and the reader's satisfaction in wrongs redressed are accomplished via the reenactment of the woman's degradation.[20]

In the Revolutionary era, shifting social contexts breathed new life into the older gendered meanings of rape and sexual assault I discussed so far. Nearly all of the notices of rape and sexual assault appearing in Massachusetts newspapers from 1765 to 1783 mentioned soldiers as the perpetrators. Accounts of rape and sexual assault underscored the depravity of British and Hessian men in contradistinction to virtuous American manhood. For three months in a row, the *Essex Gazette* ran stories of sexual assault committed by soldiers, illustrating the threat that unbridled male sexuality posed to women and social order in general. In June 1769, the paper carried two notices about soldiers who attempted sexually to assault women in Boston. One detailed an attempted rape against an "aged Woman" in the north part of Boston. The other described an attempted assault made by several soldiers against "two married Women." Both accounts underscored the violent threat to America's honor that British troops posed and used sexual assault to symbolize the political violation. The articles were introduced by a condemnation of the practice of quartering troops for the reason that it results in "Instances" of "Debaucheries and consequent Violences." The following month an account highlighted the symbolic nature of the sexual assault when it described in detail how a "gentleman" nearby attempted to rescue an innocent woman and how the scene degenerated into a near riot once neighbors faced off against other soldiers, who drew "Bayonets," threatening to place the crowd in "Barracks."[21]

During the war accounts repeatedly focused on the sexual degeneracy of British and Hessian troops, most often through stories of rapes. In early 1777 the *Continental Journal* carried several such notices. One described an attempted rape by a Hessian officer in Woodbridge, New Jersey. Another described how three women fled to the American army at the Jersey shore after they had all been "very much abused." One of the articles described the loss of Elizabeth Town in New Jersey and the fact that "Husbands and Fathers being oblig'd to be witnesses of the lustful Brute ravishing the dear object of their affections before their eyes." To underscore the depravity, the notice ended by stating that the youngest girl, "about 15, had been ravished that Morning by a British Officer." That the notices reported on the actions of officers, rather than undisciplined subordinates, further underscored the deviant sexual nature of the enemy.[22]

Occasionally the threat of sexual assault was implicit. The above articles, for example, were followed by an ominously toned report about sixteen women who had been captured by the "cruel Enemy" and "brought down into the *British* Camp, where they have been kept ever since." By following on the heels of stories about rape, the report had clear implications here. Such stories focused on the manly contest between troops, with women and children serving as symbols of control and power. In the same vein, another notice described how General William Howe "ordered all the male inhabitants of Long Island capable of bearing arms, immediately to repair to New-York, to reinforce the British army," thereby leaving the "women and children" to the "ravages of the troops left for the defence of the island." Such notices fueled the war effort by portraying the cause as one of defending female dependents against sexual assaults. These notices used sex as a symbol of assault. But they also used the issue of sexual assault to motivate the patriotic cause by playing to men's sense of honor and duty.[23]

A poem published in the *Independent Chronicle* in 1777 captured the sentiment of American virtue in the face of Hessian "wickedness and brutality."

> Our groaning country bleeds at every vein;
> New murders, rapes, fell massacres prevail,
> And desolation covers all the land!
> Who can hear this, and not with patriot zeal,
> Nobly step forth, to guard their wives and children!
> And sheath a dagger in the villain's heart
> Who'd rob us of our peace, our all, our honour!

For this author, masculine "honour" depended on the ability of patriots to "guard their wives and children." The attacks against dependents, including rapes, were attacks against the "country." The rapes were symbolic as much as actual. Paul Revere, writing to a French cousin late in the Revolutionary War, explained that one of the reasons for the break with England was Britain's use of gross force. "They have Ravished our wifes and daughters," wrote Revere.[24]

Court records, newspaper notices, and other print literature presented violent sexual assault as a crime against the masculine social order. As the following section shows, rape and seduction narratives in both print literature and court cases were also fertile ground for exploring competing, often contradictory norms of masculine and feminine sexual comportment.

Predators and Victims:
Paradoxical Representations of
Masculinity and Femininity in
Narratives of Rape and Seduction

Eighteenth-century normative masculinity was predicated on control and self-mastery. Rape and ravishment, as crimes of violent sexual disorder, stood in opposition to ideals of male authority and power properly harnessed. Young people in particular were believed to be prone to committing sexual assaults given that they had not yet learned the appropriate degree of self-restraint. *The Young Man's Guide* by Thomas Gouge, published in Boston in 1742, outlined many of the sins of "Wantonness and Uncleanness." Gouge listed rape and incest along with fornication, adultery, and polygamy as examples. By including rape with formally noncoercive sexual sins such as fornication and adultery, Gouge underscored that male mastery over sexual passion was of primary importance. Gouge framed rape, like other sexual sins, as particularly addictive: the failure to master one's desires leads step by step to excessive indulgence. Newspapers sometimes echoed the idea that rape and ravishment were crimes "fir'd by extreme Lust," produced by unleashed "libidinous Faculties."[25]

Early novels used rape and seduction to highlight the importance of moral autonomy and sexual restraint. Beginning in the 1740s, novels such as Samuel Richardson's *Pamela* and *Clarissa* were as popular on this side of the Atlantic as they were in London. *Pamela*, for example, one of the most widely read English novels of the eighteenth century, appeared in bookshops in early America almost immediately after being published in London in 1741, and by 1744 it had been published in Philadelphia, New York, and Boston. *Clarissa*, also a bestseller in colonial America, is perhaps the best-known eighteenth-century novel to center on rape.[26]

These seduction novels contained powerful critiques of patriarchal authority and also emphasized female responsibility. Historian Richard Godbeer describes the shift that occurred at the end of the eighteenth century whereby men increasingly took advantage of a loosening of parental control over courtship and shirked their responsibilities when lovers whom they did not intend to marry became pregnant. Print culture was rife with cautionary tales of women who had allowed themselves to become pregnant while believing the sweet talk of marriage intentions. One such story appeared in the *Independent Chronicle* and *Hampshire Gazette* in 1787 and described the sad tale of a young woman from Petersburg, Virginia. Seduced and pregnant, her lover had "refused to marry her." "Abandoned by her friends" and full of "shame" and "melancholy," "with her penknife [she] stabbed herself to the heart." Consider also the news carried in the *Salem Mercury* on July 29, 1788, that reported on the now famous case of Elizabeth Whitman, who died at a tavern in Danvers. She also had been duped by her suitor. She became pregnant and later died of fever. The story became immortalized in Hannah Foster's novel *The Coquette*. These stories cautioned women to protect their virtue and drew on an older model of male sexuality that was depicted as threatening and powerful. Although the dominant moral lesson for women was to be responsible, they did carry the message that men ruined themselves as well. Sanford, the responsible male party, at the end of *The Coquette* is a ruined man, financially and emotionally, and his reputation is in tatters. His wife has left him, and as the victim's female friend declares at the end, "poverty and disgrace await him!"[27]

As an antiaristocratic moral reformer, Richardson touted the ideal of moral self-governance for men and women and embraced new freedoms in courtship, but he also warned of their dangers when self-mastery failed. His rakes, especially the infamous Lovelace, but also Mr. B, Pamela's suitor, perfectly illustrate the destructive consequences of capitulation to "extreme Lust." As a man incapable of self-mastery, the rake and eventual rapist Lovelace is ruined by his own lack of emotional and sexual self-control. Lovelace, though initially plotting a mere dalliance with Clarissa, finds that he is captivated by her. In a letter to his friend, he portrays himself self-pityingly as a victim of his own desires: "She'll live to bury me; I see that: for; by my soul, I can neither eat, drink, nor sleep, nor what's still worse, love any woman in the world but her." Knowing that he will not succeed in seducing her, Lovelace balks at the task of self-mastery and contemplates rape. As he explains in a letter to his rake friend: "Oh Jack! what a difficulty must a man be allowed to have, to conquer a predominant passion, be it what it will, when the gratifying of it is in his power, however wrong he knows it to be to resolve to gratify it!" In one of his letters to his friend John, Lovelace includes a poem that takes the view that masculine sexuality was predicated on dominance and aggression.

> 'Tis nobler like a lion to invade
> When appetite directs, and seize my prey,
> Than to wait tamely, like a begging dog,
> Till dull consent throws out the scraps of love.

Here sexual aggression is "nobler" than waiting for "dull consent": seduction becomes rape. For Lovelace, manhood would be compromised if he were to "wait tamely," "begging" for intimacy. Here also, sexual desire ("appetite") is the ultimate arbiter of when and where to act, a sure sign that Lovelace is a brutish creature of appetite. Conversely, Mr. B, Pamela's seducer, at one point highlights his putative self-control in an effort to win her over: "Had I been utterly given up to my passions, I should before now have gratified them, and not have shown that remorse and compassion for you, which have reprieved you, more than once, when absolutely in my power." Expecting to be rewarded for not acting the part of the rapist, Mr. B tries to excuse his repeated attempts at seduction and to position himself as not so far removed after all from the ideal of masculine self-mastery. Of course, Richardson did not expect his readers to take Mr. B's self-congratulatory view of his own self-restraint seriously.[28]

Court testimony also reveals an emphasis on rape as failed self-mastery. Thus, when Moses Hudson pleaded with Nathaniel Hawthorne not to file charges for the rape of Nathaniel's wife, Mary, he explained his heinous actions as the result of failed self-control, stating he "had no Ill thoughts," but that when he "Saw her" he had been unable to control himself: "god had left him." A witness in the same case also portrayed that attack as a lack of self-mastery. She told the court that Mary said the attack resulted from the "Rage of his lust."[29]

Slander cases point to a positive evaluation of sexual control as a hallmark of normative masculinity. Two such cases heard in Plymouth County between 1700 and 1765 involved charges of coerced sex. In both, one man sued to save his reputation. For example, when husbandman David Orcut began "spreading" rumors that Nathaniel Hooper, a mason, had "breached" a virgin "girl," Hooper's first defense was that he had an excellent reputation for moral behavior in the domain of sex: he attributed his "good Esteem and Credit among his Majesties and Leige Subjects" to his living a life "unspoled [*sic*] from the Crimes of Adultery, fornication and all acts of unchastity Towards the female Sex." He portrayed himself as a model man in Thomas Gouge's sense: one who has been capable of lifelong restraint. This reputation would, of course, be utterly destroyed if he did not rebut the rumor that, he said, had already "brought him into disgrace and Contempt among all his Majesties good Subjects." Hooper also complained that the circulation of the story had made his "life uncomfortable with his wife and family," and thus sought vindication through court action. In the second case, the tanner George Asken sued widow Mary Richards in 1764 for one hundred pounds for "uttering" "false and scandalous words" that he had exposed himself and offered her money for sex.

On two separate occasions, Asken complained, Richards had "publicly said 'that the plant. [plaintiff] Took out a Johannes [coin] inn one hand and pulled out his Secret parts and held them naked in his other hand and offered to give her that Johannes if she would let the plant. [plaintiff] Have the Carnal Knowledge of her Body." Asken contended that he "had a fair prospect of a reputable advancement in the World" and that the statements were intended to "render him forever infamous... and to render him odious and miserable for life." The jury appeared to agree and awarded him twenty-five shillings and costs.[30]

Men who failed to master their own desires paid a certain price. Newspaper accounts of men who suffered for their actions could serve as moral lessons offering a broader teaching on the importance of male virtue. Consider, for example, an account from Newbern, North Carolina, published in the *Essex Gazette* in 1769, about a young woman who was courted by an insincere "gentleman" who had proposed marriage but was unwilling to go public. She trusted him and continued the relationship, finally giving birth to their child out of wedlock. He, as a "man of pleasure," began to deny the child was his and one night went to her house with the "avowed intention of using her ill." "Thinking himself able to subdue her to his will, as heretofore, boldly entered the house, by breaking open the door," despite her threat to shoot him if he did so. She, true to her word, "shot one of his arms off," mortally wounding him. Thus, the article opined, he fell "victim to female vengeance, which he had justly provoked." The article concluded: *"A sad warning to these plunderers of female honour!"* Other articles also carried graphic depictions of female vengeance such as the following: "The bargirl at an inn on the Cambridge road [London], being pregnant by a Squire in the neighbourhood, after assuring him of her condition, and he showing more than indifference, she pulled out a pair of small-pointed scissars, and stabbed him to the heart." In all such cases the bodily harm that men suffered by getting themselves into dangerous situations served as a symbol of the loss of masculine honor and self-control.[31]

Paradoxically, at the same time that men were to control and restrain their passions, idealized masculine sexuality was informed by a dominant, aggressive model of male authority. Consider again Lovelace's self-serving lines that "'tis nobler like a lion to invade" than to wait "tamely, like a begging dog." He even declares that women "are born to be controlled," that they love rakes because rakes "know how to direct their uncertain wills, and manage them," and that "a tyrant-husband makes a dutiful wife." Here Richardson's rake is a mouthpiece for views of masculinity that the author condemns but finds it necessary to embody for the sake of female readers who need to be put on their guard.[32]

Court records suggest that a notion of masculine pride in sexual conquest was at work among some of the accused. On April 3, 1729, Thomas Proctor entered Abigail Kindall's house when her husband was away and "ravished her," "committing carnal copulation with her against her will." After the attack, Proctor "told her he believed he had gott her With Child & Went away & Left her." Folklore and popular belief still generally held that a woman required orgasm to conceive. Thus, Proctor's statement expressed pride in his virility, in his reproductive and sexual capabilities. He also self-servingly assumed that her initial wishes had no bearing on his capacity to give pleasure. Likewise, John Bryant, who, in a case we have already seen, brandished a "cutlass," exclaimed to his victim "by God he would Get a Bastard." These men expressed notions of masculinity that relied on sexual supremacy and the wholly one-sided ability to impregnate. Paradoxically, they believed they could forcibly give pleasure. The court ordered Bryant to be whipped twenty-five stripes "at the Corner of Some of the Most publick Streets in Plimouth." Proctor, however, received no punishment, as the plaintiff was unable to prove lack of consent.[33]

Operating alongside the idea that men were expected to exhibit strength and authority in sexual matters was the long-standing view of women as lustful and seductive. Carol Karlsen and Laurel Ulrich have found that the idea that women were actually the more passionate sex was still prominent in the early eighteenth century. Women were still seductive "Eves"; only gradually did Eves become virtuous Pamelas, capable of preserving their moral virtue and modulating their own (in any case more temperate) passions. Although this view of women's hypersexuality was not the only one available to New Englanders, it was the basis for most misogynist writing in the eighteenth century. As Kenneth Lockridge and others have suggested, such writing was suffused with the idea that a "combination of female lust and cleverness" was a "deadly power that women wield over feeble men."[34]

As Richardson knew, the male seducer was likely to take a dim view of those he preyed upon. Despite their virtue and their resourcefulness, their would-be seducers call both Pamela and Clarissa "charmers" and say they are unfeeling women who hold great power over them. Pamela's seducer, for example, exclaims, "I believe this little slut has the power of witchcraft, if ever there was a witch; for she enchants all that come near her." He also describes women as the "cunning sex." When his advances are rejected by Clarissa, Lovelace, who once again seeks to excuse his own machinations, uses tired old stereotypes to stigmatize Clarissa, calling her an "arrogant creature, revengeful, artful, enterprising, and one who, had she been a man, would have sworn and cursed, and committed rapes, and played the devil."[35]

Given that in the older view women had to negotiate contradictory ends —their immoderate sexual desires and their socially circumscribed roles— women were also expected to manipulate and deceive. Medical manuals and popular literature certainly promulgated this idea in the early 1700s (in part because many were reprints of books first published in the seventeenth century). *Aristotle's Masterpiece,* for example, contained the following tidbit: a woman could literally imprint the visage of her husband on a child conceived with another man by imagining her husband's face at the time of conception and thus could conceal her infidelities. In this view, women retained considerable power over fertility and sex, powers threatening to the very men who were assigned the responsibility for governing and guiding potentially disruptive women.[36]

Given such sentiments, the female rake occasionally appeared in publications circulating in Massachusetts. In 1732 a series of extended excerpts from George Lillo's London play *The London Merchant; or, The History of George Barnwell* were reprinted in the *New England Weekly Journal*. They appeared in fifteen pages of newsprint, occupying nearly all of the issues of the *Journal* from February 14 to March 6, 1732. The play had been published just one year earlier in London, and its appearance in the *Journal* indicates that the provincial Boston publication managed to be quite up-to-date. The *Journal*'s printers believed the play to be worthy of a place in their readers' personal libraries and suggested that readers "stitch" the set of papers together.[37]

The female rake in the play, Millwood, manages to manipulate the eponymous character, George Barnwell, into killing his uncle to steal money for her. Her power is clear. Barnwell laments: "Without Money Millwood will never see me more, and life is not to be endured without her:—She's got such firm possession of my Heart, and governs there with such despotick sway;—Aye, there's the Cause of all my Sin and Sorrow." In short, Millwood has corrupted the naive and lovesick Barnwell, who is then sentenced to death for the murder. Millwood's justification for her behavior—that it is a form of vengeance for a prior lover's manipulation and abandonment of her—is one standard account of motivation in narratives of male rakes. Millwood's female rake is not a simple gender inversion, however. Not only does she pine away of grief and presumed guilt for her treachery after Barnwell is executed, the vengeful female rake emerges in the end as a figure of righteous retribution called forth by the prior failures of "barbarous" and "flattering" men who routinely seduce and "ruin" women. The following poem, placed at the end of the third installment, appears to have been spoken by Millwood herself and addressed to men generally:

> With cruel Arts you labour to destroy:
> A thousand Ways our Ruin you pursue,
> Yet blame in us those Arts, first taught by you.
> Oh! May, from hence, each violated Maid,
> By flatter'ring, faithless, barb'rous Man betray'd;
> When robb'd of Innocence, and Virgin Fame,
> From your Destruction raise a nobler Name;
> To right their Sex's Wrongs devote their Mind.
> And future Millwoods prove to plague Mankind.

Although the female rake as a stock figure was rare, she represented a lingering belief that women's sexuality and deceitfulness could pose a threat to male sexual mastery. At the same time, she highlighted the ease with which women could be corrupted and even operated as an indictment of male seducers.[38]

Misogynist fear of the power of women appears to have landed some women in court. Thus, in 1759, Anna Donham found herself brought before the Plymouth General Sessions for "having a wicked and diabolical Intent to corrupt and debauch the morals of divers of our good Subjects and to accite them to commit Fornication and adultery." The charge heard by the court was that on several occasions she would "in a wicked and devilish manner Entice and seduce divers of our good subjects, being Young men to the Jurors unknown." Here the charge evoked the image of a sexually threatening witch; it described Donham's actions as "wicked and devilish." The formal complaint continued: she "did freely and voluntarily retire" "into Barns, roadhouses, and other out houses and places of Secresy to the encouraging and promoting of Lewdness, debauchery and uncleanness." Apparently by not resisting male sexual advances ("did freely and voluntarily retire"), Donham could be accused of "encouraging" and even "promoting" "debauchery and uncleanness." Her sexuality was disruptive to both normative courtship practices and established marriages: it incited both "Fornication and adultery." And she committed these transgressions outside the regulating gaze of the moral community in "out houses" and "places of Secresy." The court ordered Anna Donham to pay a fine of twenty shillings and to be publicly whipped ten stripes, but no men were ever indicted. Four years later, now a widow, Donham again was brought before the court. This time, the presentment charged that as her husband was "lying extreme sick and drawing near to death," she at "diverse ... days and nights" again set out to seduce and to "excite" the men of the town "to commit lewdness, Fornication and adultery with her." Once again her sexuality threatened the sexual self-mastery of other men in the community. The citation of her husband's mortal illness suggests that the court attributed her promiscuity in part to the failure of the marriage bed to provide the necessary sexual outlet—but also that it viewed her with contempt for failing to offer wifely comfort and support to her husband in his final days. The court again found her guilty, this time raising her fine to forty shillings.[39]

Women who were lascivious by nature, and hence potentially socially disruptive, needed to be firmly guided by male guardians and masters. As the misogynist literature's portrayal of men threatened by women's power suggests, however, this was a tall order. Men clearly had to be on their guard against such women. Some advice literature was explicit about this. Thus *Look e're you Leap; or, A History of Lewd Women* used misogynist portrayals of lustful, deceitful women who were incapable of offering the companionship and faithfulness on which marriage depended to underscore to young men the potential pitfalls of courtship and marriage. In its tenth London edition by midcentury and appearing in a Boston edition by 1762, it began with a blanket indictment of women. Women, it warned, were "all contaminated by the sin of their great grandmother with vice and wickedness." The author cautioned young men to select a wife whose sexuality would not threaten his mastery. "A whorish woman is a deep ditch, and they that are abhorred of the LORD, shall fall therein." It also depicted marriage to the wrong woman as bondage: "And when a Man has married and got children; if providence be so kind as to release him from his bondage, never let him become a slave again, by marrying a second time." The text was also replete with stories of spurned women who used false accusations of rape to exact revenge. Accounts of false accusations of rape consistently played on the misogynist theme of men threatened by women's perceived sexual power and manipulation.[40]

The following skeptical account of an alleged rape that appeared in the *Weekly Rehearsal* in 1732 also made use of the comical figure of the older woman desiring sexual intercourse (who was presumably freer about her desires, now that she could not produce an incriminating child).

We have an Account from Mountown, that on Sunday last, an Old Woman about threescore Years of Age was met with in the Fields by a young Fellow; who, without much Resistance, ravished her; but she seeing some Gentlemen on the Top of the Castle, who were diverting themselves with the Scene, screamed out most heidously a Rape! A Rape! The young Man, confounded at her Roaring, fled.

In a move typical of such portrayals of older women who "without much Resistance" have illicit sexual intercourse with "young Fellow[s]," this old woman is deceitfully willing to charge "Rape"—a capital crime—as soon as she realizes that her public reputation is in jeopardy. As a "Roaring" woman, screaming "most heidously," she is a comic grotesque: open-mouthed, loud, lying, and highly sexual.[41]

The topic of false charges of rape from the "cunning sex" and how to guard against them preoccupied newspapers almost as much as protecting women from rape did. The following news item about a false rape accusation made by one Mary Gregory against A. Hamilton, both from Philadelphia, detailed a scenario that every innocent man would have feared and that every rapist could use to his advantage:

It appear'd upon the Tryal, from a great Number of Witnesses, that the whole was a villanous Forgery, contriv'd against the said A. Hamilton to extort Money from him: that the said Mary is a Person of a most abandoned and infamous Character, and that she had the like Attempts against sundry other Persons of unblemished Reputation in this City.

The whole narrative creates a gender inversion that underscores Mary's power and men's vulnerability. Although Mary and her husband were named as defendants, only her character is described, highlighting her active criminality. She is a "villanous," even "infamous" con artist (terms typically used to describe men who dupe other men) who victimizes the men in her city by using false charges of rape to threaten their "unblemished Reputation." In using terms like "most abandoned," the author could suggest sexual depravity as well as social treachery.[42]

Indeed, in accounts of false accusations of rape, the theme of male vulnerability to women's sexual power and manipulations was, as the following newspaper notice indicates, quite pronounced. An account from London described a case where a seventy-two-year-old man had been falsely accused of raping a fourteen-year-old girl, the daughter of his landlady. Only a very clever examination in court and presentation to the jury acquitted the man and criticized the girl. The girl had claimed that she did not scream out because the man had kept "his lips so close upon her lips, that she could not open her mouth." The article detailed how the court used a wooden beam joined at a pivot to argue that a six-foot-tall man could not simultaneously penetrate the girl and place his mouth on hers, given that she was only four feet tall. The jury acquitted the elderly man, but the cautionary lesson was clear: without the technologically resourceful tactics of his defense, the man's fate may have been otherwise.[43]

Court records reveal a similar concern for male respectability at the hands of unscrupulous women. Thus, in 1754 Shribal Standen, a blacksmith from Tisbury, complained to the sheriff of Dukes County that Ann Swain, a fourteen-year-old girl, had been spreading lies "in the hearing of many People." According to Standen's complaint, Swain told people that "in the night time" he had assaulted her. He had "attempted her chastity by severall words and actions," including "uncovering her in the night" and "attempting to have Carnall Knowledge of her Body." Moreover, he claimed, Swain had told people that Standen had questioned her morality by allegedly stating, "If she should prove with Child there were young men Enough to Lay it to." For Standen it was outrageous, given that the charges were "false," but it was worthy of court action because the accusations were "uttered with an Intent to Defame him and Take away his good Name & Cause Differences to Arise between him & his wife." Standen sued to protect his reputation and to preserve the stability of his marriage and household.[44]

Men accused of rape in eighteenth-century Massachusetts typically simply denied the charge. Given the difficulty of proving rape in the absence of damning evidence of force, most men apparently did not feel the need to resort to the strategy of openly stating that the alleged victim had enticed them or had simply made the whole thing up. We can speculate that a simple denial, which created a "he said, she said" stalemate, may have relied for its effectiveness on the cultural familiarity of the figure of the deceitful or lustful woman. In one extreme case, Emanuel Lewis, a Boston laborer accused of sexually assaulting a child, admitted to the sexual encounter but nonetheless claimed innocence on the grounds that the child had not just consented but had, in fact, seduced him:

> The Child put its hand into his Breeches and asked the Examinant to lye with it. That he took the Child into his lap laid its face upon his Breast, denied that he attempted to have Carnal knowledge of it that the Child did not Cry when he lay with it but asked him to do it more—That the Child pulled up its Coats—put his yard to its body but nothing further.

The court, however, found Lewis guilty of attempted rape, and he was sentenced to be tied to a cart, carried to the gallows, and whipped.[45]

These narratives of rape and related crimes reveal paradoxes of gender and are replete with gender inversion. Men who raped were guilty of failing to master their sexual passions, yet dominant, almost overpowering male sexuality was at times eroticized and idealized. The norms of masculinity that stressed active, even aggressive prowess made it possible for the accused rapist to fancy himself virile and acting within the bounds of normative masculine sexual comportment. Competing images of women likewise abounded. Women were victims—the vulnerable prey of unbridled male sexuality. But female sexuality was also dangerous. Women's sexuality could lead entire communities of men astray, and their false accusations of rape could jeopardize a man's purse and reputation. The hyperbolic, misogynist imagery of sexually rapacious and deceitful women who preyed upon men is symptomatic of the tensions around the masculine norm of moderation and responsibility for women's sexuality. These entanglements of power and weakness, found both in print and in court discussions of rape and seduction, indicate tensions in eighteenth-century norms of masculine and feminine desire and comportment. As the following chapter shows, these norms and understandings of manly sexual desire and comportment figured in creating important bonds in the community of men.

CHAPTER 4

Sex and the Community of Men

I N THE SUMMER OF 1744, Benjamin Walker, Junior, was out strolling in the South End of Boston when a young man overtook him and struck up a conversation. Talk soon turned to disgraced minister Stephen Roe, who the previous summer had bid his final farewell to a town that had rightfully turned its back on him. Having impregnated the daughter of his landlord, a widow living in the South End, Roe had first been gossiped about by the community, and then officially "silenced" by his church before being "discharg'd." Walker had been there when Roe left town, and he wrote in his diary about seeing Roe in the stern of a boat "with his back to ye people on ye wharf looking very pale & disconsolate" and then how he "looked out on ye people on ye wharf & just bowd his head & then put his hat on." The happenings were still fodder for gossip a year later. The young man who spoke with Walker informed him about the details of the financial settlement between the minister and the family he had wronged. At that point in the exchange, a "man following" Walker and the young man, having overheard their gossip, broke into the conversation to add that the child was born and had lived just twenty-four hours. For these three individuals, as for most men, sexual behavior was one important measure of a man's respectability. Observations about it and informal regulation of it were threads that tied the social, economic, and political community of men together.[1]

This chapter examines sex and the social order of men. It also examines how several of the topics discussed in this book, including marriage, courtship, adultery, incest, rape, racialized sexuality, sodomy, and same-sex sexuality figured in fostering and hindering relationships between individual men and the larger community, especially the larger community of men. Mutually shared understandings of normative sexuality could help forge important masculine social bonds.

But sex was also a threat to fraternal social order. Throughout the eighteenth century, court records and printed discussions presented a variety of sexual transgressions involving women, children, and servants as wrongs committed by one man against another. Sex was an important component of the formal and informal networks of men that functioned to protect household and communal stability—but also to create and sustain individual reputations.

Gossip and Talk

Although modern commentators may tend to equate gossip about courtship and marriage with women, we should be careful not to transport today's gender stereotypes into the colonial world. In the eighteenth century men gossiped. Scholarship on talk in early America has focused on slander and defamation to examine cultural norms and ideals. Some of the best studies have focused on how gossip functioned for women as a means to wield social power at a time when they were legally, politically, and economically disenfranchised. Scholarship that has looked at men and masculinity has tended to zero in on the official and the public, such as formal speeches and oratory, or it has dealt with the rough-and-tumble world of masculine politics and early American political slander and satire.[2]

Scholars have used slander cases to make the generalized claim that reputation for men was based on probity in economic concerns, while for women, sexual virtue was paramount. But the bases for slander cases do not accurately reflect the salient components of a man's or a woman's total reputation. After all, being a hardworking, productive housewife was also important for cultivating womanly honor. Moreover, for married women slander cases are not a clear measure of gendered reputation because a wife's suit would also be designed to defend her husband's honor. And we should note that married women brought charges more often than single women did. For men sexual reputation mattered. There is no clear relationship between concern for sexual reputation and the number of defamation suits brought to court. By examining ordinary talk in addition to slander cases, we can more fully understand the position of sex in the formation of gendered reputations.

Gossip is popularly conceived of as idle talk, unregulated, spread without care for entertainment's sake. But as we know from countless social histories, gossip was not just admissible in early American court cases, it was sought after. In trials people testified about individuals' reputations and testified to common knowledge. That is, they swore under oath not as *eye*-witnesses to relationships and events (something we place a premium on today) but to their own awareness of communal talk, as *ear* witnesses to gossip. Such information, which would be hearsay testimony today, was a crucial part of establishing justice. As such, gossip was not just idle talk. It had important cultural weight in public and official as well as social and personal arenas.

Being the subject of sex rumors could have a direct bearing on masculinity. Men could suffer tangible consequences distinct from the rare criminal penalties meted out for sexual transgressions, given that gossip could and did contribute to a man's biggest social failure: divorce. We should bear in mind that in eighteenth-century Massachusetts, Anglo-American manhood was largely equated with becoming an independent householder; it was tied closely to marriage. As this chapter demonstrates, sex was a part of securing and maintaining that social position. A reputation damaged because of sexual transgressions could restrict access to patriarchal entitlements, lead to divorce, limit a man's marriage options, and bring scorn from neighbors and kin.

Male talk about sex was socially a double-edged sword. Networks of men, such as those chronicled by Benjamin Walker, Junior, Benjamin Bangs, and others, point to the importance of gossip about sex for social bonding among men. It's significant that talk about intimate matters often took place in commercial and semipublic settings. Participation in such talk not only underscored the bond enjoyed by particular individuals but also reinforced their position as embodiments of accepted community norms of masculine sexuality.

Partaking in sexual gossip was a vital part of securing the networks that were crucial for a man's standing among men and in the community at large, but being the subject of sexual gossip could cause humiliation and shame and damage his social standing. In a world where marriage in particular was the central social status for men, a bad reputation could even bring about divorce, thwarting a man's ability to assume the mantle of normative manhood.

In addition to threatening his social standing, sexual gossip threatened a man's commercial connections. We know that probity was paramount for developing commercial ties. A man shown to be dishonest in his intimate relationships could not retain the strongest reputation for commercial virtue.

Men closely followed the marriage market. Not surprisingly, they did so when it concerned a relative, as in the following letter between the Salisbury brothers. Samuel wrote from Boston on February 14, 1771, to Stephen in Worcester, who had obviously expressed feeling slighted. "Miss Hannah Pain is quite mistaken in Sister Betsy being Published, you may Depend upon it she will not be married some months yet—she desired I would Inform you she was not married, nor had she forgotten she had a Brother at Worcester." Samuel took the time to clarify for his brother their sister's wedding intentions. But the letter reveals more than simply the transmission of such information. It conveys a witticism, the remark that Betsy had not forgotten she "had a Brother in Worcester," to defuse a potentially emotionally painful situation.[3]

Such concern was not reserved exclusively for family members. Men also spoke of the weddings of friends and acquaintances. While in the Continental Army, Benjamin Gilbert still maintained his networks and managed to keep abreast of such happenings. "Having heard from good authority" that his hometown friend was engaged, Gilbert wrote a letter of congratulations.[4]

Talk about sex often dealt with courtship, marriages, and bastardy and paternity. Eastham sailor and navigator Benjamin Bangs, for example, wrote in his diary in 1759 that in his "absence" two "accidents" had been "discov'd"—both of which were about women pregnant without "lawful fathers." Bangs also reported intimate details about married couples. After another trip, Bangs noted in his diary what the "news in town is": a man who had his "first daughter after being married more than thirteen years." In calling this last occurrence a "strange thing indeed," Bangs may have been commenting on the couple's good fortune, or he may very well have been casting aspersions on the couple's fertility. Either way he, like other men, wrote of local births and marriages as faithfully as a local paper in modern times. Participation in gossip networks could contribute positively to a man's reputation, apparently reflecting a man's connectedness and his awareness of happenings in his town and region.[5]

Men noted marriages, births, and marital discord, and they also observed when couples split. Bangs, for example, noted in 1754 that one Richard Hopkins and his wife did "part" and that it was the "chiefe discourse among people all over town." On March 4, 1731, Benjamin Walker, Junior, recorded in his diary the punishment of a couple in Boston for adultery, noting also that he knew of the woman's husband and father. He wrote, "a lusty man and a woman . . . both married folk, were Carried in a

Cart to ye Gallows & there sat upon it with ropes about their necks, came down, both ty'd to a cart... and whipped 39 stripes thro part of this town for being convicted of adultery." Even when public punishments were not called for, neighbors and friends still took note.[6]

Just as there were both formal and folk divorces, there were also informal marriages. Boston merchant Benjamin Walker, Junior, noted in his diary that one couple "I hear lived many years together as man & wife." Of course, chroniclers also noted hearing talk about actual petitions for divorce, particularly when the circumstances were unusual, as when in 1740 Jesse Turner petitioned for divorce on the grounds that his wife was physically incapable of intimate relations.[7]

Men relied on male friends to counter talk that might have tarnished their sexual reputation. When men were separated, correspondence between male friends and business associates took the place of talk. Benjamin Gilbert, for example, took the time to write on behalf of a friend who had apparently cheated on his girlfriend. Describing his letter as a "silent messenger," he vouched for his friend's character: "I have so good an opinion of Mr. Newhall as to think that it was done rather through Inadvertancy than any intinded infringments on the Virtues of that young Miss." Entreating her to forgive him for the transgression, Gilbert declared, "Considering his unspotted character heretofore, and unblamable Life he has ever led, I think we ought to over look it not doubting but his future good conduct will more than attone for this one piece of Imprudency." Less than one year later, the seventeen-year-old recipient, apparently having forgiven Walker's friend, married him.[8]

For many men, intimate affairs bled into commercial concerns. And relationships of trust were forged in person, as well as via ink and paper. Benjamin Walker, Junior's shop was the most common place for him to note exchanges of gossip or talk among his networks of men. In this locale, such talk seamlessly linked the sexual and romantic actions of men to business and commercial networks. Walker wrote, "Capt. Joseph White," a tax collector, "told me at me shop door" with "Capt. Wm Curtis [near]by" that Doctor Clark's son was going to be married. Noting in the margins of his diary, Walker added: "Doct. Clarks son had done ye Trick before hand," indicating a premarital affair and pregnancy. Placing such talk within the network of men he presumably had business dealings with, and in the locale of business, linked private sexual happenings, masculinity, and the public world of commerce.[9]

Sex slander in this commercially charged context was doubly dangerous given that it threatened a man's commercial reputation. In 1719 one Edward

Ellis was found guilty of slandering Reverend William Boyd by saying that Boyd had "screwed Mr. Longs Maid." Significantly, the disparaging talk took place "in the shop of Benjamin Gray, Bookseller."[10]

Male talk about sex often took place among informal but self-consciously established networks of men. Benjamin Walker, Junior noted in his diary the names of individuals who stood at his "shops door" one summer day in 1744 and shared a bawdy tale. The four men, Walker, Moses, William Rand, and Samuel Eliot, exchanged a crude but "comical story of Mr. John Morehead minister for ye Irish in ye Town." In his diary Walker recorded the names of the men in his circle of talk. Years later, when he noted how he heard about a Mr. Tuttle, a toolmaker whose daughter allegedly had been raped by the captain of a Boston man-of-war then anchored in Boston Harbor, Walker again detailed the chain of gossip: "Wm Rand Told me & Sd Laughton Junior Told him & Justice Waldo son told Laughton told Sd Rand & Far Toleman was at my door When Rusid Told us." In fact he spilled more ink on the network than on the story itself. Such talk could nurture and develop the kind of networks of trust and confidentiality crucial to commercial and trade concerns. Gossip could be good business.[11]

The subject of gossip itself could also link a man's calling with his sexual reputation. In one such example, we see that not only did sexual gossip mark a man's reputation but that reputation became welded to a material object in the memory of our chronicler, Benjamin Walker, Junior. On May 9, 1746, Walker noted that a new weathervane had been placed at Benjamin Colman's Brattle Street meetinghouse. Walker had nothing to note about the new weathervane's creator, Sherman Drown, but about the original weathervane's creator he wrote extensively. "The old one ytt was blown down," he gossiped with his diary, "was made by Benjamin Pollard then a brasier or Tincker who is now High Sheriff in Suffolk." Pollard, Walker noted, was the son of a tailor, and "I heard In days past his mother had a child by a Negro." The toppling of the weathervane jostled the memory of more than just Walker, and he gossiped about its creator with more than just his diary. Two days before the replacement vane was hoisted into place, at his shop, Walker spoke with another man about the sexual history of Pollard's family. For Walker and his circle of friends and associations, a family history of interracial sex and a child out of wedlock became fixed, like a patina, to the weathervane that graced the spire at Reverend Benjamin Colman's Brattle Street Church. When strong winds dislodged the vane, tales of sexual deviancy about the maker became fodder for male gossip. That the Brattle Street Church was somewhat tolerant of non-

Congregational theology and religious practices may certainly have nurtured the negative association.[12]

Networks of gossip about sex and marriage did not just concern affairs in the immediate vicinity. Noting that a story about a shameful frolic at which a man's wife had behaved improperly with another man, Benjamin Bangs wrote that the story had "spread all over the Cape." Writing to his mother from Bourdeau in 1774, William Pynchon noted that when he was on board a ship in Portsmouth, he ran into a passenger from Salem who informed him of the local marriage market, telling him of a recent marriage. Talk could and did spread far and wide.[13]

These men were not engaging simply in idle talk. Connections, commercial or personal, were based on trust, and even gossip made the intimate details of an individual's life into public news. It was important to speakers and writers to create circles of friendship that suggested confidentiality and discretion and underscored in-group status and moral standards. Benjamin Walker, Junior, wrote in his diary about speaking confidentially with one of his tenants, Joseph Hiller. Walker noted that the conversation did not take place until "he & I [were] alone," at which point Walker "askt him" about "Mary Sirago [and] whether she had a child lately." Hiller told him that about a month earlier she'd had a child with a young man, a joiner by the name of Vintino. Vintino had promised marriage, and the child was now in the "country." Perhaps because Walker waited for the appropriate moment to ask for the information, Hiller told him what he wanted to know, including intimate details of the couple's relationship, the father's name, status, and current location.[14]

Depositions from court records also reveal that gossip was not simply unbridled blather but managed by codes of secret keeping. Consider court depositions from the divorce case of a Dedham yeoman named Gill Belcher. In 1739 Belcher petitioned for divorce, alleging that he had been forcibly intoxicated and duped into marriage by his wife's family. Apparently they had acted to protect her good name, as Belcher had impregnated her. One man testified about the conditions under which he learned about the couple's relations, the intoxication, and the marriage. "If I would not Speake of it to any Person till I heard it Reported by others he would tell me the whole affair." Such boundaries, even within networks of gossip, underscore the importance of trust in defining social relationships.[15]

Sometimes men went to great lengths to blur the line between spreading gossip and discreetly protecting private information. Such efforts were noted by gentleman Josiah Ham of Marlborough. He took part in something of a guessing game with William Parham when the topic of a woman's infidelity came up. When Parham first spoke of the affair, Ham asked him "how he dare'd to utter such things about the woman." Parham, however, said he could prove it and so was not concerned with appearing to gossip. When Ham began to ask for more information, the answers turned the exchange into something of a coy game. Ham asked if he "knew the man (that was catched in bed with her)" but was rebuffed when Parham told him "that was to be kept a Secret." Thus Ham chose an indirect approach, asking: Is he a "Married Man"? "Yes," replied Parham. Is he a "Poor man or a Rich man?" asked Ham. "A Poorish Man," came the answer. Ham continued the volley. Does he live "near by sd Russel Knights or far off?" "Not very far off," came the answer. Through this exchange we can catch a glimpse of the presence of internal rules of gossip—underscoring that such talk was neither idle nor unbridled.[16]

The size of male networks varied, of course. And at their largest and most abstract level, the "group" could simply be the community. In this way, gossip also had the effect of joining men together in a unified moral sense. Men who spoke of indiscretions placed themselves as men in a position to judge those indiscretions. They gossiped as sexually normative men. This was referred to as "town talk." As I've mentioned, our Eastham sailor, Benjamin Bangs, liked to keep abreast of community gossip and would often note in his diary what news he had learned when returning from short excursions. If you'll recall, Bangs wrote in his diary in 1759 about the two "accidents" that in his "absence" had been "discov'd." A few years later, when a woman's father refused to consent to her marriage, the couple had trouble finding a minister who would marry them, but when they found one John Freeman of Eastham to marry them, Bangs noted: "its town talk." Our Boston merchant Benjamin Walker, Junior, also used a form of the expression "town talk" when he wrote about the awkward courtship of one Edmond Quincy and Mrs. Bayard. "Quincy courted her & as I hear was plaid [*sic*] fast & loose for another." What became even more controversial was that the young man intended to win her over "with out her parents consent." This "made much talk about Town," wrote Walker. When a minister from South Carolina debauched and impregnated his landlord's teenage daughter (the topic of discussion in our opening scene), Benjamin Walker, Junior, noted that he had heard this by "many people" and that it was "reported about this town." The idea of "town talk"—a collective outrage or fascination with a sexual indiscretion—signified to both Bangs and Walker that they were part of a cohesive community that accepted certain norms about courtship, marriage, and sexual conduct. By retelling such stories and noting that they were "town talk," the men were signaling that they were part of a moral community.[17]

We should also consider that such gossip was a form of social regulation. Throughout the eighteenth century the courts assumed less and less involvement in the policing of moral behavior. Other social and cultural mechanisms such as print partly displaced the courts as a source of moral guidance. Gossip was not only a reflection of norms, then, but also a means of producing as well as spreading and enforcing community standards. Men salvaged tarnished reputations outside the courts. In the face of a swirl of gossip, a man might speak out in defense of himself, or if absent, he could write letters to stem the tide of community opinion.

While serving in the Continental Army, Benjamin Gilbert waged a letter-writing campaign to defend his reputation after he had been accused of impregnating Patience Converse. His collection of letters reveals a circulation of letters among the principal male family members involved: Gilbert; his father; his brother-in-law; Patience's father, Colonel Converse; and her brother-in-law, Captain John Cutler. Writing to her father, he began the letters with something of an admission of guilt and a declaration of his intention to "settle the matter." As her male guardian, Patience's father was the appropriate individual for Gilbert to engage. Gilbert learned that his reputation was jeopardized by gossip in their hometown of Brookfield, when his brother-in-law wrote to inform him of this. Securing this flow of information, which he considered reliable, as opposed to the talk of "common fame" that had already tipped him to the talk, he expressed gratitude to his brother-in-law and complained that his "friends" had been "so polite as to advertise me of what had transpired."[18]

Given that much of Gilbert's correspondence with his father during the war discussed financial matters, his denial of sexual impropriety with Patience and his efforts to secure his reputation in his father's eyes must be interpreted as an effort to secure his still uncertain financial future and signals the connections between sexual behavior and commercial reputation. Complaining to his father that "so many enemies" in Brookfield "wish to destroy" his "character, Interest, and Life," he begged his father to "suspend your Judgments untill you shall se me." Gilbert's brother-in-law was also an important male family connection for him, and Gilbert acknowledged his support in a letter a few months later: "I think myself under the greatest obligation to you, for the trouble you have given yourself on my account, in endeavouring to procure every information possible relative to my character and Interest." When Gilbert returned to Brookfield at the end of the year, he was arrested and eventually settled the affair by paying thirty pounds, for which he received "a full acquital from the father and Daughter," which he then filed with a local magistrate. Undoubtedly because of his tarnished reputation in Brookfield, Gilbert moved to New York, where he began the process of reestablishing his reputation. He married several years later.[19]

Communications among men about reputations that had been threatened by sexual transgressions were not limited to single men on the make. A close examination of a divorce case illustrates how one man, facing the threat of divorce, also embarked on a letter-writing campaign to save his reputation, and hence his marriage. The case is useful to look at in some detail, given that it also illustrates the distances a reputation could travel. Moreover, it reveals the extent to which gossip about sex could be quite public and linked to familial, political, and economic aspects of a man's life. In the realm of gossip, all worlds were collapsed into one reputation.

In 1783 Puella Kelly was granted a divorce from her husband, Samuel Kelly, a mariner from Martha's Vineyard, on the grounds that he had committed adultery. Puella's decision to petition for divorce was probably delayed due to the years of letter writing on behalf of Samuel to his and her parents in an effort to maintain his reputation. Samuel Kelly had claimed that he was unable to return for court action, given his imprisonment by the British during the American Revolution and subsequent problems traveling home, but letters reveal that he was stonewalling.[20]

Three years before Puella asked the governor for her divorce, Samuel Kelly, then in Philadelphia, had gotten wind of talk about himself that was unflattering—and he had heard that such talk had hardened into the belief that while in the West Indies he had been unfaithful to his wife and would soon be the subject of divorce proceedings. On May 20, 1780, Samuel wrote from Philadelphia to his parents to stave off what he crafted as rumors: "I believe you have heard a parcel of lies about me." One week later he wrote to his wife's parents, "Sir the news that I hear greives me much to think you have So little Opinion of me. Sir I would not have [y]ou think" that I would "leave an honest wife and live with a Damd hore in the West Indies." "I must Sir have reason to think that you believe Every Damd lie you hear." He ended, "I hope Sir you'll believe no more of what you hear till I come home." He wrote that he expected to be home within two months' time. That same day he wrote to his wife denying that he was married to a woman in Martinique and telling her that he had heard that her father was going to get a bill of divorcement. He explained: "This News Comes to me from day to day by Vinyard men." He told her as well that he'd be home in two months and pleaded: "So my Dear Dont you mind what any body tells you concerning me but make your Self Easy and I will Make them all lyers." As if to rule out divorce, he ended the letter: "I am as before your well wisher and affectionate husband untill Death."

But Kelly apparently never did venture homeward to face the music, and after two years had passed, Puella, given his absence, was essentially married only to her husband's reputation, and his reputation was at best that of an adulterer and at worst that of a bigamist. So in July 1782 Puella petitioned the governor and his council to ask for a divorce. In her petition she stated that she believed the reports that he was married or at least having an affair given his reputation for "ludeness." Connecting his "ludeness" to his political character, she added that he has "forsaken his Country," "takeing armes against his Breathern." This charge of treason she claimed she could have proved if one Mr. Isaac Bunker had not drowned. In an effort to gain support for a case built on hearsay, she added that breaches of the marriage covenant are not always in "open Day Light, but in Secret, & to that it is very Difficult always to bring positive Proof." As such, she argued, direct proof would be too much to ask. Her claim also underscores the importance of reputation.

Testimony from one Richard Bunker supported her claims that Samuel was involved with other women. Bunker told the court that in March 1781, while privateering, he put in at Martinique, where he came across Polly Raimond. When she learned that he was from New England, she asked if he knew Samuel Kelly and told him that she had been a bridesmaid at his wedding. Intrigued, Bunker went with Polly to meet the woman claiming to be Kelly's wife. She confirmed the story but said that she had left Kelly once learning that he had a wife in New England and because his "Behaviour was so Scandalous both in Gaming & Drinking."

Other sailors testified to having come across people who spoke about Samuel Kelly's sexual life while in the West Indies. One Jephemiah Butler confirmed Bunker's story when he swore to the court that he was in Martinique in April 1781 and had also met the alleged bridesmaid and the woman who claimed to be Kelly's wife. Butler added the tantalizing detail that the alleged wife told him she had received a letter in which Kelly referred to her as his wife. Unfortunately the court was again asked to rely on second- and third-hand testimony, as she claimed to have burned the letter in anger. In light of such testimony, Puella's reminder to the court that open breaches of the marriage covenant often lacked "positive Proof" seems wise.

This story of a second marriage was refuted, however, by testimony of one Boston mariner, Jacob Dunnell. He testified that in 1778 he had been at Martinique with Samuel Kelly and one Mary Stevens. There, at a public house, the hostess suggested, as a party game, that Mary Stevens should get married and select a husband from the crowd. According to his testimony, the man she chose was none other than Samuel Kelly. The two joined hands and went into another room but were soon followed by another man, indicating that nothing untoward had happened. Dunnell further testified that Kelly had lodged in his room that night, so that it was quite clear it was only a tavern game, not a real marriage.

Samuel Kelly never returned to Martha's Vineyard to face the courts, his wife, or their families. Several men testified that he had venereal disease and that this kept him from going back to his wife. When John Pease spoke with him in April 1783, he was privateering in New York and had plans to go to Nova Scotia and never to return to Martha's Vineyard.

Although testimony was conflicted on whether he in fact had another wife, venereal disease, or mistresses, his reputation for such actions and the fact that he did not return to the courts to face these charges led to Puella's obtaining her divorce after years of enduring his stonewalling. Samuel Kelly's reputation for sexual impropriety had gone the oft-traveled route of sailors and tradesmen crossing from New England to the West Indies and back again. His vain attempts to mold that reputation through letter writing bought him time but in the end were not enough.

Sex talk among men, and about men, covered a variety of topics, but all had a bearing on manliness. It should come as no surprise that sometimes talk took the form of masculine boasting. Depositions in the divorce case of Andover Cordwainer, John Bragg, and Anna Bragg revealed the sexual gossip and boasting of local youths. In an unsuccessful attempt to secure a divorce, John Bragg mobilized testimony from individuals who could bolster the charge that his wife frequently committed adultery. He claimed that "it was comonly takt of that Sundry young men had us'd her as they pleas'd & some even made their boasting of it." Thus his complaint revealed the extent to which neighbors gossiped and the propensity for men (especially young men) to boast of their sexual exploits. We should bear in mind that such talk was publicly humiliating, as it indicated that a man did not govern well as a husband and household head or succeed as the sexual partner of his wife. She cuckolded him, and did so openly, or so he alleged. Boasting and lighthearted jesting could also be heard on board a ship where a captain traveling up the coast from Boston was known to be sleeping with a married woman whose husband was not on board. The men on board "bantered" Captain Hall rather than subjected him to communal rebuking. The largely male world of sailing may have lent itself to such jesting.[21]

In the similarly all-male environment of soldiering, we also hear boastful talk. On October 30, 1760, while a soldier during the French and Indian War, David Holden wrote in his diary: "Sir Williams men arrived here that Came with General Amherst—A mighty Discord amongst the Regulars this Night Disputing who had the best Right to a woman & who should have the first Go at her even till it Came to Bloos & their Hubbub Raised all most the whole Camp." Here a group of men jockeyed for the respect and admiration of their peers, based not on birthright, wealth, or intelligence but on their sexual attractiveness to women, their sexual prowess, and their sexual competitiveness in a marriage market, all of which showcased the power of their own desire.[22]

Boasting of sexual exploits was not the only way that talk about sexuality fed a man's reputation. Being the subject of gossip, regardless of the issue discussed, was a personal failing of sorts. After all, the man being gossiped about may well have committed an act of adultery, infidelity, or fornication, which many men committed. To be gossiped about, however, meant that he had been discovered. It also meant that he had been betrayed. When people gossiped, it meant that the man had failed to nurture relationships that encouraged people, including loved ones and dependents, to remain loyal and discreet, to protect his public reputation from the tarnish of sexual impropriety.

Reputations, of course, were not solely a consequence of one's actions. A wife's sexual infidelities could place a man's reputation in jeopardy, as he would publicly appear to be incapable of governing his own household. Additionally, the fact that another man had come into the picture revealed that he had also failed to create crucial networks of respect and trust among male friends.

Sex and the Community of Men

In 1788 and 1789 Captain Thomas Shreve corresponded with Paul Revere regarding Shreve's wife's apparent emotional withdrawal—but the exchange of letters would eventually turn to rescuing Shreve's damaged reputation once it became clear that his wife, Catherine, had been unfaithful. Traveling for business, Shreve lamented the fact that he had little to do with his wife and that she had shared with him almost no details of her own travels to Boston. Writing to Paul Revere in June 1788, Shreve remarked: "We have very little else than anecdotes of your & others Friendly Behaviour to her during her stay at Boston since her return." In November he wrote to Revere that he was unhappy with the manner in which Catherine had to travel—on a boat "filled with almost all Manner of Beasts, of which the Master seems the greatest"—a situation that he blamed on the scarcity of packet boats. The lecherous captain, as far as Shreve was concerned, was accountable to *him* for the "attention or innattention he may pay" to his wife. But by also sharing this concern with Revere, he partly enlisted his services as a surrogate guardian.[23]

By April 1789 Shreve again wrote to Revere, this time expressing dismay at not hearing from Revere and stating, "I was not wrong in anticipating the many mortifications Mrs S would unavoidably be exposed to in sailing in Company with a <u>Man</u>, if it is not an abuse of the Word to call one such who is as much noted among us for the Want of those common feelings characteristic of such a Being, as He is for the Want of Truth." Shreve focused on the captain as instigator and blamed him for intervening between him and his wife. Moreover, he shared this information with Revere in a manner that expected shared outrage at this violation of masculine order and impugned the captain's manliness.

Clearly cuckolded, he wrote that his wife insisted on continuing to travel with the man who had apparently expressed himself inappropriately to her. In a perplexed tone he wrote: "I am afraid I shall loose her for the best part of the Summer, however hope for the best—she has her Friend again for a fellow Passenger whose base Treatment to her last Fall, I should have supposed a sufficient inducement for her to have postponed her journey;—but as the urgency of her Business requires dispatch, she waves every other Consideration." Apparently, the man in question had attempted to seduce his wife: "You have added to the many obligations already conferred by your kind interfearance last Fall when Mrs S was so wickedly attacked by this Man whose Art seems to keep pace with his Wickedness." Shreve positioned the captain as not just his own personal enemy but as an enemy of the community of men. From a distance, Shreve relied on Revere to handle matters for him—in this instance the important business of not only protecting his wife but also of upholding his own honor as a man.

But by September 1789 his tone had changed, and Revere's task was now one of rescuing Shreve's honor at the hands of his wife, who had indeed cuckolded him by having an affair and a child with another man. Shreve wrote to Revere in appreciation of his sympathy and support but also for aid in establishing a case for divorce:

My Dear Sir, To take up my Pen to express my Feelings on a Subject so distressing as the present, can not but fill my Soul with Horror. . . . I am sensible you are capable of feeling all I could say. One Favour, my Dear Sir I am induced to ask at present; Is that you'll be so good as to collect every Circumstance of this poor unfortunate Woman's Conduct so authenticated & transmitted to me, as may enable me to sue a Divorse. . . . the Name of this vile Character she last lived with, with Facts as well authenticated as can be,—I have spoke to Capt. Myrrick agreeable to your reference and he has forgot the Man's Name (if it is not a prostitution of the Word to call him so)—I am so agitated I scarce know what I write, or how to express myself in soliciting your assistance in preventing so my & my Children's ruin by so vile a Woman.

Having reached the point of no return, Shreve turned from blaming only the captain and now enlisted Revere's help in maintaining his honor by vilifying his own wife. He focused on protecting his remaining dependents by pleading with Revere to aid him in preventing his "Children's ruin." He used the language of sympathy and affection to secure his bond with Revere and again positioned the captain outside the community of respectable men for having disrupted his marriage. Shreve relied on Revere to aid him in maintaining his reputation and his financial security and to right the injustice he had suffered. A trusted friend such as Revere was a crucial ally in efforts to maintain one's social and economic standing and to rescue damaged reputations.

Economic concerns were woven through the correspondence with Revere over the loss of his wife's fidelity. In June 1788, before Shreve suspected serious breaches of his marriage covenant, he discussed having "enclosed a set of Bills for 25 L sterling on the Treasurer of the Society." Several months later he asked Revere to assist his wife: "I wrote you some time ago both from this place & from Halifax informing you that I had inclosed a set of Bills drawn in your Favour for 25 L sterling & to be disposed of as Mrs Shreve had directed." The funds were passed through one Captain Gale, who had assured Shreve "he delivered to Mr. William Bordman," a Boston merchant. Bordman had "promised in person to deliver them to you," wrote Shreve. Concerned about their arrival, Shreve had written to Revere, adding, "hope they have come safe to Hand—as Gale still stands accountable to me till I receive your acknowledgement of the Receipt." The long chain of individuals involved in transmitting funds from Shreve to his wife underscored the importance of his broader reputation. In the same letter he continued: "I have now given Mrs Shreve another set of Bills for 25 L more drawn in your Favour, which your assisting her in negotiating & purchasing such Things as We want will be adding to favours already conferred." Thus the relationship with Revere incorporated both the assumption that Revere would share his concerns for his wife's virtue while traveling on board a ship with a lecherous captain and his dependence on Revere (and other men) for his financial affairs. His marital problems and commercial concerns were linked, and his reputation was paramount for handling his affairs from afar. In the course of their correspondence, Shreve was not only enlisting the aid of Revere for maintaining his personal honor but also asking him to handle financial matters, writing at one point, for example, "Mrs S. takes a small Bill with her which I shall be oblidged to you, to negotiate for her."

By the time he began to pursue a course of separation from his wife, Shreve relied on Revere for information but also for economic allegiance, providing him with the names of individuals who he had contacted to protect his financial well-being and to cut off his wife. Thus, in November 1789 he wrote:

> I received yours of the 12th Oct org. & am much oblidged to you for having been so particular in giving me the information I wanted. I embraced the first opportunity in forwarding it to my Mother & such of my Friends as I thought it most likely she would attempt to impose herself upon. I particularly wrote Mr Wilcocks respecting the Draft she had made upon him that I neither should pay it or any future Demands she might make upon me.

Shreve's letters to Revere reveal connections between personal conduct, shared understandings of respectable manhood, and social and economic reputation. Over the course of a short period, Shreve went from having concern for his wife's emotional distance to protectiveness of her virtue to vilification of her conduct. And economically, he went from asking Revere to assist him in establishing networks of credit for the financial support of his wife to asking Revere to aid him in cutting off the flow of funds and to help him spread information to other creditors about his wife's conduct.

Of course, the community of men was not exclusively one of talk and correspondence. Court records reveal that male community members sought to regulate sexual behavior directly. Male family members sought to protect their female dependents' honor. In her petition for divorce, Mary Smith claimed that her husband, Thomas, was unsuitable because he became involved with lewd and debauched company and committed adultery on numerous occasions. Corroborating testimony came from a David Abott, who served in the Office of the Constable and who had apprehended Thomas Smith in 1784 for getting a woman pregnant. According to the testimony, Thomas Smith "Settled the matter with the Father of said Elanor by giving a Certain Consideration." Others testified that he "paid a certain consideration." The divorce was decreed on July 6, 1784.[24]

As historian Richard Godbeer argues, the double standard seen in eighteenth-century court records, whereby women are being held accountable for fornication and bastardy and men are not, is misleading. Women often approached the courts or their church and made the issue public in order to exact support from the man. Moreover, the men often settled out of court. Women pregnant before marriage either married the father or got support from the father and married someone else. Although the courts did not seek out men in this matter, and many of them lived without damaged reputations, men who took advantage of women did risk opprobrium.[25]

Male family members sometimes responded to suitors who failed to live up to their promises. When Gill Belcher, a yeoman from Dedham, petitioned on December 28, 1738, for a divorce from his wife, Mary Finney, he claimed that he had been forcibly intoxicated by her brother, John Finney, and a group of his friends and had married against his will after being accused of fornication with Mary. A grand jury was convened to determine if the marriage violated Massachusetts law, specifically the Act to Prevent Incestuous Marriages, because the certificate from the town clerk was issued without fifteen days' notice and the wedding took place without Gill Belcher's only parent, his mother, being aware of it. Belcher contended that a warrant charging him with fornication had been issued for his arrest, resulting in his being brought to several taverns by Mary's brother on the way to being taken into custody. The warrant, according to Gill, was falsely issued. He claimed that he had never gotten Mary pregnant, even though he "frequently Kept Company with her for this seven or Eight months Last past." He was "Induced to drink So much that he was very much Intoxicated." Drunk, he was given the choice of putting up money he didn't have to secure his appearance in court or being placed in jail, before being given a third option—marriage to the woman he had allegedly wronged. Mary's brother and other male friends involved made sure that he married Mary— but the following day, Gill claimed to have been duped. He maintained that although they slept in the same bed that night, he "did with his Cloaths on that night, and left her the next morning and hath never lived with her Since." Within a matter of weeks he petitioned for an annulment. Evidently, sometimes the mechanisms of social control made alcohol the lubricant of choice.[26]

Newspaper notices and other print literature depict a broader notion of masculine community. In some cases the bond forged between men was portrayed in a favorable light and as compatible with the goal of marriage, as was the case with the following notices about a soldier who chose to be married at the spot where he fought glorious battles with fellow soldiers. Reprinted in two newspapers on the same day, the notice described the marriage of a man "who lately belonged to the Continental army" and who made a "whimsical choice of place for the marriage ceremony: a spot of ground within four yards of . . . where some of his intimates fell (in a skirmish with the Indians in the late war) whose bones and tattered garments were still to be seen." In this and other cases, men joined their feelings of camaraderie and fraternal debt with their marriage ideals. In this case, the physical presence of the bones and garments of the groom's fallen comrades symbolically joined the man's brotherhood with his wife.[27]

Newspapers also carried notices about competition in courtship. Competition between men underscored the challengers' virility and manly appeal. To the victor went pride; to the loser, shame. But in some satirical notices, if both suitors were unworthy, their sense of entitlement to compete in courtship could underscore their deviance from manly ideals.[28]

Conflict between men served to regulate egregious disruptions to household order, as in the case of adultery and sexual assault. In an article about a lawsuit in London brought by a "gentleman" against his former "steward," the author explained that the court hearing the steward's defense advised the jury to consider the fact that the gentleman had neglected his wife and essentially driven her to commit adultery with the steward, given the gentleman's "incapacity to comply with the terms upon which a lady always contracts matrimony." His drinking apparently made him incapable of engaging in sexual intercourse with his "beautiful young" wife. The article, in depicting the men's sides of the lawsuit, the judge's advice as well as ruling, and the jury's findings, portrayed the issue of adultery as a wholly male affair—in this case, one in which a lower-status servant of the household had disrupted masculine order by violating the trust of his master. In the end the jury found for the gentleman.[29]

Disordered households were an affront to the community of men. But the following two articles make the point that the community of men could sometimes go too far in enforcing standards of behavior. Although critical of violent, vigilante actions, both essays underscore the presence of a masculine culture of social regulation. In 1765 the *Boston Evening Post* ran the following story:

> Some months ago, an account was published in the News-Papers, of a company of men in Providence, unlawfully associated, and disguised, who undertook to punish all Matrimonial Trespasses that came to their knowledge, and had assaulted a man whom they suspected of wronging his wife by too great a familiarity with another woman, with an intent to make him ride *Skimmington*, that is upon a pole, carried on men's shoulders; but were prevented from executing their design, by the resolute defence of the suspected man, who killed one of them and dangerously wounded one or two more, which dissolved the Association.

This notice was directly followed by another that carried similar themes. Both stories harp on the lawless nature of the response of companies of the "Disciplinarians" who reacted to men who had dishonored their wives. In both stories the men leaped to conclusions and took action that the author implies should be handled by legal means, if not by the heads of households themselves. Erroneously believing they embodied community standards, these men placed *themselves* outside the community of householders as underscored by their disguises and their damaging actions. Both notices emphasized the right of the head of household to establish justice in his own household but underscored the threat that men who let their homes get unruly faced by the larger community of men.[30]

The community of men generally focused on sex that violated marriage, family, and households, but in rare cases accusation of sexual behavior involved sodomy. In 1730, for example, those reading the *New England Weekly Journal* might have discussed the following story emanating from Versailles:

> There has been a dirty Business carried on here between two Gentlemen of the English or Irish Nation for some time by the Arts of the Law. One swore Sodomy against his Friend, and push'd on the Procecution [*sic*] vigorously, in hopes to have him burnt; but the supposed Criminal happily escap'd, for he was acquitted; and then in his Turn he attack'd his Adversary, by charging him with hiring a Man to assassinate him; for which, he that is Defendant now is Prisoner in the Chatelet, and in fair way to be hang'd.

Sensible readers must have concluded that with a friend like this, there would be no need for enemies. It is unclear whether the story is apocryphal, but notices like this suggest that accusations of sodomy were weapons of social attack. Using false charges like sodomy to discredit or blackmail someone posed a common enough problem to lead to legislative action in England. In 1750 the *Boston Evening Post* reported: "We hear a Bill will be brought in next Sessions of Parliament, to make it Felony without Benefit of Clergy, in any Person or Persons attempting to extort Money under Pretence of Swearing that detestable Crime of Sodomy against Innocent Persons."[31]

Sodomy, while still a capital crime, at times appears to have become something more akin to a social offense. Consider, for example, a news item from Dublin about attempted sodomy; appearing in the *Boston Evening Post* in 1752, it labeled sodomy unnatural. The case involved a "person of great distinction in the *British* nation [who] has lately suffered an amputation of both his ears, by a gentleman on whom he had the impudence, as well as the enormous baseness, to attempt the commission of sodomy." In this instance it is unclear if the attempted "commission" refers to an attempted rape or merely to a proposition. In either case, by labeling the attempt a mark of "impudence" and "enormous baseness," the article underscored that sodomy was a deep affront to masculine honor.[32]

The use of sodomy to impugn manliness was not restricted to Europe. Same-sex behavior was at the core of a satire appearing in the January 7, 1751, issue of the *Boston Evening Post* lampooning Freemasons. Accompanying the notice was an engraving that depicted two gleeful men, one bent over to receive a wooden spike, the other with a hammer raised overhead, ready to strike. The poem also included several lines that highlighted the alleged group practice of loosening compacted bowels with a clyster, or enema tube. The passage used the relatively common practice of clystering to smear the Freemasons via its metaphorical associations with the charge of secretly practicing sodomy. The poem continued with lines that underscored the homoerotic nature of the Freemasons.[33]

The poem, entitled "In Defence of Masonry," although signed by "A M-S-N," was written in a style meant to lead people to believe that it was authored by the Freemason satirist Joseph Green. Green had written earlier pieces referencing "Clio," a pseudonym that functioned here to ridicule the Freemasons' pretensions to an ancient provenance (or to classical learning). But the poem's real author was John Hammock, who was apparently engaged in a dispute with Green. The scandalous poem then served not only as an attack on the Freemasons but as an attack on Green. It portrayed him as a man who taunted the Freemasons on sexual and gendered grounds. To clear his own name, Green published a notice one week later in the *Boston Post Boy* denying that he had authored the poem. A second such notice appeared in the *Boston Evening Post* one week after that.[34]

The use of humor to lodge the charge placed the author in a position of control and distance from the smear of same-sex sexuality. Far from being the shrill tone of a seventeenth-century sermon condemning such wickedness and identifying it as ubiquitous, humor did the work of masculine heterosexuality. Demonstrating the ability to joke about the issue portrayed the satirist as savvy and psychologically unencumbered by same-sex sex. Humor also removed the reader from the topic, leaving it squarely in the lap of its object of ridicule. As such, the poem outraged many Boston Freemasons, who subsequently boycotted the *Evening Post* and met with the lieutenant governor and the provincial council, lobbying them to punish the printer.[35]

Throughout the eighteenth century, sex and sexuality were not cordoned off in early America from the masculine worlds of politics, commerce, and community. Gossip about a man's sexual and marital behavior was clearly designed to suggest something about the total man. His sexual reputation was not, therefore, simply about his sexual proclivities—it was about his overall character, his general capacity for moral self-regulation. Part III looks at how character could be assessed by a wide variety of external signifiers, including physical appearance, race, physique, and social comportment.

III ➻ *Sexualities*

CHAPTER 5 ◄-◄-

"Half-men"

Bachelors, Effeminacy, and Sociability

O N FEBRUARY 19, 1758, a few weeks shy of turning twenty-eight, prominent Boston teacher and lawyer Robert Treat Paine complained in a letter to his younger sister, Eunice, of having been quite ill and told her he overheard those who were tending him remark, "tho' I was a saucy Batchelor yet I might make a good husband & so it would not do to loose me." This tongue-in-cheek comment suggests that for those around him and for Paine himself, his status as an eligible bachelor was a key part of his social identity. Several years earlier, Paine had referred to himself as a " *Weather beaten* Batchelor." This comment also indicates a cultural interest in marriage markets. A letter from his first cousin Edmund Hawes Junior, written in September 1759, underscores this. "You Wrote Nothing Conserning your Marriage and so I Conclude you to be an Honest old Bachelder. I Recommend you to Read a Sermon Entitled a Wedding Ring if you Can find it. However we must wait with Patience till Providence & Time Brings about our Marriage." Now in his late twenties, Paine's unmarried state earned him the unflattering term of "old" bachelor. That bachelors enjoyed a degraded moral status is evidenced by the need for the qualifier "Honest." Similarly, in 1782, Paul Revere wrote to his thirty-something French cousin John Rivoire, "it gives me great pleasure to find that you are in so good business in Guernsey; You did not write me word, wether you were married; if you are not; nor do not marry soon, I'm afraid they will call you an old Bachelor." Given that most men in the eighteenth century married at around the age of twenty-five, Paine's status as a twenty-eight-year-old bachelor would have branded him a late bloomer rather than a committed bachelor. For Revere, a cousin who was over thirty and still single was cause for some concern. People would begin to cluck.[1]

Although in the late twentieth century the bachelor became synonymous with martinis and endless social pleasures, throughout the eighteenth century, bachelors were a serious cause for concern. In the colonial context, bachelors were considered disruptive male types with a particular sexuality, who demonstrated the frustration of marital, moderate, heterosexual masculinity. The foppish, effeminate bachelor was also associated with deviant sexual desires and practices, including masturbation and sodomy.[2]

In the last quarter of the eighteenth century, the figure of the bachelor retained his importance but did so in the face of a broader American "sexual revolution" that increasingly emphasized greater freedom of sexual expression. Nonetheless, in Massachusetts, bachelors deviated from normative male sexuality by eschewing the only legitimate site for male sexual expression: marriage. Thus, bachelors would either remain celibate and "fry in the Grease of their own Sensuality" or be "whoremongers" and engage in out-of-wedlock sexual intimacy, intimacy that neither produced children, nor nurtured a marriage bond, nor aided in the development of a stable household or society.[3]

Bachelors and the Marital Ideal

In *A Wedding Ring*, the sermon that Hawes had recommended to Paine and that had been reprinted throughout the eighteenth century in both London and Boston, the author pointedly underscored the link between marriage and manhood: "The *Hebrews* have a Saying, *He is not a Man, that hath not a Woman*." Other sources, although different in tone and ideological outlook, echoed this basic point. "My Father says I am now a Man, and may speak to him like another Gentleman," remarked one recently married young man in a letter in the imported London serial *The Spectator*. This view had changed little by the end of the century. In 1785 the *Continental Journal* opined: "A man is in his height of dignity when he becomes a virtuous husband, and a good father." All stressed the importance of a youth marked by virtue and restraint as the precursor to the achievement of respectable manhood.[4]

Serving as a foil for articulating marital norms, the bachelor often figured as the ideal narrator for writings on love and marriage. His status as a man without dependents and without marital love rendered him capable of offering an outsider's look at contemporary society, of being an ethnographer while culturally and racially still an insider. In this regard the bachelor figured as a narrator in such publications as *The Spectator* and in regular columns on love and marriage in newspapers—for instance, "Proteus Echo" of the *New England Weekly Journal*.

Although suited for the role of a disinterested spectator, the bachelor was otherwise not yet glamorized for choosing to abstain from marital domesticity. In the spring of 1749 readers turning to the *Boston Evening Post* found the front page occupied by a lengthy letter from the "Petticoat Club," a group of women "between the Age of Sixteen and Forty" whose letter had been previously published in the *New York Gazette*. The group criticized "Old Batchelors," accusing them of being "in Contempt of the Laws both of God and Nature," of "insufferable Stupidity and Obstinacy," and of forcing women to "remain useless, and even burdensome" to society. The Petticoat Club, therefore, proposed that "all Batchelors above 26 Years of Age, may be obliged to pay a moderate Tax, which should yearly increase till they arrive to 40 . . . and if any of the aforesaid Drones shall presume to continue in their Obstinacy till the Age of 40, then we pray, that there may be some publick Mark of Distinction, that they may be known from other Men." Their distinguishing mark was to be "some publick *Badge of Disgrace*"; married men, in contrast, should wear *"Marks of Honour"* for their contributions to the "Country." The reason? God, they argued, had commanded people to *"increase and multiply, and replenish the Earth."* Blaming bachelors for placing an intolerable burden on single women, the Petticoat Club portrayed single men as feckless and unmanly. Labeling them "Drones" (bees that have no stinger and gather no honey), they characterized bachelors as nonproductive members of society, as idlers and do-nothings.[5]

The letter concluded with a poem summing up the principles of domesticity and reproduction, which bachelors eschewed.

> Were Batchelors but wise enough to see
> The Way to Bliss and true Felicity,
> How soon would they exchange their senseless Noise,
> For prattling Girls and lovely smiling Boys,
> Who round their Table would their Praise proclaim,
> Maintain their Honour and preserve their Name,
> Defend their Country, and their Fame convey
> To future Generations: Thus we pray.

Bachelors, shortsighted and stubborn, missed out on the "true Felicity" that marriage and reproduction brought, instead focusing on the pursuit of meaningless pleasures ("senseless Noise"). Their failure to assume their manly prerogative left them without "Honour," especially the sons, who could carry on their "Name" and ensure their place in society ("Fame"). Such selfishness had larger social implications as well. Bachelors not only denied themselves true happiness and family security but left their country without men to "Defend" it.[6]

The conceit of a tax on unmarried persons, which was premised on the notion that they were unproductive, appeared in articles on both sides of the Atlantic. In a 1746 article reprinted from the *Gentleman's Magazine* in the *Boston Evening Post*, a section entitled "proposal for augmenting the publick Revenue" contained the following commentary on the selfishness of both unmarried men and women: "*Old batchelors* and *old maids*, as they promise no help to the future generation, should, I think, be made of all possible use to the present." Taking a rather old-fashioned viewpoint, the essay also criticized the contemporary overemphasis on the importance of love in marriage. Thus, the author chided: "I would excuse all maids who could take a solemn oath that they had never been ask'd the question. But for her who had, and without good occasion used the man ill, keeping him still a batchelor thro' pure love, I would have the duty levied upon her for both parties, and him excused. The same upon a man, who has kept a woman single upon the same principle." Although in this case both single men and women bore the brunt of the author's satire, bachelors generally came under heavier fire, given that men were the primary initiators in courtship and marriage.[7]

Throughout the eighteenth century, many essays took on a goading tone and pointed to the shortcomings of the single life. In a 1710 essay touting the goal of more "Births in the Year 1711, than ever before known in *Great Britain*," *The Tatler* pointed to the "Pains and Penalties of Celibacy." Using similar language, a poem from the *Gentleman's Magazine* reprinted in the *Boston News Letter* in 1752 referred to the "Heart-ache, and the Thousand Love-sick Pangs of Celebacy." Others echoed loneliness as the chief affliction: "Old batchelours in general, may see their unconnected, unrelative State in Society, tottering to their Graves in a gloomy Solitude," warned the author of *Reflections on Courtship and Marriage*. Bachelors, according to that text, suffered. What every man needed was, the author wrote,

> [a] tender affectionate Companion, of similar Mind and Manners, whose *constant* Sunshine of Love, warm'd the Spring and Summer of his Days, and now with an *unalterable* Friendship and Fellow-feeling, accompanies him Arm-in Arm thro' the dreary Wilds of Winter, with the Guard

of a Son or Sons, whose filial Piety and manly Vigour, is ever ready to protect him from the Insolence of others or to defend him from those Calamities to which our feeble Age exposes us.

Here the author contributed to the developing norm of companionate marriage, playing up the value of a "tender affectionate Companion" and the "*unalterable* Friendship and Fellow-feeling" undergirding good marriages. But he also linked companionate marriage to the production of heirs and to the defense of family honor through a "manly" "Guard of a Son or Sons" who were prepared to defend their fathers' reputations and care for them in their old age. A poem in the *Boston Gazette* read more simply: "How happy 'tis to have a Wife, Rather than live a single Life."[8]

Eighteenth-century criticisms of unmarried men focused in part on procreation. In Massachusetts such concern may well have been exacerbated by the geographic mobility of young men in the eighteenth century and the associated fact that more men married outside the communities of their birth. Although in New England there was no shortage of available men overall, in long-settled communities and in eastern Massachusetts in particular there were simply not enough single men to go around by midcentury. Not marrying, according to John Cotton's oft-reprinted Boston sermon *A Help Meet*, was neither "pleasant, nor profitable, nor indeed honourable." On "Batchelours," Cotton grimly declared "they are unworthy to Live themselves who are not instrumental of giving life to others."[9]

By harping on the frivolity of bachelorhood, these accounts hoped to encourage single men to assume the responsibility of husband, father, and head of household. Youth who did not choose to live a virtuous life and head down a path toward marriage were warned that they would end up as sickly, remorseful bachelors. Portrayals of bachelorhood, in short, underscored that true manhood relied in heavy measure on marriage and reproduction.

Bachelors were sexually suspect and therefore had to guard their reputations as carefully as—if not more so than—married men. In 1769, at only twenty-three, successful Worcester merchant Stephen Salisbury found himself the subject of scurrilous gossip that suggested he led an immoral life. Although he still lived at the Chandlers' (the family his future son would marry into), a story apparently surfaced that he had moved out to live at an establishment of food and drink. In an effort to control the worry this caused for his mother, he wrote to his brother and business partner, Samuel, in Boston: "they tell you 'that I have left the Old Lady's to Board at Bigelo's.' It is absolutely false—So farr [*sic*] from being True that I have not Eat or Drink anything in Mr Bigelo House, nor even So much as been inside of his House Since Brother & Sister was up here—As to my Laying a Bed on the Sabbath day morning, I am up as Soon as I am other mornings." The apocryphal tale that Stephen had left a stable household for a tavern would have raised eyebrows. When coupled with his sleeping in instead of attending public worship, the story portrayed him as an unchurched tavern goer. As a young single man, without a wife or family, staying at the stable household of a family friend shielded him from the suspicion that life in a tavern would have generated.[10]

Bachelors who died while still engaged captured the imagination of a culture that viewed such deaths as the poignant tale of a man unable to fulfill his manly duty. In the early spring of 1769 Reverend David Hall of Sutton dolefully recorded in his diary the sudden passing of a local young man. He had died after a brief illness, and his death had special meaning for Hall given his station in life. "Had he not been indisposed," wrote Hall, "[he] was to have been Married ye evening before. O let all old and young take warning."[11]

The tragedy of this boy's story had been recognized by newspapers, which in the 1730s carried a spate of tales about young men full of promise who were cut down in the prime of their lives—just on the verge of marriage. For example, an account from Dublin appearing in the *New England Weekly Journal* reported: "On Tuesday a Son of Mr. Baggs, who lives near Archboy in the County of Meath, having come to Town to get his Wedding Cloaths made, the Taylor brought them to be tried on, and waited till he was shaved; when he was shaved he rose in order to put them on, but dropt down dead at the George Inn in Smithfield."[12]

Massachusetts, too, produced dying grooms. A *Boston Gazette* essay of 1733, "Against Drunkenness," referred to a drunken quarrel between two friends that resulted in the death of one who was "in the Flower of his Age" and "possess'd of a plentiful Estate." He had also just entered into "a Treaty of Marriage with a beautiful young Lady" who had "a considerable Fortune, the Articles being drawn and the Wedding Day appointed." In 1739 the *New England Weekly Journal* reported the story of a man who had drowned trying to cross a river on a horse. The man "was just upon marrying, his Father being at Boston buying his Wedding Cloaths." Consider the following as well: both the *Boston News Letter* and the *New England Weekly Journal* carried the sad story of a Mr. Baker's death. "We hear from *Dedham*, That on Monday last one Mr. *Baker* (Son of Mr. *John Baker* Cornet of a Troop) as he was riding home fell from off his Horse, and as 'tis tho't crack'd his Skull; he was soon taken up, and dyed on Tuesday Night, not having spoke a Word after his fall: He was a young Man, and just upon the point of being married." All of these stories used the young man's status as a would-be groom to underscore the tragic waste of potential. The stories underscore that in addition to owning property and securing a career, marriage was a pivotal marker in a man's life, as it signaled his transition to adult manhood.[13]

Much like Hall's diary entry, the stories frequently highlighted deaths that occurred virtually on the eve of the marriage ceremony, serving to underscore the tragic loss. One such example read: "A few days ago, a very desirable and hopeful Young Man, at *Watertown*, the only Son of his Parents, dy'd there the very day that was design'd for his Marriage day." Similarly, in 1729 the *New England Weekly Journal* reported on the death of Nathaniel Cushing, a graduate of Harvard College who "was seiz'd by Death the night of his Marriage." Like many news items appearing in Boston papers, tragic deaths taught a lesson: "An affecting Instance of the vanity of humane Life, even in the Bloom of Youth, and Affluence of Worldly Prosperity." In the case of the young man who died before fulfilling his manly destiny, the "vanity of humane Life" took on a very specific meaning.[14]

The tales point to the significance attached to marriage as a ceremony that marked not only the union of two individuals and the formation of a new household but also the life-altering change of status and sexual identity that marriage brought about for men. By the end of the century, this view had changed little. In 1787 a poem appearing in the *Independent Chronicle*, purportedly written by a young man "the evening before he married," described him with amazement as "Between a man and boy."[15]

In the Revolutionary era, most commentators still referred to bachelors as "dull" and "stupid," such as the essay that appeared in the *Massachusetts Spy* on March 14, 1771. A series of essays and letters printed in the *Spy* in March and April of that year drew upon a range of social and personal characteristics that bachelors supposedly possessed. Acrostics were a popular form of poetry in early American and British papers. The following example published by the *Spy* was unmistakably negative in tone:

> **B**EREFT of wisdom, learning, wit or sense,
> **A**nd crown'd with mischief, folly, impudence,
> **C**ensure like thin, it will avail thee not;
> **H**onour and justice, are by thee forgot:
> **E**nvy and malice, with ill-judging spite,
> **L**ink close in thee, in thee they all unite.
> **O** change thy conduct and reform thy life,
> **R**epent thine *errors*, bless the name of wife.

The bachelor was a thorn in the side of a stable society. He was vilified and ridiculed. He frustrated the natural order of men and women pairing off in marital harmony. Authors who were determined to correct this figure of wayward manhood deployed every literary means possible to warn men from this path and coax those on it back into the village order.[16]

Women recognized the impact that the end of the war would have on the marriage market. Elizabeth Ann, in a letter to her mother—Catherine Pynchon in Providence—dated April 18, 1783, wrote of being in Salem and going out socially with a large group where she learned that many were "going to Providence." She also wrote that one woman at the gathering, Nabby Gerrish, "in her ill natur'd manner told her if she went she would return single, for the Town was full of pretty Girls, and but few Gentlemen." Apparently Gerrish had explicitly linked the shortage of bachelors to the disruption of the war, adding, "beside[s,] the Gentlemen there were not fond of marrying for there had not three marriages taken place since the War."[17]

Abigail Adams's sister Elizabeth Shaw, like many women, took it upon herself to monitor and coax the marriage market in the postwar era. In a letter to their sister Mary Cranch, she wrote: "Why does Mr Thaseter resolve not to marry—This is certainly the voice of dissappointed [*sic*] Love. I hope he will come here soon & we may live to see him alter his mind." Even before the end of the war, she was already beginning to anticipate the impact that peace would have on the marriage market. Elizabeth Shaw, writing to her sister in the spring of 1780, commented that two local widowers were to be married. She viewed the event with righteous approval: "Mr Duncan & Mr Sparhawk have arrived at the threshold, & will very son [*sic*] bow at the Shrine of Hymen—from hence we may conclude no Widower will ever die with grief." Shaw continued by portraying recent engagements as a local movement and a return to stability and normality. "All Haverhill seem disposed to join in the bands of wedlock," she wrote, "an excellent example this in these days of peace and plenty."[18]

The Revolutionary War had inadvertently provided opportunities for men to form social and sexual attachments as transients, as men without firm ties to a local community through marriage, family, and household. After the war, many commentators heralded marriage as the correct path for men.

The issue of a tax on bachelors was resurrected during the post–Revolutionary War era, when essays on the benefits of marriage and family filled newspapers and other print sources. In an article appearing in the

Boston Gazette on February 23, 1784, entitled "An Address to Maids" and signed by a "bachelor" in "Massachusetts," the postwar situation was explicitly described. The author criticized women for using the war as an excuse not to marry or commit to men while acknowledging that a "*few* sincere nymphs have waited pretty patiently for an offer, till the conclusion of the *War*." After poking fun at a supposed bachelor tax, the author exclaimed, "no doubt that heavy taxes would remove this political and social evil, Celibacy:—interest may induce an old churl to stifle all the dictates of nature and passion; but the annual sum of twenty pounds will frighten him into the arms of Venus, and make him a good member of society."[19]

In the postwar era, bachelors stood in the way of the growth and development of stable households on which to build a virtuous nation. Their resistance to marriage and family prevented them from achieving proper manliness. An essay entitled "On Marriage," appearing in the *Continental Journal* in 1785, opined: "Single persons, who, without sufficient reason, refuse to marry, are to be considered as half-men, wanting the courage and address, the pleasing satisfaction, of performing many great duties, which Providence has beneficently prepared men for."[20]

Hopelessly attempting to balance the lopsided debate, only a handful of essays countered the negative images of bachelors. A 1785 letter to the printers of the *Independent Chronicle* appropriated the language of the American Revolution in asserting that bachelors had the right to live singly, given that "every man has a right to liberty." The letter defended bachelors against the charges of their being like "a drunkard" and "a whoremonger." Those who articulated a position that was decidedly against marriage had their voices heard, to be sure, but more often than not, they were ridiculed by the press.[21]

Bachelors, as individuals who had not yet achieved full manliness given their unmarried state, worried those who saw marriage and household order as critical for a virtuous, stable social order. In the absence of a proper sexual outlet, single men not only frustrated social order, failed to father future generations, and left women unsatisfied but were also implicitly sexually deviant. Given the close adherence to the marital sanctioning of sexual expression, bachelors were either unnaturally celibate, and therefore without a healthy masculine sexual drive, or presumed to be engaging in out-of-wedlock trysts. As I argue in the following section, figures of effeminate unmarried men, including the fop, and an array of other closely related figures or nascent types, such as the "coxcomb," "beau," and "pretty gentleman," operated within this broader critique of unmarried men. As such, depictions of the foppish bachelor echoed many of the same concerns, including his deviance from the male sexual norm.

Foppish Bachelors

For three weeks in August 1729, readers of the *New England Weekly Journal* found the front page devoted to comparisons between the "unaffected gentleman" and the "fop." The series of three essays typifies eighteenth-century discussions of masculinity found in newspapers. The essays centered on contrasting characteristics, including common sense and foolishness, humility and excessive pride, and the various ways in which these traits were said to manifest themselves in dress and social comportment. In the early eighteenth century, representations of effeminate unmarried men figured in discourses of manly comportment and character. Bostonians' concerns about the consumption of luxury goods, changing ideals of courtship and marriage, and the development of public spaces for heterosociality heightened their preoccupations with effeminacy and manliness. In their newspapers and literature, and from their ministers, Bostonians read and heard about how normative eighteenth-century men should dress, socialize, and converse and were warned against his unmanly counterparts.[22]

Additionally, there existed, more specifically, a relationship between perceived sexual licentiousness and the preoccupation with the distinction between effeminacy and (married) manliness. Portrayals of male effeminacy, especially in dress, but also in conversation and other social behavior, that circulated in eighteenth-century Massachusetts focused on social vices such as cowardice, foolishness, vanity, and idleness. On occasion, the effeminate bachelor was directly implicated in unauthorized sexuality, and all of his vices also figured in discussions of sexual deviance, in particular of nonreproductive sexuality—masturbation and sodomy.[23]

In Massachusetts the discourse of normative manliness and effeminacy remained more closely yoked to older (sexually charged) religious discourses about idleness, luxury, and pride than it was in London. This is in part because Boston remained a provincial town still influenced by its Puritan origins. Thus, early eighteenth-century London was home to molly houses, where men gathered for same-sex romantic and sexual relationships, and to a visible subculture of effeminate (usually single) men who paraded around public parks, such as Vauxhall Gardens, and congregated in theaters. In contrast, theater did not even debut in Boston until the very end of the eighteenth century; nor did the city have a promenade early in the century, let alone a visible molly house subculture.[24]

Tensions over the consumption of luxury goods were high in a culture where Congregationalist churches still dominated and where Puritan ministers and their literature still had great influence. It is true that consumption patterns in the colonies did not undergo dramatic shifts until the midcentury, when consumer goods became more widely available. Nevertheless, new patterns of consumption were significant enough even in the first half of the eighteenth century to warrant concern. In the first half of the century, Bay Colony cultural concerns were articulated as a combination of orthodox Puritan and secular views. Within this context concerns over effeminate male dress and comportment and the accompanying associations with problematic (heterosexual) sociability became linked with the unauthorized sexuality of unmarried men.[25]

The effeminate bachelor's deviance expressed itself in his interactions with women in social settings, particularly through conversation. As a man who transgressed the rules of normative gender performance, the effeminate unmarried man was socially disruptive. Discourses of the effeminate bachelor, however, also connected his social comportment to his inward moral character. A religiously saturated discourse of immorality centering on pride and vanity connected the effeminate unmarried man to deviant sexuality in particular: the effeminate man shared traits similar to those of the masturbator and the sodomite. This aspect of portrayals of effeminate bachelors highlights one particular strand of normative masculinity: good men married and avoided sexual corruption. Closely related, the effeminate man's deviance was written onto his corrupted body and physique. In the early eighteenth century, these portrayals of effeminacy pinpointed forms of gender deviance that all men, married or not, needed to guard against, yet at the same time they created an effeminate bachelor minority. By the end of the eighteenth century, that minority status would confer the specific figure of the fop a less important role in Massachusetts discussions of manly comportment, whereas bachelorhood, in general, remained a central concern.

Dress, Fashion, and Effeminacy

Commenting on Shaftesbury's *Characteristics of Men, Manners, Opinions, Times* (1711), historian G. J. Barker-Benfield concludes: " 'Effeminacy' . . .

was a derogatory term, applied to men and coupled with cowardice and weakness." Also citing Shaftesbury, Michèle Cohen rightly points out that one of the primary meanings of *effeminacy* was "excess." "Excess positioned the gentleman as effeminate, 'self-control' positioned him as manly," writes Cohen. Both scholars agree that effeminacy was associated with a capitulation to one's desire for pleasure.[26]

These scholars have shown that the specter of effeminacy played a significant role in discourses critiquing luxury and excess and their relationship to developing commercial trade networks. The association of effeminacy with critiques of excessive consumption was certainly present in early Massachusetts and was linked to an older religious discourse on gluttony, luxury, and excess that would later become closely connected with a developing culture of refinement and with critiques of the increasingly sophisticated market economies of the second half of the eighteenth century. In eighteenth-century Massachusetts, the word *effeminacy* was often used to denote moral weakness, especially in relation to love of luxury, with or without a clear emphasis on commerce.[27]

Effeminacy was at times explicitly used to denote sexual immorality. Thomas Foxcroft, in a sermon to young people, included the "Effeminate" as an "unclean Person" along with the adulterer, fornicator, and masturbator. In this case Foxcroft may have had in mind one seventeenth-century meaning of "Effeminate" when he drafted his list: the "sodomite." Cotton Mather, in a sermon to "Old Men, and Young Men, and Little Children," used the term to connote moral laxity, especially failures of self-control. He charged that many people wrongly viewed certain sins as "venial, easy *peccadillo's*." Mather singled out "self-pollution" and quoted scripture to label such harmful "filthiness" as *"Effeminacies."*[28]

The normative man did not blindly follow fashion, yet he nonetheless crafted an appearance designed to appeal. "The Medium between a Fop and a Sloven is what A Man of Sense would endeavour to keep," declared the imported British periodical *The Spectator* in 1711. Clothing was to reflect a man's station in society, yet was also to be somewhere between careless and carefree. An article on appropriate male dress and comportment appearing in the *New England Magazine* in 1758 instructed: "Do thy Affairs call thee abroad? Array thee in decent Apparel; neither respect nor condemn too much the Fashion; the one is Foppery, the other Singularity: Approach then as near the borders of the Mode as thy Fortune, thy Condition, and thy personal Figure permit thee. Follow not the Examples of Numbers, who purchase the being ridiculous at a vast Expence." Thus, one was to dress in a manner that appropriately reflected one's personal wealth and status, but also with regard to the general injunction to avoid luxury and excess.[29]

The stress was on the importance of crafting an appearance that accurately reflected one's social position and demonstrated good taste. The *New England Weekly Journal* clearly promoted this message in its three-part series of 1729. In the final installment, the paper contrasts the man of "good sense" with the "affected man":

> Whereas your Gentlemen of good Sense are for doing what is natural and agreable to common Custom; they are for every thing out of the Way, extraordinary and distorted. They fancy it will wonderfully recommend them if they appear something singular to the World. This makes them affect either intirely to differ from the Fashion in their Dress, or else to go so much to the Height of it as to be taken Notice of for being the greatest Beaux's of the Species.

"Distorted" and "singular to the World," the affected man was an unnatural member of his "Species" and a figure against which normative manhood could be clearly defined. Through dress, speech, and comportment, the "unaffected man" indicated his awareness of social position and his sensitivity to "common Custom." Overall, the series declared, "The unaffected Gentleman is one, who at the same time he is truly humble, knows what belongs to him: When to condescend, and when to assume. His Sense is his own. He is Master of it, and lets you see he understands himself in whatever he says."[30]

Thus, dress and comportment were supposed to operate as visible markers of gradations in social status. Deviations from normative dress signified social disarray as well as individual aberration. Some British accounts, such as the following piece reprinted in the *Boston Evening Post* in 1757, bluntly articulated anxieties surrounding changing fashion and its capacity to erode social distinctions: "Now Dress is so blinded that there is no real Mark to know a Gentleman." Increase Mather, too, condemned the poor, who though they had "scarce Bread to Eat," would yet be "Fine and Fashionable." In so doing, they commit the sin of pride, he said, wrongfully going "above their Quality, above their Parentage, and above their Estates."[31]

The fop's ostentatious display and failure to know his social position tended to be expressed as a violation of natural order. "Nature in her whole Drama never drew such a Part; she has sometimes made a Fool, but a Coxcomb is always of Man's own making." Men who affected effeminate behaviors and adopted fashionable clothing outside the bounds of normative manliness were said to be a "graft upon Nature" or to have become a "Race of Coxcombs." Indignant about an advertisement that had appeared in his *Essex Gazette,* which read "a Person from London, dresses Hair at Salem in the newest Fashions," one reader submitted a poem that makes a similar point about calibrating dress to nature's dictates. He wrote: "Nature first taught Simplicity of Dress; / Clean elegant Attire, free from Excess; / Unmix'd with foppish Ornaments." More generally, the author of the series on the "affected Gentleman" exhorted his readers, "let us study Nature: that is the genuine Pattern and Rule to which we should conform our Actions." "What is unnatural," the article warned, "presently becomes monstrous, and ridiculous." By raising the specter of the "monster," though a monster more "ridiculous" than frightening, the author underscored his emphasis on the unnatural.[32]

Sociability and Conversation

As Michèle Cohen observes, by the end of the eighteenth century "'free communication between the sexes' was an index of the refinement and polish of a nation." But even in the early eighteenth century, praise of the normative man could include his "unaffected Behaviour in Conversation." Many accounts pointed to the effeminate bachelor's stilted and empty conversation. "It is not without the greatest Indignation that I always behold *Will Formly,* " reads one such example from the *New England Weekly Journal.* "He is the most exact in his Apparel of any Man breathing; had learn'd to Dance exquisitely well; can adjust his Body to the Best Rules of good Manners; and always affects to be seen with the most fashionable Gentlemen of the most polite Sense: But I scarce ever knew him to say anything, except, *Ladies, it is very fine Weather! Gentlemen, can you tell what a Clock it is? Madam, will you please to take some of my Brazil?*"[33]

The fictitious Will Formly and other "coxcombs" were generally portrayed as bachelors who were aware of the social importance of conversational skills and who therefore tried but failed to pass themselves off as appealing, intelligent men to both sexes. "An easie Manner of Conversation is the most desirable Quality a Man can have; and for that Reason Coxcombs will take upon them to be familiar with People whom they never saw before," began one article in *The Tatler.* "These People are the more dreadful, the more they have of what is usually called Wit: For a lively Imagination, when it is not governed by a good Understanding, makes such miserable Havock both in Conversation and Business, that it lays you defenceless, and fearful to throw the least Word in its Way, that may give it new Matter for its further Errors." In short, such men lacked social tact and spewed disruptive nonsense speech.[34]

Such sentiments were echoed in Boston papers, which charged affected unmarried men not only with ignorance but also with a lack of self-awareness: "If they are talkative they will deafen your Ears with such a loud Din of Words, that you cannot bear to hear them any longer, yet they imagine they have fully made you sensible they are Men of large Understanding." Thus, while the affected, fashionable man plunged into conversations and attempted witticisms, the results—as with his other social endeavors—were comically inept: he disrupted polite conversation and subjected himself to social humiliation.[35]

The effeminate, single man was portrayed as a failure in the polite social world of networking and courting. In some accounts, such men were vilified for prejudicing the minds of young women against more virtuous manly types, in part through flirtatious talk. "A Coxcomb flushed with many of these infamous Victories shall say he is sorry for the poor Fools, protest and vow he never thought of Matrimony, and wonder [that] talking civilly can be so strangely misinterpreted," wrote one female complainant to *The Spectator.* In reply, the editor asserted: "They whom my Correspondent calls Male Coquets, shall hereafter be called *Friblers.* A Fribler is one who professes Rapture and Admiration for the Woman to whom he addresses, and dreads nothing so much as her Consent." In short, such men took pleasure in leading women on through insinuating banter.[36]

But unlike the rake, the effeminate bachelor mocked polite company by soliciting the affections of women without intending to follow through. In this respect, the "Male Coquet" was very much the heartless and vain, but impotent socializer. Such a figure resonated loudly at a time when changing ideas about courtship and companionate marriages made heterosociality a heightened concern. Through their manipulation of appearance and gesture, bachelors posed a calculated threat to the undiscerning woman's heart. So suspect was their banter that *The Guardian* could underscore a woman's virtue and powers of discrimination by pointing out her indifference to such company: "She is in no Familiarities with the Fops, her Fan has never been yet out of her own Hand, and her Brother's Face is the only Man's she ever look'd in stedfastly."[37]

The foppish, witty bachelor was said to be popular in certain circles, but he could not win approval as a serious suitor or future husband. Criticizing the *Boston Gazette* for carrying an article that provocatively stated that "Fools and Coxcombs are most acceptable to the Ladies," one woman, in a lengthy letter printed on the paper's front page in the winter of 1731, re-torted that "Men of Sense are scarce." "Must we resolve never to Converse with the opposite Sex, or go under the Reproach of favouring Coxcombs?" she queried. She elaborated: "It may be said we love Fops and Fools, be-cause we play with them, and so we do with Parrots Monkeys and Owls." In a covert criticism of Boston's pool of eligible bachelors, she explained why women tolerated the company of such creatures: "if we cannot procure Ob-jects of Admiration and esteem, we divert ourselves with those of Ridicule and Contempt." "But, Oh, Sir," she wrote, giving a nod to the unaffected man, "if you knew the exquisite Pleasure that we Women receive from the Conversation of a Man of Sense." Such praise of the "Man of Sense," complete with his power to produce "exquisite Pleasure" through well-conducted social "conversation" (a term with a sexually laden double meaning), endorsed a model of manhood that emphasized true refinement. Meanwhile the letter equated the effeminate bachelor with "Parrots" and "Monkeys" who mindlessly copied others, and with inarticulate "Owls." In his foolish, promiscuous, yet enticing talk, he was far removed from the normative manly ideal, despite his superficial success in social circles.[38]

By contrast, the normative man was clearly a man of moderation, capa-ble of regulating his social self-presentation, mastering his body, and or-dering his mind. He was truly cultivated—a far cry from the "coxcomb," who merely simulated such cultivation and more often then not betrayed himself in polite company through foolish excess. One letter to *The Specta-tor* from a sixty-seven-year-old woman distinguished between true feeling and mere posturing in courtship and love. "The Gentleman I am Married to made Love to me in Rapture, but it was the Rapture of a Christian and a Man of Honour, not a Romantick Hero, or a Whining Coxcomb: This put our Life upon a right Basis." The bachelor's nonsense, and sometimes se-ductively misleading talk, served as a foil for the "Man of Sense," who was capable of the unaffected conversation that promoted harmonious social in-tercourse associated with courtship and marriage.[39]

Youth, Idleness, and City Sins

In the early eighteenth century, if preening self-display and excessive attachment to fashion were sometimes associated with an effeminate mi-nority, they could also signal a more widespread form of overweening self-regard or pride. From this vantage point the foppish bachelor was not so much—or not just—a foil against which normative manliness could be defined, but rather a figure that represented in an extreme form the vices to which all were prone. Thus references to prideful love of appearance were frequent in the sermons on Sodom and Gomorrah. Increase Mather, for example, included the wearing of *"Strange Apparel"* as one reason for the destruction of Sodom and Gomorrah. In 1723 the front page of the *New England Courant* declared that among the "Sins of Sodom" already appearing in New England were "abundance of Pride, in Heart Behaviour, and Apparel." *The Burning of Sodom,* a Boston publication of a sermon preached at Charleston, South Carolina, after a fire destroyed a large part of the city in 1740, similarly warned that "The PRIDE of *Sodom*" has "appeared in our *Dress* and *Address,* in our *Mien, & High Looks,* and *supercilious Language.*" *The Burning of Sodom* also explicitly singled out sodomy as one of the causes of the destruction of Sodom. The effect of this text and other sermons that focused on the sexual dimension of Sodom's fall was also to associate vain social display with the taint of sexual corruption. When the suspicion of "city sins" was coupled with a desire to protect youth, the result could be a cautionary tale about the lifelong consequences of idleness and the sexual and social vices that it encouraged.[40]

In 1713 *The Guardian* took a similar tack, connecting vain living with a propensity to commit sinful and "unnatural" sexual acts. "Gay Characters, and those which lead in the Pleasures and Inclinations of the fashionable World, are such as are readiest to practise Crimes the most abhorrent to Nature, and contradictory to our Faith." Here the pursuit of the "pleasures" of the "fashionable World," including ostentatious dress, is directly linked to a propensity to engage in "Crimes the most abhorrent to Nature," a phrase typically used to allude to the sexual sins of masturbation and sodomy.[41]

Young people, and young, single men in particular, were the special concern of those who wrote sermons and tracts warning of extravagant living, excessive attachment to fashion, and associated sexual temptations. Consider the following warning in a sermon of 1725: "Idleness," which included "Mirth and Jollity, impertinent Visits, unprofitable vain Conversation," and "over curious Dressing," "is likewise a Sin that Young Persons are exceeding apt to fall into." One notices that the pastimes and vices to which the young were especially prone were also the ones associated with fops: "vain Conversation," "impertinent Visits," and, of course, love of fashion. This is also true of Samuel Phillips's sermon. Noting that "Young People are prone, above others, to be puff'd up with *Pride,*" he said that such pride is revealed "Sometimes by their *Gesture* and Behaviour, as in their Gate [*sic*] and manner of Deportment. Sometimes by their *Garb* and *Dress,* in which they are oftentimes Extravagant." He also said of ostentatious dress or *"Extravagance in Attire,"* in particular, that it is "Another Sin, which some *Young Persons* are fond of, and which they *entice* one another unto." "Extravagant" "Garb," "Gate," and "Gesture" were social manifestations of the sin of pride that carried the special danger that they could be easily spread by youthful mimicry. Idleness was also a *"City*-Sin," according to Thomas Foxcroft's sermon on Sodom. *"Idleness,"* he wrote, "was the Iniquity of thy Sister *Sodom*: Abundance of Idleness was in her, & in her Sons & Daughters. It is very much a *City*-Sin, and a Sin of *Youth*.... Idleness is a common Inlet to many other Sins: it's seldom that those who are idle, are *only* idle: they are at Leisure to attend the *Devil's* Motions, and often go of his Errands." Here Foxcroft linked the growing concern over leisure-time activities associated with city life with the youthful propensity for idleness and the sins that it bred.[42]

The cultural sites and practices typically associated with what Thomas Foxcroft called "City-Sins" were not as extensive in eighteenth-century Massachusetts as they were in London in large part because Boston ministers continued to construe the sin of idleness expansively to demand a ban on theater (which would last until 1790) and restrictions on public dances and celebrations. Meanwhile, critiques of luxury and consumption that had currency on both sides of the Atlantic featured a close association of foppery with London's masquerades, balls, and theatergoing culture. This association did not go unnoticed in Boston; in addition to the ban on theater, dances and dancing schools were subject to alarmist criticism by those concerned with regulating social interactions.[43]

Urban centers in particular raised eyebrows when provincials from Massachusetts left the region. William Palfrey, while on a diplomatic tour of London in 1771, was shocked to see graffiti in the city and made the effort to record what he had read. For Palfrey every public place seemed to be marked with the words of an immoral population. Glass etchings, according to Palfrey, included "obscenity and prophanity." For this Massachusetts man it seemed that "A Diamond and Glass Is pen & Ink for every Ass." Similarly, when clergyman Benjamin Guild left Boston to visit New York in 1774, he included the "many young rakes & beaus" among his physical description of the city; he also noted the water supply, colleges, churches, and streets. For Guild the nature of relations between the sexes was as important to the city as its infrastructure.[44]

Some forty years after the demise of the Puritan commonwealth, newspapers such as the *Boston Weekly News Letter* still carried in their pages critiques of a generation gone awry. The following appeared on the front page as a letter from an alarmed "gentleman" who wrote "for the Benefit of the Publick," after he had been handed, as he walked past the Town-House in

Boston, a piece of paper advertising a monthly "assembly" or "Entertainment of Musick and Dancing." He wrote: "When we look back upon the
Transactions of our Fore-Fathers, and read the Wonderful Story of their
Godly Zeal, their pious Resolutions, and their Publick Virtues; how should
we blush and lament our present Corruption of Manners, and Decay of Religious & Civil Discipline?" He linked his general lamentation about the
decline of public "Virtues" explicitly to the popularization of dances, or
so-called assemblies. The author continued: "But this their Posterity are
too delicate to follow their sober Rules, and wise Maxims, and crying out
for Musick, Balls and Assemblies, like Children for their Bells and Rattles;
as if our Riches flow'd in so fast upon us, that we wanted ways to dispose of
them: Whereas it is too well known how our Extravagance in Apparel, and
Luxury at our Tables, are hastening the ruin of our Country, and are evils
which call loudly for a Remedy." Here a vision of the pious Puritan past was
used to critique the excesses of unregulated appetites stimulated by riches.
"Musick, Balls and Assemblies" were associated with "Extravagance" and
"Luxury" and roundly condemned. Speaking of the monthly dances, the
writer continued, "I could not read this Advertisement without being star-
tled and concern'd at the Birth of so formidable a Monster in this part of
the World." By branding the dances as a "Monster," the author called upon
eighteenth-century discourses of unholy and unnatural occurrences that
could be both threatening and instructional. While it was assumed that in
London vice was rampant and tied to such activities as strolling around
parks, attending the theater, and dancing in public balls, Bostonians reacted
with all the force of the jeremiad against such new sites of urban sociability
and associated them with depravity.[45]

At the same time, idleness and the specific pastimes associated with
youthful idleness were also very closely linked to sexual immorality. As we
have seen, "balls" and "assemblies" in particular were believed to arouse
sexual passions that most could not resist. Published sermons had long used
historical and biblical references to illustrate how dance stimulated unbridled sexual urges. In an early sermon against mixed-sex dancing, Cotton
Mather explained: "Some when they were inflamed at the *Dance,* went from
the *Dancing-school* to the *Brothel house.*" In a diary entry on a ball he attended for Governor William Shirley's departure in 1756, Robert Treat
Paine included remarks on the passions stirred by dance and costume:
"every Appetite becomes fir'd, & every faculty moves briskly to the infat-
uation of its charms. Nor can we leave the dear delusion at once. Our rebel
Passions must have time to cool ere they consent to reinstate Reason on
the Throne & extirpate the ill weeds of Vice." The notion that public gath-

erings could stir up vanities and desires that even the hardiest of persons could not control seems to have held sway for much of the eighteenth century.[46]

Thus, while it was understood that young single men were prone to idleness and its twin, sexual licentiousness, such behavior was not excused as an acceptable part of growing up. Rather, these sexual activities could poison a life. "THAT Sins committed by Persons in their Youth often prove long after, a great grief and heavy burthen to them," was a commonplace belief. The *Boston Gazette* expressed a similar theme, with an emphasis on the degenerative and debilitating effects of effeminate living, using the figure of the foppish old bachelor to make its point. In 1730 the paper's front page reprinted an article in letter form from the British *Gentleman's Magazine* on the "Vanity of affecting to be tho't younger than we are." The editor's commentary condemned such men in now-familiar language: "*dressing Coxcombs, and ridiculous Fops.*" But his emphasis was elsewhere. He also wrote that they were "old decay'd *Debauchees,*" who "having consumed their Youth in *Vice* and *Vanity,* have no Relish in their old Age for any Thing but the Gratifications of Sense which they cannot enjoy." Thus, the letter warned young people that indulging in youthful vice led to a lifelong downward trajectory. The end result would be physical enervation and decay: the old "Debauchee" was so much at the mercy of his desires after a lifetime of indulgence as to suffer a kind of social and physical impotence. The following section examines perceived causal relations between effeminacy and the corrupted body.[47]

Weak Bodies and Degenerate Natures

While property ownership and becoming an independent, married householder were important markers of adult manhood, overlooking the physical and sexual components of manliness flattens the complexity of gender ideology. As the discussion of commentaries on marital sexuality has shown, the male body was indeed both sexualized and idealized in eighteenth-century Massachusetts.

Ideals of male physique often emphasized stature, especially height and musculature, but also at times facial appearance. One letter reprinted in *The Tatler* satirizes prevailing bodily ideals by playing on the feeling that women were too hard to please: "'Tis my Misfortune to be Six Foot and a half high, Two full Spans between the Shoulders, Thirteen Inches diameter in the Calves. . . . I am not quite Six and twenty, and my Nose is mark'd truly Aquiline. For these Reasons, I am in a very particular Manner her

Aversion." Though a satire, the essay provides a list of early eighteenth-century physical ideals, even as it exaggerates them; they include muscular calves, a broad chest, tallness, and such racialized traits as an aquiline nose. Strength figures prominently among such ideals. Comparing men and women, the *New England Weekly Journal* informed readers that the "Male-World are distinguished with a stronger Form and Constitution, as well as an Air that is bold and rugged."[48]

The satire also puts in play a broader commentary on heterosexual attraction. In Bernard Mandeville's 1709 essay *The Virgin Unmask'd*, which was set as a dialogue between an older woman and her niece on love, marriage, and morality, one of the central characters responds to seeing a man she once loved: "Being grown taller and more Manly, in Spight of all her Vertue, *Leonora* could not forbear being charm'd with the Sight of him." According to Mandeville, at any rate, physical appeal was a legitimate feature of courtship. In the same work, Mandeville described one hopeful suitor as follows: "He was a Tall, Well-made, Proper Man, and *Aurelia's* Father seeing a Gentleman of his Mien, well Dress'd, with a Couple of Footmen in good Liveries to attend him, received him very civilly." Here Mandeville connected idealized physical attributes—"Tall" and "Well-made"—with indications of gentility ("well Dress'd" and "Proper," not to speak of an entourage of footmen).[49]

But such physical attributes were not purely about looks. The state of the body was a manifestation of the moral man within. Josiah Cotton, for example, recorded in his diary on the occasion of his brother's death in 1691: "as to his Person, he was rather less than tall, of a ruddy Countenance a very handsome Face of a good Mien & Gesture, and much of a Gentleman in his Garb and Actions." Similarly, about his father, Josiah wrote: "As to his Body he was of a Handsom Ruddy, yet grave countenance, of a Sanguine Complexion, a middling Stature, and inclined to Fatness." Such descriptions emphasized a healthy complexion ("Ruddy") and other physical features, conjoining them with appropriate dress and comportment ("a Gentleman in his Garb and Actions"). In some cases the descriptive language blended looks and temperament ("grave countenance").[50]

A handsome face or pleasing build was believed to reflect the inner man. Writing to her sister, Abigail Adams remarked that their cousin's suitor was both physically and spiritually appealing—the ideal man inside and out. "His Face, you know," she wrote, "the more you behold it, the more it shines." Still appraising his looks, she continued: "his Shape is very fine." She then linked his physical attributes to his comportment and character. "His voice agreeable—his Manners easy—attentive and polite." The sisters counted their cousin a lucky woman to have found a man who appeared to be such a promising husband. As far as they were concerned, she would be a "very happy Girl, if she can love & be loved by a Person of so worthy a character." This view was captured by a poem printed in Jacob Cushing's almanac of 1781. Published by Isaiah Thomas, the poem was entitled "The Maid's Description of the Man She Would Choose." Linking both physical and interior states, it began with the stanza "Give him a form that may delight. / My inward sense, my mental sight; / In every outward act, designed / To speak an elegance of mind." Finally, consider the description of an eligible bachelor in *Roderick Random*: "He was about the age of two and twenty, among the tallest of the middle-size; had chestnut coloured hair which he wore tied up in a ribbon; a high polished fore-head, a nose inclining aqualine, lively blue eyes, red pouting lips, teeth as white as snow, and a certain openness of countenance." One of the female characters also referred to his modesty and sincerity: "He spoke little, and seemed to have no reserve, for what he said was ingenuous, sensible, and uncommon.... His behaviour was modest and respectful." Here the description of an ideal suitor linked key physical attributes, such as height, with valued character traits such as modesty and intellect.[51]

Great leaders were often the subjects of a physical scrutiny that underscored their strength of character. The *New England Weekly Journal* in 1727 devoted the front page to a discussion of "illustrious Heros" in history. The essay included the following description of how "the commonality delight to hover over the Ruins of Greatness, as the *Grecians* did over the Body of *Hector*." There they admired "the Beauty of his Face, his manly Limbs." In an anecdote designed to amuse a friend, Robert Treat Paine referred to Gardiner Chandler, who was selectman, treasurer, and finally sheriff of Worcester, as "the *Duke of Limbs*" and described him as "gracefully tall" and "his Limbs" as "of a most manly proportion wch. Gave rise to his title." He proposed "himself for the Standard of a well proportioned Man," concluded Paine. Commenting on an officer's universal appeal, Revolutionary War soldier Joseph Plumb Martin wrote, "This Colonel Stewart was an excellent officer, much beloved and respected by the troops of the line he belonged to. He possessed great personal beauty; the Philadelphia ladies styled him *the Irish Beauty*." George Washington had a kind of physical appeal. One anecdote from the *Hampshire Gazette* in 1790 told the story of a gentleman traveling in Massachusetts who refused to sleep on sheets that the landlady explained had been used the previous night by the president. He was promptly given another room, but a "young lady" arriving on the same night, upon being offered Washington's former bed, declared: "*she would sleep in the sheets,* and if she could not be where he *was,* was glad to be where he *had been.*"[52]

Occasionally looks could mislead, though. A 1748 article in the *Boston Evening Post,* sentimentally describing the execution of a counterfeiter in England, remarked: "Those of the softer Sex, who attended the Ceremony, lamented that so comely and well-*timbered* a Man, should come to so untimely an End." Similarly, an essay that warned that reading novels was said to mislead women highlighted the distractive nature of male beauty. The author argued that reading spoiled the minds of young women with "luxuriant fancy" by depicting "a young man in perfection in body and mind."[53]

If the ideal man was married, strong, and controlled, the effeminate single man was known not only by his dress and gesture but also by his physique. The "beau" in the poem "*Monsieur* A-LA-MODE" had "lank Calves" and "to add to his Height," wore his breeches so that they did "not cover his knees." The focus on well-developed calves as a synecdoche for the general emphasis on musculature and its association with masculinity explains the early modern fashion of wearing fake calves of wool.[54]

Weak bodies were considered evidence of degenerate natures. Although the association of immoral behavior with weakened bodies applied to both sexes, effeminate men were more often singled out because masculinity was so closely tied to robust physical strength and sexual performance. The youthful vigor displayed at his Boston wedding reception by an elderly man who married a younger woman "shews," wrote one commentator, "the great Advantage of a *plain* way of living." In contrast, the "many who live after a *luxuriant* manner, are of puny Constitutions, and their Days contracted." Depictions of men given up to luxury and idleness highlighted their lack of manliness and associated it with their underdeveloped musculature. According to the 1752 *Boston Evening Post,* "Dressing, Drumming, Routing, Playing, [and] Masquerading...turn Youth, Bloom, and Beauty, into ghastly, palled, and unwholsome Complexion." Men who engaged in such "pleasures" had "lost that masculine Aspect worn by their Ancestors." "Is it not frightful, as well as lamentable, to behold so many young Fellows enervated and wasted into Skeletons, thro' an inordinate Gratification of their sensual appetites?" asked the *Evening Post,* expressing concern over young unmarried men's loss of strength and the weakening of their moral and physical constitutions.[55]

In addition to the connection between sickly bodies and immoral living generally, a scrawny physique was associated specifically with sexual dissipation, most often with masturbation. According to *Onania*, too many young people were unaware of the "Bodily Sufferings and infirmities" that masturbation could bring. "Licentious Masturbaters" physically resembled the effeminate bachelor; they had "meagre Jaws, and pale Looks, with feeble Hams, and Legs without Calves." They lacked "Robustness or Strength." Cotton Mather echoed this sentiment in his tract on masturbation. Men given over to the practice were described as being "emaciated," "reduced into a woful *Consumption*; his *Visage* Pale and Leane, and *Stomach* Depraved, and his depauperated *Blood* fill'd with acid, and acrid Particles." "Many young Men," explained *Onania*, "who were strong and lusty before they gave themselves over to this Vice, have been worn out by it, and by its robbing the Body of its balmy and vital Moisture, without Cough or Spitting, dry and emaciated, sent to their Graves.... That used when young, it so forces and weakens the tender Vessels."[56]

Onania also warned that masturbation could rob single men of their abilities to marry and reproduce. According to the author, when such young men "come to Manhood, it renders them ridiculous to Women, because impotent, a Curse half tanti to Castration; many of them not being able to touch a Woman.... In some Men of very strong Constitutions, the Mischiefs may not be so visible, and themselves perhaps capable of Marrying." But even those men, according to *Onania*, would almost certainly be infertile, or, if "by Nature's extraordinary Helps, they should get any Children, which happens not often, they are commonly weakly little ones, that either die soon, or become tender, sickly People, always ailing and complaining; a Misery to themselves, a dishonour to humane Race, and a scandal to their Parents."[57]

As their lack of physical strength might suggest, effeminate men were also thought to be cowards. Appearing in the *Boston Evening Post*, the poem entitled "*Monsieur* A-LA-MODE" included the line "he to Cowardice shews he's a Slave!" Bravery figured as an important component of manliness in part because it was considered a necessary quality for heads of household and masters of dependents. Effeminate men, such as "pretty fellows," lacked the bravery needed to protect dependents.[58]

As a foil for normative manhood, then, the foppish bachelor was not merely a figure who condensed norms of social comportment by negation. He was a nascent type, possessing a character structure that explained his social buffoonery and disruptiveness and which marked itself upon his dissipated body. As a character type, he was unmanly through and through: he was not merely foolish; like the bachelor, he lacked "natural sense." To refer one last time to the three-part series run by the *New England Weekly Journal* in 1729, the "affected man" or "fop" was "half-witted" and had "little Share of natural Sense." Similarly, a midcentury poem described the "beau" as "a Creature that Nature has form'd without Brains, Whose Skul nought but Nonsense and Sonnets contains." Or, consider the following: "Nature having set them out half-witted, you may depend upon it, all their Actions will be parti-coloured, and bear the Stamp of Wit and Folly." The effeminate bachelor was incapable of self-regulation, and his body bore the imprint of his disordered mind. As one account from London reprinted in 1734 summed it up: "the Imperfections of his Mind run parallel with those of his Body."[59]

His folly was compounded by excessive self-regard, of which his foolish preening was only a symptom. The poem "*Monsieur* A-LA-MODE," written by a "LADY," appeared on the front page of the *Boston Evening Post* in 1754. She described "*Monsieur*" as possessing "a Mind where Conceit with Folly's ally'd, Set off by Assurance and unmeaning Pride." This self-regard marked the entire character. "This Pride," explained another author writing on the "fop" some twenty-five years earlier, "possesses their Soul, mixes it self with every one of their Actions, and sits enthroned upon their Countenance." In this instance, pride was portrayed as an aspect of inner being ("Soul") and of "Actions," and it marked the body through physical expressions ("sits enthroned upon their Countenance.")[60]

The fop's self-regard revealed his lack of interest in women and highlighted, by way of contrast, normative male sexual attraction to women. In eighteenth-century Massachusetts, traits in women that were assumed to cause "excitement" in men could be found in newspapers, essays, and popular literature. Such essays, which circumscribed the ideal traits of womanhood, simultaneously defined normative male sexual interests. Consider, for example, one item appearing in the *American Herald* in 1789 entitled "Advice to Unmarried Ladies." This item was a veritable laundry list of idealized female traits, including demureness, modesty, and avoidance of confrontation in conversation. By defining in a male voice what women should be like, the essay represented male sexual desire. The emphasis on physical traits, especially in young women, such as a "pretty foot," "good teeth," "pretty hands and arms," the "finest voice," was coupled with social qualities such as avoiding outward envy, being "gentle," and lodging "blame" only with "reluctance." This conveyed the qualities that normative men were to desire in a mate. Similarly, an open letter to "LADIES who affect shewing their WHITE STOCKINGS," printed in the *Boston Gazette* in 1782, chastised women who wore white stockings for their lack of modesty, but it hinged the critique on normative, racialized male sexual desire, declaring "A Lady's Leg is a dangerous Sight in whatever Colour it appears." The specific problem related to white stockings was that given their color, they were "next to shewing us them naked." The letter was sprinkled with references to suggest that all men felt this way: "our view" or "gives us such Offense" and "puts our Virtue into so much Danger." Here the pronouns signal that this letter described heteronormative masculine standards of sexual desire. Popular songs also repeated this cultural work. Consider, for example, the song "Sally," reprinted in the *Massachusetts Magazine* in the summer of 1799, which sketched the ideal young woman as "fair as the flow'rs," "sweet as the rose after show'rs," and elegant and graceful. Such qualities lent themselves to complementing the ideal male physical desires as well as his social role as head of household, governor of their marriage.[61]

To say that there was an emphasis and fixed interest in the male physique in this culture is not to equate that interest with any focus on women's bodies. Eroticized male bodies, such as open faces, had important implications for the eighteenth-century male world of reputation and personalized networks of commerce. Hands and shoulders symbolized force, strength, and mastery. Male bodies were not simply abstractly appealing under the female or male gaze. Male bodies could be eroticized because they were thought to display qualities so prized in eighteenth-century men.

The foppish bachelor's enervated body stood in contrast to masculine ideals of physical robustness. His physicality was associated with an emasculating cowardliness and unearned self-regard. He was associated with a dissipated sexuality and deviant social disposition that amounted to a refusal to participate in productive adult sexuality with women. The foppish man's body, as well as his dress and comportment, revealed an inward disposition and character that stood in opposition to eighteenth-century Anglo-American norms of heterosexual and social masculinity.

Eighteenth-century discourses of normative masculinity were forged in relief, through discussions of deviant male figures, particularly in social settings. By focusing on the wasted potential of unmarried men, these accounts of bachelors and foppish men hoped to encourage single men to assume the responsibilities of husband, father, and head of household. Those men who did not choose to marry were warned that they would end up physically weakened, spiritually bankrupt, alone, and full of regret. Negative depictions of unmarried men underscored that true manhood was based on marriage and family. Standards of male dress, physicality, and social comportment took shape, in part, around a constellation of repudiated unmarried effeminate figures, including the fop, coxcomb, and beau.

Social traits associated with fops and effeminate men clearly had sexual connotations, including masturbation, impotence, and even sodomy. The "monstrous" nature of effeminate men, including fops, was deduced primarily from their visible transgressions of gender codes: their effeminate "gate," "garb," and dissipated body. These visible violations of gendered norms indicated deeper character flaws and suggested an unorthodox sexuality. Through visible social affect, effeminate bachelors revealed their deviant dispositions. As the following chapter shows, race and ethnicity could also signal deviate male sexuality and sociability.

CHAPTER 6 ◄◄ ◄◄

"*When* Day *and* Night
Together Move"
Men and Cross-Cultural Sex

I N 1705 THE GOVERNOR, COUNCIL, AND REPRESENTATIVES of the General Court outlawed intimate relations between blacks and whites with the enactment of a statute entitled "An Act for the Better Preventing of a Spurious and Mixt Issue, &c." The act distinguished Massachusetts from other New England colonies, none of which had statutes prohibiting interracial sex. The act contained eight sections: four pertained to interracial unions, three covered requirements to register and pay duties on "All negroes imported," and one defined whipping as the penalty for a "negro or mulatto striking a Christian." The penalties for interracial fornication were severe: if "any negro or molatto man shall commit fornication with an English woman, or a woman of any other Christian nation within this province," both parties were to be "severely whip'd" and the man was to be "sold out" of the colony. If such a liaison were to produce a child, the woman would be unable to rely on town support for that child. The punishment to be meted out to "any Englishman, or man of other Christian nation within this province, [who] shall commit fornication with a negro, or molatto woman," was also severe: as in the case of a black man or white woman convicted of interracial fornication, the man would be "severely whip'd." Moreover, the statute added to the degradation of public whipping the heavy fine of five pounds.[1]

By passing the act, the council created a special category of fornication —interracial fornication—and thus drew on and reinforced racial boundaries. For all parties tried under this statute, the legally allowable punishments were more severe than for simple fornication. For example, a white woman committing fornication with a white man that resulted in a child could expect community support if the man absconded, but the same woman found guilty of fornication with a black man could find herself sold into servitude if she could not support her child. A white man convicted of interracial fornication could be sentenced to suffer both a "severe" whipping and a very large fine; a white man's conviction for fornication with a white woman usually resulted in only a small fine. For a black man or woman convicted of interracial fornication, being sold out of the colony—usually to the West Indies—would underscore his or her degraded status and threaten his or her life, given the conditions of slavery there. Finally, the act provided financial incentives for masters to regulate their slaves' intimate relations because a master faced the prospect of having to sell a slave found guilty of fornication with a white woman.

The act also forbade all whites in the colony ("her majesty's English or Scottish subjects" or "of any other Christian nation") to "contract matrimony with any negro or molatto," thereby removing the possibility of officially legitimating a union between blacks and whites. Here the Bay Colony saved its harshest fines for those who solemnized such marriages—a fifty-pound fine for "joining any such in marriage." At ten times the fine levied against a white man who produced an illegitimate child with a black woman, the penalty underscored the importance of preventing anyone from offering an official blessing on an interracial relationship. Half of that unusually high fine was paid to the government, but the other half went directly to the person who sued and brought the couple to court. The law thus created a financial incentive for colonists to police behavior. By not distinguishing between free and enslaved blacks, the act also underscored the salience of racial distinctions rather than degrees of servitude. Overall, by preventing legally sanctioned interracial marriages, this statute dramatically reinforced racial boundaries. It did the same when it created special penalties for interracial fornication rather than allowing the general law against fornication to cover such cases.

An exchange of letters between the Lords of Trade and Governor Joseph Dudley expressing concerns over the statute some five years after its enactment indicates the central role of sexuality in discourses of social control. In an exchange over the clause concerning duties paid "upon Negroes imported," the governor used the specter of interracial sex to placate the Lords of Trade, who were concerned that the import duty was being levied in order to discourage the importation of Africans into Massachusetts. In his letter, the governor stated that the act was passed not to prevent the importation of Africans per se but because of "several complaints that several Negroes had lain with white women." The Bay Colony enacted such regulations in an attempt to preserve what they regarded as sexual, social, and racial purity, which was threatened by the presence of Africans. In so doing, they legally codified and thus reinforced understandings of racial difference and African inferiority.

Unlike most of the British colonial empire, eighteenth-century Massachusetts was a remarkably homogeneous English society. Non-English people did not make up a significant portion of the population at any point in the eighteenth century. The first Massachusetts census, taken in 1764, showed that Indians made up less than 1 percent of the colony's population, and blacks, only 2 percent. By 1790 the numbers had changed little; blacks made up 1.4 percent of the population, according to the official census.[2]

As a consequence, the scholarship on sex and gender in New England has tended to overlook the salience of race in constructions of norms and ideals of sexuality and gender. Studies of sex examine interracial unions in less homogeneous regions. Studies of manhood in New England focus largely on elites and pay scant attention to nonwhites or to racial attitudes and their impact on white masculinity. But recent scholarship on interactions between the English and the Indians in late seventeenth-century New England suggests that the comparative homogeneity of eighteenth-century Massachusetts' population did not lessen the importance of racial and ethnic categories. Along with the recent scholarship on the effects of protracted warfare with the region's Native American population, a moment's reflection on Boston's participation in the Atlantic slave trade suggests an additional reason that racial categories were culturally salient in eighteenth-century Massachusetts. Whereas most studies examining the nexus of race and sexuality in the colonial era focus on southern slave societies, this chapter shows that even in mostly white regions, race mattered and that constructions of sexuality were a significant component of discourses of racial difference.[3]

Moreover, this chapter reveals a discourse of sexuality by examining the perceived connections between race and ethnicity on one hand and inner sexual and moral selves on the other. In colonial Massachusetts the black rapist symbolized general human depravity—and threatened specifically the colonial masculine ideal of self-control and social order. Newspaper accounts that focused on the social disruption that sexual abuse by a black man caused developed a racialized sexuality while illustrating a general Puritan-influenced concern.

Indians, Blacks, and Christian Sexual Morality

In the early eighteenth century, Massachusetts ministers continued their seventeenth-century mission to Christianize and civilize blacks and Indians living in the Bay Colony. By the third quarter of the seventeenth century, the missionary John Eliot had established fourteen "praying towns" for Christian Indians. As Jill Lepore explains, Eliot hoped that converted Indians would prosper and live in these towns "free of the cultural influences of their non-Christian peers." Only four such towns endured into the eighteenth century, in part because of the devastation of King Philip's War and its decimation of Indian populations. Boston merchant Benjamin Walker, Junior, noted in his diary the declining Indian population. In 1726 he recorded that there were only 509 Indian men in 23 tribes from Boston to Nova Scotia, down from 4,310 men in 1690. Religious instruction was the centerpiece of the Christian civilizing mission and displayed the tensions characteristic of assimilationist racial doctrines. In many ways these teachings resembled the general catechism taught to every English colonist as part of the continuing Puritan mission. But although Christian doctrine emphasized that individual souls were ultimately free of ethnic or racial markers in the eyes of God, religious education also served to justify social and racial hierarchies.[4]

In Massachusetts assimilationist racial doctrines emphasizing the importance of the Christian civilizing mission continued to be influential well into the eighteenth century. Assimilationist racial doctrine, especially in the hands of evangelizing ministers, contained a tension. On the one hand, the status of Indians and blacks as heathens and as savages living without the benefit of civil order or Christian morality justified imperial domination. Portrayals of sexuality had an important place within this scheme: the sexuality of exotic peoples around the globe and of Indians and Africans in the Americas in particular was one sign of the moral and social gulf that separated the savage from the European and the heathen from the Christian. Such portrayals reinforced a sense of English superiority and racial difference. On the other hand, the Christian civilizing mission held out the hope of eventual assimilation; the ultimate aim of a Christian education under the benevolent tutelage of English masters and provincial officials was to lift Indians and blacks out of a state of savagery. From this vantage point assimilationist racial doctrines stressed potential likenesses. After all, the English were once barbarians themselves: only divine providence (as Puritan ministers would have it) or the civilizing process itself (as more secular views of history might put it) separated the fortunate English from those under their care. In matters sexual, as in other aspects of moral life, English rule and Christian care would erode difference.[5]

Concern over Indian morality peaked in the decades surrounding the turn of the century as border wars and frontier threats weighed heavily on Massachusetts residents' minds. As Richard Gildrie points out, the greatest frontier disruptions took place in New England between 1690 and 1720: the increased attention to Indian morality in this period was not accidental. The English viewed Indians as at once corrupt and suitable for civilizing, as capable of becoming proper Christian subjects of the British Empire. Discussion of sexual mores constructed distinctions between Christians and non-Christians but also reminded Massachusetts readers of their own sinful natures. Indians were corrupt, but so were the English.[6]

Cotton Mather spelled this out in an election-day sermon preached to the governor and General Assembly in 1700. For Mather, English "Ancestors," whom he described as "rueful Pagans," were once as "wretched" as contemporary Indians. According to Mather, the English nation was superior to others, both European and non-European, only because God had arbitrarily chosen them (through "the meer *Soveraign Grace* of . . . God"). His sermon called for a recognition of God's role in making the English free of "plagues and woes." At the same time, Mather did accent a contrast in the present between the English and everyone else, including the Indians who are now "forborn, wretched," and "rueful" because they lack access to true Christianity.[7]

Indian adoption of Christian moral law under the jurisdiction of the Bay Colony would put a stop to, for example, cruder forms of Indian justice such as the type of revenge described in a letter appearing on the front page of the *New England Weekly Journal* in 1733. The article was an excerpt from a letter by James Oglethorpe, founder of Savannah and one of the original trustees of Georgia, to imperial officials in London, remarking on the "Door opened to our Colony towards the Conversion of the *Indians*." In his letter, Oglethorpe made several comments about Indians' understanding of adultery and retribution: "They hold, that if a Man commits *Adultery*, the injur'd *Husband* is oblig'd to have revenge, by cutting off the Ears of the *Adulterer*, which if he is too sturdy and strong to submit to, then the injured Husband kills him the first Opportunity he has so to do with Safety." Playing the role of ethnographer, Oglethorpe reported that Indians shared the Christian prohibition against adultery, but he underscored for Massachusetts readers the barbaric nature of Indian social customs and reminded them of the continued need for conversion and governance by the English.[8]

Of course, not all Massachusetts residents shared the assimilationist perspective on the Christianization of Native Americans. Massachusetts did not lack for Indian hating, and many commentators depicted a more threatening view of Native Americans. In particular, the captivity narratives were rife with portrayals of Indian brutality. Thus, captive Mary Rowlandson described Native Americans as "merciless heathens," "barbarous creatures," "savage," and "bruitish." She also directly cast doubt on the ability of Indian "hell-hounds" to become true Christians, describing even a "praying" Indian as "so wicked and cruel as to wear a string about his neck strung with Christians' fingers."[9]

As scholars have noted, however, depictions of specifically sexual atrocities committed by Native American captors are absent from nearly all early captivity accounts. Rowlandson, in her otherwise scathing account of her captors, took pains to point out that she had remained unmolested. Rowlandson, perhaps responding to the English recognition of rape as a weapon of war, declared that she never suffered "the least abuse of Unchastity." Likewise, captive Elizabeth Hanson stated that Indian men were "very civil toward their captive women, not offering any incivility by any indecent carriage." Other accounts bolstered Rowlandson's portrayal of Indian men as sexually chaste by emphasizing a general ethos of sexual restraint. Such accounts constructed an image of Indian men who, though capable of great cruelty, especially in war, were not given to committing sexual atrocities. Neither was sexual assault a major feature of newspaper reports of Indian raids. Indians were not generally viewed as sexual predators.[10]

Ministers for the most part viewed the moral education of Indians as a Christian responsibility. Indians were more often than blacks singled out as the group to be molded by Christian sexual teachings. Matthew and Experience Mayhew, for example, were influential missionaries on Martha's Vineyard who endeavored to bring Christianity, including sexual mores, to Indians. Their publications include an assortment of pamphlets designed to inform white residents of Massachusetts of the colony's Christian mission among the Indians.[11]

In the late seventeenth century John Eliot, the Massachusetts missionary who established praying towns of Christian Indians, translated the Bible into Algonquian. The Eliot Bible represented an attempt to bring Christianity to Indians in a local language. Just as numerous English children learned to read and write using the Christian Bible, so did many Indians. Extant Eliot Bibles reveal that many different hands traced characters on the printed pages as Indians learned to form the letters of the English alphabet while reading in their own language the messages of Christianity.

Thus, Christian morality, including sexual morality, was taught along with basic skills in reading and writing.[12]

Translated margin writings in the surviving eighteenth-century Eliot Bibles indicate Anglo-Christian sexual values. Scrawled in the margins of one such Bible is this gloss by its Indian reader: "You, Thomas, remember: do not fornicate." To be Christian was to control one's sexual passions, to avoid fornication. In the margins of another surviving copy, another Indian wrote: "I Banjom Kusseniyeutt caught [?] a Negro Man and a White Woman." "Banjom" connected his identity as a Christian Indian to his capacity to identify and judge immoral sexual behavior in others. Making his own name part of the notation suggests an assertive pride in his capacity to detect transgressions against Christian morality. Such writings serve to remind us that the transferal of English language and religion included an emphasis on redefining sexual morality among converted Indians.[13]

Preachers endeavored to teach Anglo-Christian values of sexual propriety to Indians through published sermons appearing in Massachusett, the Algonquian language of eastern New England Indians. Thus, Cotton Mather's 1705 publication, which appeared in English and in Massachusett, singled out a number of laws "by which the Magistrates are to punish Offences, among the *Indians* as well as among the *English*." The fifteen-page publication included four pages that focused on sexual crimes. Mather singled out and translated each crime one by one: "Rape," "Buggery," hiding the birth (or death) of a "Bastard Child," and having "Two Husbands, or Two Wives." Other noncapital crimes included adultery, "Incest," and "Fornication," all of which were to be punished with "Scourging." Thus, the publication linked English-language instruction with Christian teachings and the legal code of the Bay Colony, warning Indians that they were subject to legal punishment for transgressions against the same Christian sexual code that applied to all residents of Massachusetts.[14]

Bilingual publications also instructed Indians how to read English and their own language. They may also have been used to teach English readers Massachusett. *The Indian Primer*, first published in "Mushauwomuk" (Boston) in 1720, declared itself to be the *First Book by which Children May Know truly To read the Indian Language*. The text was published together with the often-reprinted John Cotton catechism titled *Spiritual Babes* (first published in 1646). Page numbering was continuous, and the two texts made up a bilingual catechism. The seal of the colony of Massachusetts, engraved on the inside cover of the 1720 edition, depicts the Indian as a man who pursues hunting and agriculture, not war. Suggesting his primitive state, the Indian figure stands in a field, holding a bow and arrow, dressed in only a loincloth. A border tightly bounding the scene and the cross at the top of the image symbolize the promise of English Christianity for containing the savage influences of Indians in Massachusetts.[15]

Published in Massachusett on the left side and English on the right side, *The Indian Primer* used biblical injunctions, including those that governed sexuality and marriage. Thus, the left page—"Nat. *Uttiyeu nesausuk tahshe Anooteamoonk? Namp.* Mamuhsehkon"—was translated on the right page into English as "Quest. *What is the seventh Commandment? Ans.* Thou shalt not commit Adultery." The text also included a section titled "Against Uncleanness," which brought together passages from biblical chapters presented as a coherent whole. Reading from the left and right pages, one could learn that "Mamuhsehkon" meant "Commit not Adultery," and "Nanwunnoodsquaausuenung kah mamussuenuog God pish oosumuh" meant "Whoremongers and Adulterers God will judge." Such texts were designed to bridge cultural gaps through language instruction. At the same time, they endeavored to bring Indian readers into the fold through the instigation of sexual self-control and self-regulation under Christian theology.[16]

By the turn of the eighteenth century, Massachusetts had "enacted into law... recognition of the Negroes as different and inferior." Because slaves in Massachusetts usually lived as household dependents directly subject to their masters' supervision, ministerial efforts to Christianize Africans emphasized the need to preserve household order and focused on masters' asking them to look to Christianity as a means of ensuring moral order and social hierarchy. Although the terms "servant" and "slave" were often used interchangeably in the writings of the period, their context most often indicates a distinction between black slaves, who inherited their status as servants for life, and other forms of service by whites, blacks, and Indians. Teachings aimed at Christianizing blacks, unlike those aimed at civilizing and Christianizing Indians, nearly always linked their ethnicity to their status as bond servants and to the importance of preserving social order within households.[17]

A broadside anonymously published by Cotton Mather in 1714 outlined Christian "Rules for the Society of Negroes." To become the "Servants of that Glorious LORD," the broadside contended, the society should insist on nine rules of behavior for its members, including regular prayer, catechism, and ministering to other blacks in the colony. In addition, the rules laid out specific prohibitions designed to preserve orderliness in relations between servants and "Owners." Members were required to obtain permission to attend meetings and were specifically prohibited from lying to their masters about attendance at these meetings. Mather also required that a "Wise and Good Man of the *English* in the Neighborhood" guide the group and enforce the rules through his "Presence and Counsel." Members were also required to adhere to a strict code of sexual behavior. Thus, they were to avoid *"Wicked Company,"* and if any member were to "Defile himself with *Fornication*," he was to be banned from the group for at least six months. To underscore the Christianizing mission, Mather also warned that any servant committing fornication would have to provide "Exemplary Testimonies of his becoming a *New Creature*," before being allowed to return to the group.[18]

Mather also "expected from every one in the Society, that he learn the *Catechism*." He singled out three publications. One of them, *The Negro Christianized*, first published in 1706, exhorted masters to give their black slaves a Christian education and provided a sample catechism for masters to use. The reward for doing so, the essay promised, was that "Your *Negroes* are immediately Raised unto an astonishing Felicity, when you have *Christianized* them.... Tho' they remain your *Servants*, yet they are become the *Children* of God." The sample lessons also reminded readers of the specific Christian values that black men would be taught should they be converted. The author argued overall that Christianity would make blacks less likely to commit a wide range of "sins," including the sexual sins that concerned readers of that time. Mather also neatly expressed the tensions within assimilationist doctrine. The "Negro" is now "Wretched" and *"Bruitish"* but could, with proper supervision by Christian masters, have "their Minds Healed" of their spiritual and moral insensibility.[19]

An early anti-slavery sermon delivered by a Quaker in Nantucket in 1729 and published in 1733 also emphasized the master's responsibility to Christianize his servants and maintain household order: "Let not your Families of Whites and Blacks be like *Sodom* and *Gomorrah*...lest sudden Destruction come upon you, and the Lord root you out, as he did them." In particular, it cautioned against allowing "servants" to "take Husbands and Wives at their Pleasure, and then leave them again when they please," and suggested that the master's laxity in this regard "may bring the Judgments of God upon you; yea, this manifests your Families to be unclean and adulterated Families." Thus, this sermon emphasized the importance of Christian marriage and associated the preservation of household stability with monogamy. The message, however, was not just about the sexual morality of Africans and the integrity of their families. Ministers articulated the benefits to English masters of Christianizing African servants and slaves and, in this unusual early case, even of abandoning the practice of slave-holding itself. The moral status of "Families of Whites and Blacks" and of their white guardians and masters was at stake.[20]

File papers concerning a divorcing African couple reveal that some masters made efforts to preserve household order by overseeing black servants' marital affairs. In 1741 Jethro, a "Negro Servant" "belonging to" Boston merchant Edward Bromfield, petitioned the court for a divorce from his wife on the grounds that she had committed adultery and had given birth to a "Molatto" child. A deposition from one John Gyles attests that Hagar and Jethro had been his "servants" at the time that Hagar was "delivered of a Female Molatto Child" and that she had told him shortly after the birth that the father was a soldier, William Kelly. In an apparent effort to keep the couple together, Gyles testified that he "used all possible Endeavours to reconcile the said Jethro & Hagar but to no purpose." Gyles's testimony is interesting because it reveals that he attempted to "reconcile" the couple despite her adultery. We can speculate that his motive was to protect the stability of his household. However, the court, hewing close to the law, which included adultery as grounds for divorce, granted Jethro's request.[21]

Other sermons emphasized that slaves should be Christianized because Christian morality would protect social order against potential threats from unruly blacks. Thus, an appendix added for the publication of a sermon preached in 1763 at the execution of a slave, Bristol, who had murdered his master's sister, neatly summed up two important lessons to be learned from the tragedy. The first lesson applied to all readers, that of the "Weakness of human Nature, the horrid Effects of our ungovern'd Passions." The second main point, however, was aimed at masters and served to distinguish "Negroes" from whites. The execution sermon explained that Bristol gave no reason for his crime "but that he was prompted to it by a Negro Boy of his Acquaintance, who threatened to kill him if he did not do it." Thus, it suggests that Bristol and his peers lacked a moral conscience. Unsupervised, the "barbarous Disposition" of Bristol and his fellow slaves made them vulnerable to their passions and were a threat to community order. Because of this "Disposition," blacks required proper governing. At the same time, however, this polemic in favor of reformed slaveholding holds out the hope that a Christian education would eventually result in moral self-regulation.[22]

Interracial Unions, Racism, and Manliness

Massachusetts' unusual step of codifying anti-miscegenation sentiment reinforced the low status of Africans and African Americans and reveals a concern with racial degradation. Consensual intimate relations between whites and blacks and Indians in eighteenth-century Massachusetts endured both official and popular condemnation, and they carried a stigma. Such concerns underscore the important role of sex and sexuality in English efforts to give meaning to racial difference and to stabilize social hierarchies founded in part on racial distinctions. For most white and Christian Native American men, interracial unions revealed a lack of manly self-control. For most black men, the reverse was probably true. The ability of black men to choose a white partner signified masculine independence in defiance of broader social race-based restrictions.[23]

Condemnation of interracial unions was not simply about racial purity. It was specifically about policing the border between whites and nonwhites. Although relationships between blacks and whites drew the closest scrutiny, the most common cross-cultural relationship was between Indians and Africans. And relationships between Native Americans and African Americans only increased as the eighteenth century progressed. Historian Daniel R. Mandell has demonstrated the prevalence of black-Indian intermarriage in the second half of the eighteenth century. In particular he found that the "rise of intermarriage among Indians before the American Revolution paralleled the development of complementary gender imbalances among Natives and Africans." Throughout the eighteenth century the numbers of Indian men declined due to disease and warfare. By contrast, African men always outnumbered African women. Thus Mandell saw a gender imbalance that provided a further impetus for cross-cultural relations—one that complemented shared experiences as socially, culturally, and legally disenfranchised people of color in Massachusetts.[24]

It is difficult to estimate the prevalence of consensual interracial unions, since many Indians, blacks, and poorer whites married outside the legal system. Such unions, even where not legally prohibited, left few written records for historians to make numerical estimates. Moreover, the most obvious evidence of interracial sexual unions, offspring, is generally lost to the historical record, given that the racial nomenclature of English did not systematically classify individuals of mixed ancestry.

In general, tolerance of sexual relationships between English and any non-English people was hard to come by. Stephen Salisbury of Worcester,

for example, wrote to his brother about his concern that their sister was involved with a "Scotchman." "I am Sorry that Betsy undervalues herself so
much as to throw away herself to a Scotch Man," he wrote, "for it is a Rare
thing to find a Scotchman that is worthy of the name of a True Gentleman."
Similarly, in 1784, when Jeremiah Higgerty petitioned for a divorce from
his wife, he charged her with adultery with a "Spaniard" and with "diverse
other foreigners." Jeremiah's fourteen-year-old son testified to having seen
three men at the house one June day. After tea that afternoon, his mother
took one by the hand and went upstairs with him. Suspicious, Jeremiah
went up after a half-hour and found the door locked, but he pushed it open
to find his mother in bed with her clothes over her head and the "frenchman" upon her with his breeches down. Jeremiah then "ran" to the stairs,
called for everyone else to come up, and threatened to tell his father. According to his testimony, Jeremiah's mother said, "She did not care if I did
& that a frenchman was better than an Irishman."[25]

But the greatest concern was over relationships between blacks and
whites. And the courts and the community at large monitored this social
border most rigorously. In Massachusetts slaves and free blacks were found
primarily in the colony's wealthiest areas: not surprisingly, throughout the
eighteenth century the largest number lived in Boston. In 1742, for example, about one-third of all blacks in Massachusetts lived in Boston, where
they made up about 8 percent of the city's population. Lower-court records
for Suffolk County indicate that the port city of Boston housed a community of lower-status whites and blacks who eschewed popular and official
pronouncements against interracial sexuality. Convictions for interracial
sexual relationships were at their height in the first third of the eighteenth
century. This coincides with the era of the greatest expansion of the slave
trade in Massachusetts. In the period 1700–1730, one-third of all cases of
fornication and one in eight cases of bastardy involved interracial couples.
Additionally, half of the cases involving disorderly houses include charges
that specify that blacks and whites socializing together had contributed to
the case against the household.[26]

As scholars have long pointed out, British culture had a long history
of embracing and promulgating a negative association with blackness. It
should come as no surprise, then, that whites filed slander charges when
accused of sexual misconduct with nonwhites. The accusation that an Englishman had sex with a black or Indian woman carried with it a stigma. In
Plymouth County, for example, defamation suits filed by white men involving accusations against them of sexual misconduct disproportionately
included the claim that the plaintiff had sex with a non-English woman. Of

the eight sexual-slur cases filed between 1738 and 1755, four involved sex with an Indian or black person. The numbers are small but noteworthy, nonetheless, as blacks made up roughly 2 percent of the population in Plymouth County, and Indians only 1 percent.[27]

For white men, sex with women of color was culturally an Anglo-American prerogative enjoyed by their counterparts in slave-society colonies and used to control and subordinate black men and women. The specter of white men engaged in sexual unions, consensual or coerced, in eighteenth-century Massachusetts, however, most often signaled a lack of manly self-control, considered unbefitting of white masculinity. Given that virtually all whites believed blacks to be inferior, a relationship based on pure and proper motives was all but ruled out. The presumption was that white men engaged in relationships with blacks to satisfy carnal urges that they had failed to master.

Sexual misconduct in general signified loss of manly self-control. Such failures were particularly offensive when the alleged partner was not white. Thus, for example, Ichabod Soul filed charges against an Indian woman for saying "publicly" that he had offered her a "yard of Cloath, if She would Consent that he Might lay with her." The court awarded him twenty-five pounds. In 1737, when Ruth Sergeant, a "Minor Spinstress," told people that labourer Godfrey Mackswaney committed "fornycations with a Negro woman," Mackswaney filed suit to protect his "name and Carecter," albeit unsuccessfully. In 1755 Henry Merritt, a gentleman, filed charges against housewright William Southworth for stating loudly that Merritt had "Carnall Copulation" with Sarah Comsett, an Indian woman," "three times at least."[28] Merritt also charged that Southworth's wife, Rachel, had spread the same story to "'Divers of our Good Subjects.'" A jury apparently agreed and awarded Merritt twenty pounds.[29]

White men who engaged in relationships with women of color risked losing their good reputations. According to Governor Thomas Hutchinson's account of the Salem witchcraft trials published in his history of Massachusetts in 1768, the fact that one John Alden consorted with Indian women triggered the accusation of witchcraft and his subsequent trial. Hutchinson described the accusation and Alden's arrest as follows: "All were ordered into the streets and a ring made, and then she cried out, *there stands Alden a bold fellow with his hat on, sells powder and shot to the Indians, lies with the squaws and has papooses &c.* He was immediately taken into custody of the Marshall and required to deliver up his sword." At the trial, one woman testified: "he sells Powder and Shot to the Indians and French, and lies with the Indian Squaes, and has Indian Papooses." As a sailor, Alden delivered goods between Boston and other harbors along the northeastern coast. As Mary Beth Norton points out, the presumption that he was trading with Indians or the French made him suspect. The accusations of sexual relations with Indian women highlighted his deviance.[30]

The focus on white male resistance to temptation was the lesson of a poem published in the *Boston Gazette* in 1735, which captured many of the negative perceptions of interracial relationships. Entitled "On a Negro Girl making her Court to a fair Youth," the poem depicted the black female as a seducer. In its entirety, it read:

> My charming Youth! Why fly's Thou Me?
> Who in Loves flames consumes for Thee.
> I'm *black*, tis true, and so is Night;
> And Love doth in the Dark delight.
> The World it self, but shut thine Eye,
> Will seem to Thee as black as I.
> Or look, and see what sable shade
> Is by thy lovely Body made.
> Which 'ere attends, where 'ere you go,
> Oh! who allow'd, wou'd not do so.
> Let me forever come so nigh,
> And then you'l need no shade but I.

Here the African servant desires the white man—a common justification for the exploitation of servants and slaves. The reader is encouraged to partake in this forbidden pleasure through the poem's emphasis on romance, desire, and physicality. "Loves flame consumes for Thee," "Love doth in the Dark delight," and "thy lovely Body" underscore the powerful feelings of the "Negro Girl" and her sexual and emotional availability. In a poetic response, directly below the poem, was printed "The Boy's Answer," in which he refers to the secret nature of their sexual relationship. Here the white "Boy" hides his relationship, given the legal and cultural prohibitions against their union. His reputation, or "Face," requires as much. The oppositional relationship of black and white is underscored with italics as "*Day* and *Night* together move." What is remarkable about this work is the graphic nature with which it discusses interracial coupling. The poem intersperses beautiful imagery with negative commentary. The "Communion of our Lips" reads like a line from traditional love poetry but is shut down as "an Eclipse" and a "Horror."[31]

The rhetoric of Revolution may ultimately have sparked an abolitionist sentiment in Massachusetts, but it did not translate into a clear decrease in negative attitudes toward interracial unions. In 1774 Asa Hunt wrote to the Warren Association of the Third Baptist Church in Middleborough about a woman who was seeking to join the church:

> An English woman that has lived as a wife with a Negro desires to joine to the chh. We are well satisfied that she is a meet subject [for membership] only as we suppose it is not lawfull for such to be married together and the above persons upon a justice of the Peace Refusing to marry them Took Each other as husband and wife and have dwelt together Ever since. We Request your advice and counsel in the Case.

As William McLoughlin, in his history of the Baptists in New England, writes, the fact that Hunt wrote at all suggests a measure of tolerance as well as uncertainty.[32]

That hesitance may suggest a willingness of Massachusetts to consider a new path, but it stood in contrast to continued disdain for blacks as the colonial era came to a close. Massachusetts-born Revolutionary War soldier Joseph Plumb Martin expressed a certain disdain and disgust when he happened upon an interracial family while traveling through Delaware. On an errand to find some liquor, Martin wrote that he had stopped at a house where a woman was alone. When her husband returned, Martin stated, he was "thunderstruck" to see that the white woman was married to a "great pot-bellied Negro man." He focused specifically on her term of affection for him—"My dear"—and "hastened off" in disgust. Exclaimed Martin: "Being fearful that I might hear or see more of their 'dearing,' for had I, I am sure it would have given me the ague." Showing his Massachusetts roots, he chalked the relationship up to regional custom: "However agreeable such 'twain's becoming one flesh' was in that part of the Union, I was not acquainted with it in that in which I resided."[33]

During the Revolutionary era, newspaper notices occasionally used the specter of interracial sex to smear enemies. On May 28, 1770, the *Boston Gazette* published a letter from a British soldier written shortly after the Boston Massacre, defending British troops against such charges ("associating with the Negroes of the Town"). Referring to Crispus Attucks, the first individual killed in the Boston Massacre, the author pointed out that among the dead "it is to be remembered that one of them was only a . . . *Mulatto.*"[34]

On May 24, 1776, the *Massachusetts Spy* carried a letter from New York that began: "As the public were a few days since informed of the honour done General *Gage,* by naming a child after him, it may not be amiss to let it be known, that Lord *Dunmore* also comes in for his share in the same way." The letter continued to express the rage that British Americans felt over Lord Dunmore's Proclamation, which offered freedom to servants and slaves for service to the Crown in putting down the American rebellion. Indeed, that the Crown had "excited domestic insurrections amongst us" was one of the grievances used to justify ending the colonial relationship with England as listed in the Declaration of Independence. "On Monday the 8th instant, a lusty likely NEGRO WENCH was delivered of a male child, who in memory of a certain notable NEGRO CHIEF, is named DUNMORE." The letter was capped off with a four-line poem:

> Hail! doughty Ethiopian chief!
> Thou ignominious Negro-Thief!
> This BLACK shall prop thy sinking name,
> And damn thee, to perpetual Fame.

Suggesting a connection between the black woman and Lord Dunmore and the carrying on of Dunmore's name, the letter attacked his manly character by bringing together Revolutionary concerns on one hand and the racist fear of interracial mixing and a free black population on the other.[35]

The British also used the charge of interracial coupling to denigrate American men. In January 1776, during the nearly yearlong standoff between British and American forces around Boston, none other than General John Burgoyne, who would later be captured at the pivotal battle of Saratoga, wrote a farce entitled *The Blockade of Boston.* A broadside published later that year included several songs performed at the conclusion of the play, including one entitled "FANFAN," sung by a black woman who mocked male Bostonians.

> YOUR Pardon my Massa's one Word to intrude,
> I'm sure in my Heart you won't all tink me rude:
> Tho' in Public you scoff, I see many a Spark,
> Woud tink me a sweet pretty Girl in the Dark.
> Thus merily runs the World on with Fanfan,
> I eat good salt Pork and get kiss'd by white Man:
> I do Misses Business, the pleas'd and I paid,
> Egad I no tir'd of Boston Blockade.

Both sides underscored a weak moral fiber by pointing to the hypocrisy of white men who engaged in sex with black women.[36]

This disdain for consensual interracial sexual coupling would only crystallize as the eighteenth century unfolded. Toward the end of the eighteenth century, when future first lady Abigail Adams wrote from London to her sister Elizabeth, she expressed what would have been a typical revulsion at interracial sexual relations. She wrote that she had been to see Shakespeare's *Othello,* a play that historian Winthrop D. Jordan reminds us is "shot through with the language of blackness and sex." As Jordan points out, Iago tells Brabantio that "an old black ram / Is tupping your white ewe." The play also commented on Iago's emasculation: "I hate the Moor, / And it is thought abroad that 'twixt my sheets / He has done my office." Adams wrote that she saw Mrs. Siddons, a celebrated actress, in the play. Despite the strength of Siddons's performance, Adams confessed the following: Siddons, she wrote, was

> interesting beyond any actress I had ever seen: but I lost much of the pleasure of the play from the sooty appearance of the Moor. Perhaps it may be early prejudice but I could not seperate the affrican coulour from the man, nor prevent that disgust & horrour which filld my mind every time I saw him touch the gentle desdemona, nor did I wonder that Brabartio [*sic*] thought some Love potion or some witchcraft had been practised to make his Daughter fall in Love with what she scarcely dared to look upon.[37]

What shards of evidence we have suggest that interracial unions naturally held different meaning for Native American and African American men. For Christian Native American men, interracial unions took on political and cultural significance as the eighteenth century progressed. The increasingly common relationships between Native Americans and African Americans did not garner condemnation from white society in Massachusetts but did generate concern among some Native American men. For those men, increased adherence to Anglo-American ways meant a general increase in the condemnation of mixed marriages and of traditional polygamous marriages. According to John Sweet, an Indian minister at Gay Head on Martha's Vineyard conducted a census at the end of the eighteenth century that distinguished between Native Americans of "pure" blood and those who were "part white" or "part black."[38]

For black men, the freedom to choose a sexual and romantic partner, of whatever background, could be an undeniable masculine prerogative. In 1705 Cesar, a man enslaved by one Captain Hill in Boston, was convicted of fathering a child with a white woman named Mary Goslin. Each was sentenced to be whipped ten times. But according to court records, when Cesar was whipped "he behaved himself impudently." Cesar rejected the court's imposition on his sexual behavior "and swore that he would be again guilty of the same crime." Moreover, he challenged the court's ability to restrict his choice of partner, declaring that he would not only commit the "same crime" again but would do so "with the sd Goslin." As a result of his defiant stance, he was returned to the whipping post and whipped an additional twenty-five times.[39]

The court records surrounding his case reveal a network of white and black individuals working and living together in the port city of Boston in defiance of the norms of the day. One Abigail Trott was fined for having allowed Mary and Cesar's child to be born at her house, for hiding the identity of the mother, and for receiving money and "other things" from Cesar in exchange for the child's maintenance. Several months later Cesar was again brought to the court and this time sentenced for stealing. At that time Sarah Wallis, a widow, was fined for purchasing New England cheese from Cesar, which she knew he had stolen in order to raise funds to pay for the maintenance of his child.[40]

Similarly, in 1755, when slaves Phillis and Mark were executed for poisoning their master, the depositions in the case revealed that a derailed black masculinity played a significant role in the justification for the murder. As John Sweet explains, the two decided to poison their master only after he denied their "own, independent family lives."[41]

As Daniel Black has demonstrated, precolonial West African manliness shared with colonial Massachusetts many of the same positive evaluations of male authority and independence. And as Daniel Pierson argues, "Black Yankees" to a large extent adopted the norms and ideals of Anglo-Americans in Massachusetts. The adaptation was a successful survival strategy in a society dominated by whites, but it was facilitated by the semblance of a traditional African family structure that shared major traits with Anglo-American patriarchy and manly independence. What evidence we have suggests that some African American men fought hard to embody the ideal of providing for one's family and directly challenged the authorities' right to deny the masculine prerogative of selecting a sexual and romantic partner.[42]

But, as I show in the following section, African American men asserted this independence in a cultural context that portrayed them as hypersexual and threatening; it also depicted them as incapable of making such decisions based on rational thought and supposed that these relationships would be forged on impulse and uncontrollable biological urges.

Sexual Assault and Black Male Sexuality

Late one October evening in 1768, Dr. Hill made his way from Worcester to Boston. His carriage was spotted in Roxbury before daybreak. Its cargo, the body of twenty-one-year-old Arthur, a black man executed for rape the evening before, would have been a horrific sight—a physical symbol of the crime that Arthur had committed. Hanging would have caused his eyes to bulge out and his face to swell as he slowly asphyxiated. Those who were hanged could suffer for up to an hour, for this was an era of executions before the development of the "humane" hangman's noose and higher gallows that snapped one's neck almost instantly. Perhaps he was still wearing the "cap" that was pulled over his face as he stood upon his own coffin, just before the cart was rolled out from beneath his feet. The sermon preached at the execution echoed the broadside and newspaper essays that had linked his criminal actions to a life of immorality and depravity. It repeated his warning to "those of my own colour" to avoid desertion from their masters, drunkenness, and lewdness.[43]

The execution had different meanings for different individuals: for the victim, a middle-aged widow named Deborah Metcalfe, it was against her wishes. She had attempted to negotiate a private settlement. For one Nathaniel Jennison, the individual who seems to have taken it upon himself to seek a warrant for Arthur's arrest to prevent him from being sold out of the colony, the execution would have been a triumph of his white masculine honor. For Dr. Hill, the opportunity to have a body to examine would have been welcomed. For Arthur, the desecration of his body would have been part of the punishment. For Reverend Thaddeus Maccarty, of the Congregational Church of Worcester, the execution was a chance to preach to a "great Multitude" a sermon "which was afterwards printed, Luke 23:42:3." Reverend Maccarty had in fact baptized Arthur two days before his execution. For one Stephen Salisbury, the death meant business. As was the custom, the execution had been a well-attended spectacle. According to Salisbury, his shop had been busy all day until the time of the execution, when it cleared out. Some "4 or 5 Thousand Spectators" attended the execution and afterward filled his shop. Salisbury wrote in his diary: "When it was over Till Candle Light I had the Shop full as it could Hold and Took L160."[44]

In the first two-thirds of the eighteenth century, the courts disproportionately tried and convicted blacks and Indians on charges of rape and sexual assault. Prior to 1765 one-third of all men convicted of rape and the lesser crime of sexual assault were nonwhite. Overall, the death penalty was also meted out disproportionately on the basis of race: of six men executed for rape in eighteenth-century Massachusetts, four were black, one was Native American, and one was Irish. In the early eighteenth century, rape accusations and convictions disproportionately involved cultural outsiders and highlighted transgressions of hierarchies of race, ethnicity, and household order. In the last third of the eighteenth century, the trend was reversed and relatively few blacks were tried for attempted rape or were the subject of rape notices in newspapers. Convictions from 1767 to 1790 for rape and attempted rape involved twenty cases, and only one defendant was not white.[45]

Black male sexuality signified broader concerns about racial purity and the perceived threat that black men posed to white households. In 1763 James Bowdoin, who would become governor of Massachusetts, wrote in letters that his slave named Cesar had "been engaged in an amour with some of the white ladies of the Town." However Bowdoin may have felt about the discovery, Mrs. Bowdoin refused to let Cesar back into the house. The threat of black male sexuality was not to be overlooked. Although the relationship was described as consensual, Cesar was considered a threat to the household and the immediate community. He was soon sold in the West Indies—an often fatal move for slaves, given the unhealthy and harsh conditions of slavery there.[46]

As a group, newspaper notices of rape and sexual assault reveal a particular view of black male sexuality. Mirroring the racial background of defendants in local rape cases, in the first two-thirds of the eighteenth century, newspaper accounts depicting black men make up a disproportionate number of the stories of rape and sexual assault. Of the thirty-four cases of rape and attempted rape appearing in Boston newspapers prior to 1765, nearly half involved black men.

In newspaper mentions of rape and ravishment, English attackers were never labeled rapists. In reports without any identification, one presumes that all the assailants were English. But even if that presumption were proved wrong, it would still be true that Englishmen were never identified as such, never linked in print with rape. The result was that the (non-English) racial or ethnic identity of the accused became associated with the sexual (and often "barbarously" violent) crime. All newspaper accounts of rape involving black men described attacks on white women or girls; none concerned black men attacking black or Indian women.

The threat of black male sexuality may have been heightened by the demographic situation. Throughout the first half of the eighteenth century, women outnumbered men among whites and Indians in Massachusetts. The reverse was true among blacks; male slaves throughout New England outnumbered female ones. In Massachusetts there were 1,500 enslaved black males and 855 enslaved black females in 1755. The cumulative impact of the newspaper reporting produced an image of black male sexuality as predatory and unbridled. This image was far different from the ministerial literature that emphasized black and Indian potential for Christian assimilation and suggested, instead, an inherent depravity and an inability to become Christian and/or civilized.[47]

In the last third of the eighteenth century, the image of the black male rapist faded from newspapers. In 50 newspaper accounts of rape or sexual assault printed between 1766 and 1790, only 3 involved perpetrators identified as black—47 were unidentified and presumably involved whites. Although most scholars point to the post–Civil War era as the period that gave birth to the figure of the black rapist, it seems clear that in early eighteenth-century Massachusetts the image was culturally significant. This is not to argue, however, that the figure had the same meaning in both times. On the contrary, the figure appears at different times for different reasons. In Philadelphia, as Clare Lyons has demonstrated, concern over black male sexuality did not develop until the Revolutionary era. Similarly, Leslie Harris locates the figure in early nineteenth-century New York City, where anxiety about black hypersexuality and interracial relationships coincides with developing controversy over the ability of individuals to be virtuous citizens in a new republic.[48]

Unlike the discourse of Native American male sexuality, print accounts of sexual assaults involving black male perpetrators consistently drew a connection between racial background and the propensity to commit violent sexual acts. Contrary to the trend in later newspaper reports, execution sermons reveal a particular view of black male sexuality as prone to committing sexual assault. As literary scholar Richard Slotkin has demonstrated, the image of the black rapist operated in New England execution sermons throughout the eighteenth century. According to Slotkin's analysis of events prior to 1765, all New England criminal narratives concerned property. But after 1765 only three out of twenty did not concern rape or interracial sexual relations. The last execution in Massachusetts, that of Arthur, linked his crime of burglary in 1786 to his own mixed-race heritage and particularly to his depraved character, as evidenced by his sexual immorality, including adultery and sex with white women.[49]

Consider the description of an incident involving a black man and a child. Readers looking over the *New England Weekly Journal* in 1727 might have come across the following grisly tale in a section devoted to news from Boston:

> We have an Account, that on the 6th Instant at *Tiverton*, a Negro play-ing with a Child of about Five Years Old, (Daughter of the late Capt. *Constant Church*) as he was tossing her up & down, a Knife which he had in his Breeches Pocket, lying with the Point upwards, entred her Body near the groin, and gave such a Mortal Wound, that the Child Dyed within about three Hours.

Notice the close focus on the knifepoint and the groin. Even in a pre-Freudian era, this story about a "Negro" accidentally impaling a fatherless young girl on his knife implies that despite the appearance of friendliness, a black man was sexually dangerous. A second story appearing in the *Boston Evening Post* in 1743 portrays a double castration: the first was that of the victim, the second came in the form of judicial punishment of the black offender. "We hear from *Hartford* in *Connecticut*, that the Negro Fellow who some time ago castrated his Master's Son; has lately been tried for the Fact, and being found Guilty, was sentenced to be whipped, then sit upon the Gallows, after that to be castrated, and then to be sold out of the Colony." The two stories together express the anxiety surrounding the presence of the black man in Massachusetts. As a man of unbridled sexual energy, he posed a threat to women and girls and to white men's patriarchal prerogatives. The black male as rapist challenged his master's authority. The case from Connecticut was unusual only in that the emasculation of the master (through his son) was literal.[50]

Boston's newspaper printers selected and reprinted a number of stories of rape and sexual assault from neighboring colonies, which had the effect of suggesting that the scope of the problem of protecting Anglo-American households from black men was wide. In 1737 the *New England Weekly Journal* grouped three stories together, giving the impression of an epi-demic in New York.[51]

Newspaper accounts also contained commentary that suggested a rela-tionship between race and an innate predisposition for sexual assault. In 1734 the *New England Weekly Journal* reported on a fifteen-year-old girl who, as she was "coming from a Neighbor's House" one evening, was thrown to the ground by a black man who "made an attempt to Ravish her."

This particular story from New York also detailed his sentencing and remarked that the "Negro" was reported to be prone to sexual attacks, having made a previous attempt on another woman. The author of this report also highlighted the special "Act of Assembly" that created a special court to *"try and convict Negroes transgressing the Law."* His sentence (to "be *burnt alive*") was also draconian for a conviction for attempted rape. The act itself, of course, reinforced the color line. The newspaper's report of this and other cases and the punishments associated with them highlighted sexual crimes committed by Africans and African Americans and the stereotypes about black sexuality that such cases conjured up. Consider one final example from London in the *Boston Evening Post* in 1750:

> Our Papers have taken some Notice of the Condemnation of one Toby Gill, a Black, at the last Assizes for the County of Suffolk; but the Enormity of his Crime, which was Murder, has not been sufficiently made known. He was a Drummer in Sir Robert Rich's Regiment and a very drunken profligate Fellow. He met, or overtook, the poor Woman he murdered upon the Road, and on her refusing to comply with his lewd Proposal, strangled her with her own Handkerchief, and then abused her dying and dead.

Here the papers state that their aim was to alert the public to the "Enormity of his crime, which was Murder," but the story pivots on his brutality and sexual perversity ("abused her dying and dead"). It is also worth noting that he was, like many assailants depicted in newspaper notices, a transient. The cumulative impact of the overreporting of sexual assault by black men, especially when coupled with frequently gruesome details, was to associate black men with an emerging stereotype as a sexual predator and rapist.[52]

Newspaper accounts also explicitly commented that the public nature of punishments would serve as a warning to other blacks: such public punishments and the printing of reports about them were inflicted as a terror to others. For example, a newspaper story about a Boston rape case involving London, a black man, noted that "it is earnestly desired by many, that his Body may be hanged in a Chain, either upon the Neck or some other conspicuous Place, to deter all, but especially the insolent Tribe of Blacks from the like wicked Attempts for the Future." Another paper reported on the same case: "On Monday last a Negro Man named *London,* was Executed here pursuant to his Sentence for a Rape by him committed; at the Place of Execution he confess'd the horrid Fact, and desir'd those of his Colour wou'd be warn'd by him."[53]

When published and circulated by colonial newspapers, these scenes of execution and their warnings also helped to construct for readers an image of a black male population prone to sexual attack. Newspapers propagated the cultural notion of black men as a sexual threat to white women and girls. Such notices operated as one component of a larger discourse that associated differences in moral character with racial differences. They then proposed vigilance and warnings of swift and stern justice as a solution to the alleged threat that black male sexuality posed. One final example underscores this point:

> Boston from New London, Feb. 20th past, By certain Information from a Gentleman we are assured, that some Weeks ago to the Westward of that place, a very remarkable thing fell out, (which we here relate as a caveat for all Negroes medling for the future with any white Women, least they fare with the like Treatment,) and it is this, A Negro Man met abroad an English Woman, which he accosted to lye with, stooping down, fearing none behind him, a Man observing his Design, took out his Knife, before the Negro was aware, cut off all his unruly parts smack and smooth, the Negro Jumpt up roaring and run for his Life; the Black now an Eunuch is alive and like to recover of his Wounds & doubtless cured from any more such Wicked Attempts.

Here popular rule complements official punishment. In this case a single man acted to protect an "English Woman." The tale was reprinted, readers are told, to inform "all Negroes medling for the future with any white Women" that the authority of Anglo-American men would prevail.[54]

Colonial-era newspaper accounts, through the overreporting of sexual assaults by black men on white women and girls, nurtured a cultural association between black men, violence, and rape. Moreover, explicit commentary about public punishments and their efficacy as a warning to other blacks about swift and brutal penalties for sexual assault reinforced this developing association between race and sexuality.

In addition to the debates about the timing and location of the emergence of the myth of the black rapist, what is important here is the general lesson that in colonial Massachusetts racialized sexuality reinforced and fostered notions of difference while simultaneously developing a particular view of the sexuality of African American men. These portrayals utilized the sexual as symbolic of greater differences between self and other and emphasized inherent depravity that linked a specific sexual act, rape, to black men's per-

sonhood. As I discuss in the final chapter, the figure of the sodomite followed the same uneven chronological trajectory in print and shows that
sodomy and same-sex sex could similarly at times be linked to character,
disposition, and inner states of desire.

CHAPTER 7 ◄┼ ◄┼

"The Paths of Monstrous Joy"

REVEREND JOHN CLEAVELAND, during his first year at Yale, awoke one January morning in 1742 concerned about his spiritual devotion. When he wrote in his diary about his "bacsliding from god," he used an older expression, referring to God as his "first husband." Some thirty-six years later, one George Sherman petitioned the governor for a divorce from his wife "of some years," Phoebe. By that time, Sherman refused to live with his wife, claiming that she was not a "proper Woman in all her parts," and that she was not "fitting and suitable for the Use of a Man as a Wife." In addition to the testimony of three midwives, an official letter was submitted on behalf of George Sherman's case asserting that the divorce should be granted, given her sexual inability, "for it is no better than for one man to be Married to another." In January 1781 the divorce was decreed. For some modern readers, such anecdotes might raise questions of sexual orientation. In the eighteenth century, in the absence of such a concept, they need not have raised such thoughts. [1]

Both examples, with their offhand references to same-sex coupling, could be used to support the argument that in early America, same-sex sexual behavior was not yet understood to be a component of sexual or romantic identity. Following this line of argument, in the late nineteenth century sexual behavior became not only associated with desire but a defining characteristic of an individual. Sodomy, for example, became an act symptomatic of a larger personality. Broader character traits and qualities of personhood became linked to a person's sexual proclivities. In the words of French historian and theorist Michel Foucault, the sodomite had become a species. [2]

The evidence presented here supports the handful of scholars who argue that in early America sex acts could be viewed as related to identity or personhood. This chapter also draws on the work of Stephen Shapiro, who has theorized that sexuality in the eighteenth century was a mix of both the earlier model of acts and the later model of psychological interiority. Shapiro points to the lack of institutions in eighteenth-century America that later would give rise to understandings of modern sexuality. One institution, the public sphere, does develop in the eighteenth century and figures heavily in my discussion of the role of print culture and cultural understandings of same-sex sexuality.[3]

Although the modern heterosexual-homosexual bifurcation had not yet fully developed, this was not a period without an understanding of sexual selves. As I have demonstrated in previous chapters, figures such as bachelors, impotent men, eunuchs, fops, and black rapists illustrate that discourses of male sexuality assumed that interior desires and moral states could be revealed by bodily and social comportment. The nature of these depictions underscores the centrality of marital, procreative sexuality in ideals of eighteenth-century manliness. This chapter also examines normative male sexual desire. It finds that even in the early modern era, male sexual attraction to women undergirded evaluations of proper manly sexual interests.

Evidence from court records and from religious discourses generally reveals an understanding of sodomy as an act—an act that could and should be punished, an act that could bring retribution down upon an individual and a community, and an act that indicated not necessarily a person's sexual desires but rather his moral failings. Sodomy in this regard was not so much a marker of the person's interior state but a transgressive act, and the transgressor could be reformed. However, sodomy, as a nonreproductive sexual act was also at times linked to character and personality. Sermons, newspapers, court records, and imported literature also reveal an eighteenth-century ambiguity regarding sodomy as an act or sodomy as a marker of an orientation.

On May 26, 1697, the General Council first published *Acts and Laws* to reflect the incorporation of Plymouth colony and the end of the Dominion of New England. "An Act for the Punishment of Buggery" in its entirety read:

> For *avoiding of the detestable and abominable Sin of Buggery with Mankind or Beast, which is contrary to the very Light of nature;* Be it Enacted and Declared by the Lieutenant Governour, Council and Repre-

sentatives in General Court Assembled, and by the Authority of the same. It is Enacted, That the same Offence be adjudged Felony, and as such Order and Form of Process therein to be used against the Offenders as in cases of Felony. And that every man being duly convicted of lying with mankind as he lyeth with a Woman. And every man or woman that shall have carnal copulation with any Beast or bruit Creature, the Offender and Offenders in either of the cases beforementioned, shall suffer the pains of Death, and the Beast shall be Slain and Burned.

Although the statute's language is draconian, the court system and the public were not especially concerned about sodomy as a criminal matter. Despite the colony's increase in population, eighteenth-century Massachusetts' courts heard only three sodomy cases. The lack of court cases, although striking when compared with much of Europe in the same period, is consistent with the experience of the other British mainland colonies. According to findings by Jonathan Katz and John Murrin, courts along the Eastern Seaboard heard only eight cases in the first half of the eighteenth century. Although a capital crime, sodomy and buggery charges resulted in the execution of only two men in this period, one in Pennsylvania for bestiality and the other in Massachusetts for heterosexual rape. Indeed, the absolute numbers of sodomy cases heard by the courts dropped in the eighteenth century. In the seventeenth century, some fifteen cases had been heard in New England, most of them in Massachusetts.[4]

Scholars have proffered different arguments to account for the paucity of cases, including a lack of same-sex activity among men, a new code of tolerance among men, the prolonged absences from women imposed by frequent wars, and a changed court system that was less concerned with policing morality than had been the case in the Puritan era. As a capital crime, sodomy, like rape, would have been heard by the Superior Court, a body that did not pursue or root out cases but simply responded to charges brought by the public. Sodomy probably did not differ from other moral crimes in that so long as the violations remained discreet, community members were hesitant to disrupt social cohesion by trudging off to the courts to trigger a hearing, particularly when the guilty party was socially prominent or occupied a position of power. As in the case of rape, this reticence was probably compounded by an unwillingness to put a man who was not otherwise a social outcast to death, unless for a heinous crime. In short, the public appeared reluctant to pursue punishment of sodomy through legal means.[5]

Although the court system was not the primary locus of eighteenth-century discussions of sodomy, the handful of sodomy cases the Superior Court heard offer a glimpse of legal attitudes and sexual practices that complements the print discourses analyzed in this chapter. Of the three men accused of sodomy in the Superior Court—a black servant, a white servant, and a gentleman—only the black servant was executed. The other two cases were dropped, probably because of the stringent legal standards of proof in capital cases. These cases all involved force and, thus, reinforce the point that the concern was not with sodomy per se but with violence, especially against the underaged or those deemed incapable of consent.

The buggery statute was used in at least one instance to prosecute a man for sodomizing a girl. In January 1712 Mingo, a "Negro Man Servant to Captain Jonathan Hawse," mariner of Charlestown, was convicted of "Buggery" and sentenced to be "hanged by his Neck" until dead. Court records charge that Mingo had attacked Abigail Hawse, a girl "between thirteen & fourteen," "Having thrown her down upon the Ground," "Contrary to the Ordinance of God & Contrary to Nature defiled & Carnally knew" her. Mingo was convicted of "Lying with & Entering her Body not after the Natural [use?] of a Woman, but in a detestable & abominable Way of Sodomy a Sin Among Christians not to be Named." Here sodomy figured as the nameless sin, contrary to "Nature," even though it was not a case involving two men. Mingo had disrupted the order of Hawse's household by raping the captain's daughter. Moreover, he had violated the "natural" order by sodomizing her.[6]

"Buggery" was also the term used in a case that the courts heard in 1714 involving an "Infant boy." In this case, "buggery" clearly referred to (forced) sexual intercourse between males. Court files tersely remark on the charges against Stephen Ropier, a servant:

> The Jurors for Our Sovereign Lord the King upon their Oaths present Stephen Ropier a Young Man servant to Jonathan Simpson for that on the 10th of July last past he willfully & feloniously made an assault on the body of James Woodward an Infant boy & he buggered & Carnally knew that Sd Infant by entering the posteriors or fundament of the Sd infant with his the Sd Stephen Ropiers yard or privy member. To which he pleaded Not Guilty.

Unfortunately, no other records survive to tell us who brought these charges. The jury found Ropier not guilty, presumably on lack of evidence about such a serious charge. Nonetheless, the trial itself underscores the social disruption caused by a servant attacking the "Infant" son of a master.[7]

A final court case, and one that did use the term "sodomy," involved Stephen Fessendon, a "gentleman" who was accused in 1740 of attempting sodomy with one of his pupils. Fessendon had lived in Roxbury for some time but had moved to Cambridge by the time these charges were brought. He was charged with several counts of attempting to sodomize his student.

> [Fessendon] with force and arms the Body of Thomas Brinley a male youth of the age of thirteen years or thereabouts, and his Pupill, did wickedly assault with an Intent to commit the Detestable Crime of Sodomy & to have carnal knowledge and Copulation of the Body of the Sd Thomas Brinley contrary to natural affection, and other Enormities and Injury's the sd Stephen Fessendon then and there did to the sd Thoms Brinley in Evil Example to others Contrary to Law and also to the Peace Crown and Dignity of our said Sovereign Lord the King.

Here the language of the court record focused on the unnaturalness of the crime: sodomy was a "Detestable" act "contrary to natural affection"; Fessendon had committed various "Enormities." What may have made this case sufficiently disruptive to warrant an arrest and trial was that Fessendon had violated the special trust between student and teacher—or more accurately between parents and teachers. Teachers, like others entrusted with the care of youth, were under a special obligation to act as moral guides and exemplars for students. Fessendon turned this obligation upside down, setting an "Evil example to others" by corrupting a child in his care.[8]

There is no evidence that Fessendon later suffered from a tarnished reputation after being accused of sodomy shortly after his graduation from Harvard. But it is difficult to know. When Ebenezer Parkman mentions being at dinner with a Dr. Breck, he notes that Fessendon was there, too. And he does so without any opprobrium. This was only five years after Fessendon was brought up on a capital charge of sodomy. That same year Parkman notes spending most of the evening at Fessendon's before lodging at Dr. Breck's. He notes that Fessendon had written a poem on the taking of "Louisbourg," to be read to Governor William Shirley on his visit to Worcester in 1747. We should note, however, that Fessendon died by 1749 intestate, presumably unmarried, and with little in this world except for his house, "a green bag, and a library which contained more literature than law."[9]

All three cases fitted well with what other scholars have argued about court prosecutions against sodomy. Citing Alan Bray's influential study of the meaning of sodomy in his *Homosexuality in Renaissance England*, Jonathan Goldberg, for example, points out that the "accusation of sexual misbehavior" in early modern London occurred only when the social status of the parties made the act a "violation of the social order." The cases examined here all involved forcible sodomy, and each one upset orderly hierarchies of race, age, and status among men: Ropier, a servant, violated a master's infant son; Fessendon attacked his student; and Mingo, a slave, who suffered the only execution on record, sodomized his master's young daughter. As violent sexual assaults, these sodomy cases are akin to the rape cases. No other records survive to tell us who brought these charges, witnessed the attacks, or first told the stories. There seem to be no prosecutions of consensual sodomy in the existing records of the eighteenth century. Could this mean that when instances of consensual relations between men were made known, community members did not view them as worthy of court action? It would seem so. Given the severity of the official position against sodomy, it also seems likely that those who engaged in same-sex sexual behavior took great care not to be discovered. Cautiousness and carefulness should not be underestimated.[10]

Other evidence from church records lends further support to the conclusion that sodomy within certain limits was more tolerable than official discourse would lead one to believe, given that it was viewed as only an act and that the individual could repent and be reformed. In 1732 Ebenezer Knight was punished by the First Church for "a long series of Uncleanness with Mankind." Knight was reinstated to full membership six years later, which suggests that the community tolerated "uncleanness," or same-sex activity in this case, and did not believe it to be a marker of a man. A second case, that of Steven Gorton in Connecticut, also indicates a community's unwillingness to convict men accused of same-sex activity and its preferred use of less severe religious sanctions. Gorton, a New London minister, had been accused in county court in 1726 of same-sex activity. The case was dismissed for lack of evidence. Thirty years later the General Meeting of Baptist Churches did punish Gorton for his "offensive and unchaste behaviour, frequently repeated for a long space of time." But the penalty was fairly mild. The council barred him from communion for a period of several months.[11]

Both cases suggest that sodomy, in certain cases, enjoyed a popular tolerance incongruent with the draconian language of sodomy statutes and was not always distinguished from other forms of "uncleanness." That Gorton and Knight appear never to have been brought to court lends further support to the conclusion that sodomy, whether understood in the particular case as sin or orientation, in popular views did not necessarily warrant court intervention. One other example of this comes to us from the diary of John Adams. Adams wrote the following about one Deacon Savil, his first cousin once removed: "Lately Deacon Savils Affair has become public. An old Man 77 Years of Age, a Deacon, whose chief Ambition has always been Prayer, and religious Conversation, and sacerdotal Company, discovered to have been the most salacious, rampant, Stallion, in the Universe—rambling all the Town over, lodging with this and that Boy and Attempting at least the Crime of Buggery." The case seems never to have made it to the courts; nor was it mentioned in the newspapers or made an issue by his parish. The surprising lack of corroborating information on Savil leads one to speculate that given the nature of the case ("Attempting") and the accused's advanced age, the case may have never been pursued. In the unfinished entry, Adams portrayed sodomy as one of a range of sinful behaviors rather than a particular mark of individuality. Trailing off, he wrote "Thus Adultery, Buggery, Perjury, are..."[12]

Sermon literature echoes this ambiguity in the belief that sodomy was just one of a range of sins under the rubric of uncleanness. Eighteenth-century Massachusetts' courts did not hear many sodomy cases, but that should not lead us to conclude that same-sex sexuality was culturally a non-issue. *Everyone* in Massachusetts would have been aware of the story of Sodom and Gomorrah because it was frequently invoked in sermons, newspapers, and conduct literature. As the setting for a biblical cautionary tale, the city of Sodom figured heavily in discourses of sin and retribution. Contemporary scholars continue to debate the biblical meaning of the story of Sodom and Gomorrah, some highlighting the same-sex component of the story, others arguing for the primacy of social sins and vices. In Massachusetts, as we shall see, same-sex sexuality certainly figured in the general understanding of the lesson of Sodom's destruction. That sodomy was also linked to other sinful and destructive behaviors, sexual and nonsexual, did not lessen its importance. Rather, these links broadened sodomy's significance; the use of sodomy in general discussions of sin heightened the sexual connotations of vice and corruption.[13]

The story itself comes from Genesis 19:1–12, which describes God's decision to destroy the city of Sodom because he deemed its residents "unclean." Before he does so, he sends two male angels in human form to the city to warn Lot, Sodom's only resident worthy of redemption, so that he and his family can escape. The night of the angels' arrival, a large crowd of men gathers at Lot's house. Filled with the lust of the damned, Sodom's residents menacingly demand that Lot turn over the angels. The crowd more specifically demands to "know" the male visitors and does not desist, even though they are offered Lot's virgin daughters in their place. As Lot and his family flee the city, fire and brimstone rain down from heaven.

The relevant scholarly debate centers on two points: first, whether or not the crowd's intentions (to "know" the angels) were sexual, and if so, whether the biblical condemnation of the crowd supports the view that homosexuality is a transhistorical phenomenon. The verb *to know* has been a focus of debate for scholars. Some say that it indicates an intention of homosexual rape; others argue for a social rather than sexual interpretation. Those scholars rejecting a sexual interpretation have pointed to the subsequent references in the Bible to the Sodomites who emphasize their violence rather than their sexual immorality.[14]

My examination of the Sodom and Gomorrah story does not seek to uncover an original meaning. Rather, it focuses on how it was interpreted in the eighteenth century. The sins of Sodom and Gomorrah were above all sexual, and references to them often included a range of acts under the general rubric "uncleanness" that were meant to address the desires and temptations of the majority of Bostonians along with the minority practice of sodomy. Thus, Samuel Danforth's 1674 *Cry of Sodom* explained: "The sins of *Sodom* were many and great, but that which was the most grievous of all was their abominable *filthiness* in all manner of *Uncleanness*." "Abominable Uncleanness," Danforth explained, included "whoredome," "self-pollution," "adultery," and "incest," as well as "sodomy," and "bestiality." Still, his sermon included a specific warning against *"going after strange flesh."* In Danforth's account, *"sodomy,* filthiness committed between parties of the same Sex; when Males with Males, and Females with Females work wickedness," had a special status signaled by its very name. "This sin raged amongst the *Sodomites,*" he wrote; "to their perpetual Infamy, it is called *Sodomy.*" Sodomy was the central point of reference, the special sin that stood for the rest and branded its practitioners with "perpetual infamy" via their special association with the cataclysm befalling their namesake city.[15]

As in Danforth's text, many eighteenth-century sermons did single out sodomy and treated it as especially representative of the sins that were indicative of the city's collective spiritual jeopardy. The Boston publication of Josiah Smith's sermon, first preached at Charleston, South Carolina, after a fire destroyed a large part of that city in the fall of 1740, used Charleston's disastrous experience as an object lesson. It opened with a preface by Boston ministers Benjamin Colman and William Cooper, who warned that their city would suffer God's wrath as had Charleston and Sodom if Bostonians did not reform. *The Burning of Sodom* enumerated among its *"Lusts of the Flesh,"* "that *unnatural* one, which must offend a modest Ear." Thus, same-sex activity was part of a broad range of sexual sins, but with this difference: it was "unnatural."[16]

It is true that some eighteenth-century Boston ministers referencing the story did not always see the need to refer to sodomy specifically, or, in some cases, even to sex, when discussing the sins of Sodom and Gomorrah. Increase Mather, for example, in the wake of Boston's fire of 1711, warned that in Sodom the sin of "Pride" had been punished with "Fires" and "Burnings." When an earthquake rattled Boston in 1727, some sermons again pointed to the lesson of Sodom without specifying sodomy as a reason for its destruction. In his sermon *The Terror of the Lord*, which went through three editions, Cotton Mather focused on the "Sins of Unchastity" and warned that "If an *Earthquake* do unspeakable things upon us, let the Impurities of *Sodom* stand indicted for it." Perhaps the most widely published sermon to invoke the lesson of Sodom and Gomorrah was Michael Wigglesworth's *Day of Doom*. By 1751, long after his death in 1705, it was in its seventh edition. It did not explicitly single out the practice of sodomy.[17]

Other sources reveal that sodomy in eighteenth-century Massachusetts was viewed as a marker of personhood, tied to an understanding of a man's sexual desires, and distinct from other vices, given this connection to the inner man. Gorton's case suggests that even in the eighteenth century popular views inconsistently meshed with official views of sodomy as a discrete act, not a marker of permanent disposition. In Gorton's case the General Meeting of Baptist Churches in Connecticut concluded that his "'offensive and unchaste behaviour, frequently repeated for a long space of time,'" resulted from "'an inward disposition.'" Sermon literature, newspaper accounts, and popular fiction all reveal evidence of understandings of sodomy as a marker of same-sex sexuality, rather than simply an isolated act as articulated by court actions and many religious discourses that focused on reform.[18]

Literature read by Bostonians that used the Sodom and Gomorrah story did single out sodomy as an unnatural sin. Benjamin Keach's very popular *The Progress of Sin*, first published in London in 1684 and in its sixth edition by the time it was published in Boston in 1744, included same-sex sexuality among the *"unnatural* Lusts [my emphasis]" of the city of Sodom, which were said to be "Whoredom, Incest, Sodomy, and Buggery it self." He elaborated: "The Men leaving the *Natural* Use of the Women [my emphasis]," explained Keach, "burn'd in Lust one towards another, even Men with Men, working that which is unseemly and abominable." Similarly, *The Oeconomy of Love*, a London publication appearing in Boston in the 1730s, warned that the "Men of *Sodom*" had "sought the Paths of monstrous Joy," "Leaving the *natural* Road [my emphasis]" and engaging in sex "Man with Man."[19]

Urban vice was a central component of the story of Sodom and its lessons, and sodomy was often associated especially closely with city sins. When Smith chastised the inhabitants of Charleston after the fire there, his cautionary tale held up both Sodom and London as negative type cases and associated a climate of same-sex desire with both cities. According to Smith, London resembled Sodom before its destruction by fire and brimstone. Why? In part because in both places "Men burned in their Lust one toward the other; Men with Men, working that which is unseemly." The special association of sodomy—or the "unnatural" vice—with urban environments was enhanced by newspaper reports on Europe's campaigns to rid its cities of inns and houses where men gathered for sex with each other. A *Boston News Letter* article about the prosecution in London of some "20 Houses... which entertain'd Sodomitical Clubs" in 1726 associates London and its vices with Sodom and Gomorrah via the fact that both harbor a sodomite subculture. Here sodomy is associated with the vices of the city and especially with the cosmopolitan and commercial cities of Europe.[20]

Eighteenth-century Bostonians focusing on the biblical lesson of Sodom and Gomorrah heard warnings that their vices, especially their sexual vices, were threatening to destroy their way of life. The lesson was designed to instill a fear of divine retribution as a means of strengthening parishioners' resolve to lead Christian lives. But among the catalog of sexual sins united under the category of uncleanness, same-sex sexuality had at times a special status. Sermons, conduct manuals, and newspapers treated sodomy as emblematic of the sins that destroyed a whole city. Further, sodomy figured as "unnatural," giving it a different status in the eighteenth century than run-of-the-mill debauchery or capitulation to the appetites. But once again, we should not take sermons as indicators of the prevalence of same-sex sexual behavior.

Historians Randolph Trumbach and Alan Bray have written about the emergence of an effeminate minority of sodomites in early eighteenth-century London. Much of the evidence comes from various accounts published in 1709, 1714, and 1729 detailing so-called molly houses, places where men gathered for ritualized cross-dressing, intimacy, and sex. While scholars have recently begun to debate how best to interpret these sources, we do know that in London arrests and prosecutions of men and boys allegedly congregating to commit sodomy were very high in this period. In contrast to seventeenth-century arrests and to the colonial cases, the eighteenth-century European cases included prosecutions of consensual sex between adult males.[21]

Massachusetts newspapers published accounts about the arrests resulting from the antisodomy campaigns begun in the early decades of the eighteenth century as part of London's Reformation of Manners movement. Massachusetts' newspapers also reported on the antisodomy campaigns in the Dutch Republic throughout this period, where as many as 250 men were prosecuted and some two dozen executed. Printers selected these stories because they carried the general Puritan-influenced lesson of depravity that still resonated in early eighteenth-century Massachusetts. Newspaper printers in Pennsylvania, by way of contrast, apparently did not carry as many of these stories.[22]

For Bostonians sodomy was linked to personhood through an emerging understanding that certain men were disposed to desire other men sexually. This view was reinforced by the increased public awareness of European men who created social organizations, such as sodomitical clubs, that centered on a shared interest in intimacy with other men. For example, the *Boston News Letter* reported in 1726: "Seventeen Persons charged with Sodomy have been taken up lately, and on Monday last were examin'd at the Bell Tavern; Westminster, by several Justices of the Peace, who committed some of them to Newgate, some to the Gatehouse, and others to Bridewell."[23]

Early-Boston newspapers point to notions of the propensity to commit sodomy as a character trait. The *New England Weekly Journal* in 1732, for example, printed a notice from Rochester, England, suggesting that a man accused of murdering his wife was engaged in a long-term adulterous sexual relationship with his own male servant. Indeed, his violence was provoked, according to the newspaper notice about the case, precisely because she impudently "call'd him a Sodomitical Dog" and his servant "his Dog of a Boy" and refused her husband's bidding to "make his Bed," presumably because doing so would be to abet his continuing adultery and her own humiliation. What is significant for our purposes here is less his rage at having his authority as master disregarded than that her slur—"Sodomitical Dog" —created a (debased) character type based on a deviant sexual proclivity or taste.[24]

Although most European notices of criminal raids treated sodomy as an act, for example by referring to those convicted as "guilty of Sodomitical Practices" or to the accused as "Persons charged with Sodomy," there coexisted a notion that acts of sodomy could be indicative of the desires of a particular type of man. Thus, men charged with sodomy were at times named by their crime. At least three foreign notices specifically refer to their subjects as "sodomites." The *Boston News Letter* report on "nocturnal Assemblies" of over "20 Sodomitical Clubs" in London, dubbed the men who gathered in those assemblies "English Sodomites" and highlighting their "Aversion to the Female Sex." The following year the *Boston Gazette* reported on the arrest of "John Harwood & Mary his Wife," who were accused of "keeping a disorderly House" for the purpose of "entertaining Sodomites." In an accompanying article about a man arrested for sodomy, the paper included mention of his alias, stating parenthetically after his name that he "used to go among the Sodomites by the Name of Queen." By creating a type, the "sodomite," these and other reports like them clearly suggested that these men were oriented primarily toward sex with other men and that their "Clubs" were organized precisely around such proclivities. When the reports also featured the spaces in which the men congregated and the slang and nicknames they purportedly used, the articles hinted at the development of a shared subculture around these desires.[25]

Several of the cases tried in London were published in a 1734 volume of cases. *Select Trials for Murder, Robbery, Burglary, Rapes, Sodomy, Coining, Forgery, Pyracy, and Other Offences and Misdemeanours, at the Sessions-House in the Old-Bailey* was widely circulated in the colonies and was apparently available in Massachusetts for decades. The book made numerous cases of sodomy part of library collections, supplementing the accounts already published in newspapers.[26]

According to *Select Trials*, in some cases the accusation presses hard on an eighteenth-century understanding of same-sex behavior as indicative of a permanent orientation toward men. One Thomas Rodin, for example, was accused of assaulting and sodomizing a drunk stranger while at a bawdy house. The attack came in full view of a witness who often lodged at the house. The witness heard Rodin say "he took more Pleasure in lying with a Man, than with the finest Woman in the World; and that he had not touch'd his Wife these nine Months." Thus, as evidence of his guilt, the accusation pointed to his sustained preference for sex with men. Rodin was convicted of attempted sodomy.[27]

More often cases used defenses that employed a similar conception of propensity and inclination based on one's sexual history. One Thomas Andrews's defense focused on his evident virility and heteronormativity.

When accused of attempting to sodomize his house guest, Andrews's daughter and others testified on his behalf that he had four children, had been married for over twenty-five years, and had twelve times gotten his wife pregnant. Although the court found him guilty and sentenced him to death, he was eventually pardoned. Similarly, the defense for Patrick Malcolm, who was eventually acquitted, stated that he "was a kind Husband to his Wife, a careful Father to his Children," emphasizing his ability to serve the normative role—but linked it to sexual desire by concluding, "and always preferr'd the Company of Women to that of Men." The defense further offered evidence that relied on the notion of a permanent disposition. Thus it was noteworthy that "some Men who had often lain with him, deposed, that he never offer'd any Indecencies to them." In one final example, we see the same connection between the ability to be a normative husband and father with a permanent sexual and romantic interest in women generally. Thus, the defense of another man mentioned: "Several of both Sexes appeared to his Reputation. They deposed that he had been married 12 or 13 Years; that he bore the Character of an honest sober Man, a kind Husband, and one who loved the Conversation of Women better than that of his own Sex." All of these cases point to an understanding of sexual behavior, with one's wife or with another man, as indicative of a broader sexual orientation. Thus, individuals defending themselves against charges of sodomy would argue that they were predisposed to desire women and therefore would not have engaged in sex with another man.[28]

Newspaper notices about the persecution of sodomites were part and parcel of debates about public executions and harsh punishments in Europe. At the same time, they also characterized sodomy for their provincial readers. These articles sometimes explicitly used vehement antisodomy rhetoric as well as reported the use of such rhetoric by others. The authors referred to sodomy as a "detestable Sin," as "abominable" and "Atrocious." In the same vein, the notices described sodomites as "vile Wretches," "vile Persons," and "horrid Company." Newspaper articles, at times, reinscribed official condemnation of the act of sodomy and characterized sodomites as worthy of the punishment of death.[29]

Since sodomy was viewed in both Europe and Massachusetts as an emblem of society gone awry, such alarmist tones must have fanned concern over the pace and direction of social and cultural change. Judging from the notices of foreign sodomy cases carried by Boston newspapers, at any rate, Massachusetts residents perceived a close relationship between sodomy and the strengthening of commercial empire in the first half of the eighteenth century. Such wariness would have been especially consonant with local, long-standing Puritan beliefs about the vices accompanying urban development and commerce. The articles also suggest that as the eighteenth century progressed, sodomy ceased to be viewed as the exclusive practice of a select few debauched aristocrats and instead was seen as being as widespread as commercial empire itself.

In addition to the newspaper accounts, midcentury English novels that circulated in Massachusetts offer evidence of print-culture depictions of same-sex sexuality. These novels included lengthy descriptions of men characterized by pursuits of sodomy. In 1748 Tobias Smollett's *The Adventures of Roderick Random* was first published in London. The novel included a character named Earl Strutwell, a man "notorious for a passion for his own sex." The book, a near best seller in the colonies, circulated widely in Massachusetts in the second half of the eighteenth century and remained popular for decades. John Mein's circulating library on King's Street in Boston included *Roderick Random* in its catalog of some twelve hundred volumes in 1765. Other booksellers regularly ran newspaper advertisements that included the book in the 1770s and '80s.[30]

In one scene the protagonist, Roderick, discussed the homosexual reputation of a mutually known writer that Strutwell had queried him about. The passage reads: "I own (replied the Earl) that his taste in love is generally decried, and indeed condemned by our laws; but perhaps that may be more owing to prejudice and misapprehension, than to true reason and deliberation." This passage captured the eighteenth-century ambivalence in references to his taste in love as "that Passion," the repeated references to "it," and to sodomy as a "vice." The earl continued with his remarkable defense of sodomy, exalting it above the more problematic sexual release of heterosexual fornication. He, therefore, reinforced the notion of sodomy as a vice or an act. Referring to sodomy as the "practice of this passion," "Nay, I have been told, that there is another motive perhaps more powerful than all these, that induces people to cultivate this inclination; namely pleasure attending its success." The earl reveals himself to be an immoral man with his defense of sodomy and echoes the view of sodomy as a "passion" or desire that is an "inclination."[31]

Roderick responded to Earl Strutwell's lengthy discussion of sodomitical practices of the ancients with some concern:

From this discourse, I began to be apprehensive that his lordship finding I had travelled, was afraid I might have been infected with this spurious and sordid desire abroad. . . . I argued against it with great warmth, as an appetite unnatural, absurd, and of pernicious consequence; and declared my utter detestation and abhorrence of it in these lines of the satyrist: 'Eternal infamy the wretch confound, Who planted first, this vice on British ground! A vice! That spite of sense and nature reigns, And poisons genial love, and manhood stains!' The Earl smiled at my indignation, told me he was glad to find my opinion of the matter so conformable to his own, and that what he had advanced was only to provoke me to an answer, with which he professed himself perfectly well pleased.

Once informing him that the discussion was merely a test of Roderick's opinions, the duplicitous sodomite departed. Roderick discussed Strutwell's reputation with a friend shortly thereafter. Smollett wrote: "Strutwell, who was so notorious for a passion for his own sex, that he was amazed his character had never reached my ears." Roderick also learned of Strutwell's general corruption. He was described as a man who spoke of political and social connections he did not have, often stole from the men he flattered, and "very often of their chastity; and then leave them a prey to want and infamy."[32]

In addition to evidence from newspapers and print literature reporting on the development of urban subcultures of men whose primary romantic and sexual interests were with other men, evidence reveals that when sodomy served as a political weapon, it was indeed connected to character.[33]

The use of sodomy in satire reveals its connections to character and suggests a view of sodomy as a marker of the sexual and total man. Early American and London Grub Street political and social attacks frequently fomented sexual scandal. The eighteenth-century New England satirist's arsenal of sexually charged social and political weapons included sodomy as a smear tactic. Although scholarship on early satires of the Freemasons has largely overlooked its sexual dimensions, the earliest published polemics centering on the Freemasons in Massachusetts clearly reveal the use of sodomy to smear men enmeshed in public controversy.[34]

Shortly after they formed in Boston in the 1730s, Masons marched through the streets in celebration. Individuals such as Benjamin Walker, Junior, took note. An organization that was founded in London in 1717, the group fascinated residents with their dramatic public displays of music and dress. The group also triggered anxieties by maintaining, along with their public processions and foreign origins, secrecy about their practices of initiation and membership. Such secrecy made Masons vulnerable to charges of illicit collusion at a time when their membership was largely confined to elite merchants and gentlemen. The Masons' parades offered members a ritual and symbolic means to celebrate publicly their status as colonial elites. Public displays, for example, utilized such traditional status symbols as swords and rods and combined them with markers of wealth and commerce, such as decorated ships. According to historian Stephen Bullock, unlike their nineteenth-century incarnation, whose members sought only to "sequester themselves from the world," the early Masons were colonial gentlemen who had joined to "establish their place" and to "emphasize their elevation above common people."[35]

Such elaborate, visual posturing came at a time of sustained social conflict in Boston. The city struggled with an economic depression from 1741 to 1760. The 1740s were marked by a general mood of unrest by the lower orders. Mobs took control of the city several times in the 1740s and '50s. Furthermore, as Marcus Rediker points out, Boston had developed a "subculture of apprentices, journeymen, servants, slaves, laborers, and sailors" that "revolved around common work experiences and a common cultural life of revels, masques, fairs, May Day celebrations, street parties, taverns, and 'disorderly houses.'" By the time the anti-Mason satire discussed here appeared in print, a culture that was fascinated by wealth, but that vilified displays of aristocratic pretension, was firmly in place.[36]

Sodomy was explicitly linked to these anxieties crystallizing around Freemasonry in the January 7, 1751, issue of the *Boston Evening Post*, which ran a full-column poem alongside a scatological engraving. Although sex slander and gossip were fairly common, satire that included posterior-centered tropes such as enemas or direct smears of homosexuality, however, was rare in the colonial era. Caricatures were also relatively unusual prior to the Revolution. The engraving was one of the earliest to appear in a Boston newspaper and the first time that Boston readers had ever seen an engraving accompanying a poem in their papers. The novelty of an engraving in itself would have drawn the attention of readers; the content of the image must have been doubly shocking. It depicted two smiling men, one bent over with his pants pulled down to receive a treenail, or wooden peg, the other, with a hammer raised overhead, ready to strike.[37]

The poem included several lines that highlighted the alleged group practice of penetrating members with treenails, or trunnels.

> I'm sure our TRUNNELS look'd as clean
> As if they ne're up A—se had been;
> For when we use 'em, we take care

> To wash 'em well, and give 'em Air,
> Then lock 'em up in our own Chamber,
> Ready to TRUNNEL the next Member.

The passage smears the Freemasons with metaphorical associations that charge them with secretly practicing sodomy. That treenails (commonly used in eighteenth-century shipbuilding) effectively joined timbers because they swell when wet, furthered the metaphor with an added emphasis on sexual arousal. Notice that the word "trunnel," which clearly stood in for the male member, was twice singled out for the reader by appearing in capital letters. That the trunnels looked unused underscored the charge of deceptive appearances and fear of secrecy that made the closed community of the Freemasons suspect. Secrecy hid the Freemasons' true purpose and illicit activity. The care and attention given to their trunnels also hinted at a kind of phallocentric and homoerotic self-regard.[38]

The poem continued with two lines that underscored the homoerotic nature of the Freemasons' society: "You see I have put our ARMS above, / To shew you that we live in Love." By equating the engraving with arms, the author reinforced the Masons' association with sodomy and mocked the aristocratic and gentlemanly pretensions of the group, revealing to the viewer the sordid reality that such pretensions disguised. The final line, "To shew you that we live in Love," created a double entendre that relied on the ambiguity of the language of fraternal love. The Freemasons' supposed rituals and celebratory practices of anal penetration perverted the norms of fraternal bonding by blurring the distinction between male friendship and loyalty and sexual intimacy. The poem also declared that "we don't use TRUNNELS with a Sister," thus portraying the men as sodomites who reserved their favored sexual rituals for men alone.[39]

Local satirist John Hammock made it look as if his rival Joseph Green was the author because of Green's other satirical pieces. In an anti-Mason poem of 1755, Green also used tropes centering on "Posteriors." The following poem depicted the fetishization of "flogging" in such a way as to emphasize its parody of, and deviance from, heterosexual intimacy.

> His mighty Force in flogging well.
> Thy blanch'd Posteriors lash'd so much,
> Blush high, protuberate to the Touch.
> The modern Beauty thus displays,
> Those Charms, that Top contracted Stays;
> Thus they thro' all Confinements move,
> Thus bound those Hemispheres of Love.

The references to "Beauty" and "Love" in this situation portrayed the Freemasons' supposed indulgence in pleasurably sadistic homosexual acts as a perversion of the aesthetics and feelings associated with normative heterosexual manhood.[40]

Significantly, Green's satires about other subjects, including, for example, a currency crisis in New Hampshire, do not use scatological humor; it was not Green's or Hammock's automatically preferred form of ridicule, but rather the fraternal order of Freemasons specifically that elicited such symbolic references to sodomy. Sodomy was generally associated with a number of qualities for which Green wished to attack the Freemasons: their elite membership, foreign origins, and international nature. Given sodomy's long history of negative associations with aristocracy and its more recent links to foreign vices that accompanied commercial wealth and consumption, sodomy was a particularly useful device for satirizing Freemasons.[41]

The year before "In Defence of Masonry" appeared in print, Green's popular *An Entertainment for a Winter's Evening* went through two editions in Boston. It emphasized anal intimacy between the men and also used the analogy of clystering to evoke sodomy. The poem also used the imagery of a banquet to link sex to Masonic initiation rules, this time with an accent on international fraternization of an illicit kind.

> Where's honest *Luke,* that cook from *London,*
> For without *Luke* the LODGE is undone.
> 'Twas he who oft dispell'd their Sadness,
> And fill'd the *brethren's* hearts with gladness.
> For them his ample bowls o'erflow'd,
> His table groan'd beneath it's load;
> For them he stretch'd his utmost art;
> Their honours grateful they impart.

Here, Luke, a "cook from London," is a sodomite upon whose "ample bowls" (read: "bowels") the Massachusetts Freemasons lavish their "grateful" "honours." Indeed, without him "the LODGE is undone." His symbolic posterior fills the men's "hearts with gladness" and "oft dispell'd their Sadness."[42]

The stanza continued with a commentary that appears to ridicule the Masons by suggesting that they pervert the principle of fraternization between manly peers.

> Luke *in return is made a* brother,
> As *good* and *true* as any other,
> And still, though broke with age and wine,
> Preserves the *token* and the *sign*.

By cozying up to Luke, the elite membership allow themselves to be seduced by their "brother" from overseas. Their new "brother," in turn, is debauched in the end by the excesses of the Freemasons: "broke with age and wine."[43]

In the winter of 1777 a series of letters printed in the *Boston Gazette* echoed the sentiment that Freemasons, because of their homosocial secrecy and ritual, elicited concerns about same-sex behavior. In December 1777 a response to a "Lawyer who pronounced an Oration to the Free Masons" said to be written by a "Lady" expressed the following:

> You said Sir on a late Occasion,
> When speaking forth your fine Oration,
> Ladies could never Masons be,
> Alass! They fail in Secrecy.
> Then with your *Brothers* pass your Life, Sir,
> Without a Mistress or a Wife, Sir;
> Lawyers with Masons ought to dwell,
> For both have much unfit to tell.

The poem impressed one unidentified diarist sufficiently to prompt the chronicler to record the poem in its entirety, preceded by this explanation: "The following lines written Extempore by a Lady. To the Lawyer who pronounced an Oration to the Free Masons on Saturday the 27 Day of December 1777." The charge of sodomy turned the image of the Freemasons as manly participants in orderly civic rituals upside down. As a marker of their deviance, it operated to define their character. And they stood as men who lacked normative desire for women and who deviated from heterosociability.[44]

By the mid-eighteenth century, through newspaper accounts, some sermon literature, and imported fiction, Massachusetts' print culture was no stranger to discussions of a minority population of men who preferred sexual romantic contact with other men. But then an interesting thing happened. In Massachusetts the apparently proto-homosexual subject largely evaporated from broad public discussions. The enduring Puritan cultural message of general depravity that gave local significance and meaning to reports of molly houses and sodomites in Europe had waned by the Revolutionary era. That this earlier message was influenced by the Puritan cultural climate of early eighteenth-century Massachusetts is suggested by the fact that Pennsylvania newspapers, for example, did not print as many of these notices. Massachusetts printers selected these stories because they resonated there. By the Revolutionary era, stories of sodomites no longer symbolized the need for all men to guard against sinful excesses, but rather described a minority concern irrelevant to the Massachusetts social setting.

For much of the eighteenth century, although official discourses of capital crime and sin viewed sodomy primarily as an act deserving punishment, popular conceptions of sodomy could view it as a feature of character. However, it would not be accurate to say that eighteenth-century Anglo-American popular culture had an understanding of sexual subjectivity that equated the sodomite with the modern medicalized and psychologized homosexual subject. Rather, the various discourses examined here joined sexual proclivity or taste to specifically religious ideas about corruption and immorality. What evidence we do have on sexual practices suggests that long-term practitioners of sodomy were characterized by their deviant sexuality; it was viewed as an aspect of their personhood, as a proclivity or taste.

⤙ Conclusion

SEXUALITY IS NOT A TRUTH of human nature or human psychology discovered in the modern era. Sexualities are broader meanings given to sexual acts and desires and linked to personhood. Sexualities arise at different times for different cultural purposes and are historically informed. Fops, bachelors, the black rapist, sodomites, impotent men, and others are all instances of periodic sexualities. But such sexualities did not just define deviant male figures and stereotypes. Indeed, arguably, deviant figures serve *primarily* to underscore normative desires and behaviors, defining normative male sexuality by contrast.

Although the colonial male stereotypes that I began this book with are rarely associated with sex, or sexuality, it was a key component of normative Anglo-American manhood throughout the eighteenth century in Massachusetts. Sex was one dimension of properly assuming the mantle of patriarch and head of household. The highly stylized figures of the lifelong bachelor and the young man who died on the eve of his marriage symbolized incomplete manhood. Men, as heads of households, had always been thought to be responsible for overseeing a satisfying and appropriately expressed sexual relationship between husband and wife. A wife's infidelity signified the husband's failure to regulate her conduct and to provide sexual pleasure. And as companionate marriage ideals became more pronounced, the pleasure-based component of marital sexuality became more closely linked to mutual intimacy: marital love was becoming eroticized, and this too became part of the manly sexual ideal.

The Puritan regime officially ended with the inauguration of the new royal charter in 1692, but Puritan cultural influences remained strong in Massachusetts throughout the colonial era and had a deep impact on the role that sexuality played in a range of social, cultural, economic, and political arenas. Puritans had viewed sexuality as potentially dangerous unless expressed within the confines of marriage and directed toward its proper ends, the reproduction of Christian heirs and the strengthening of the marriage bond. They also held men, once married, accountable for regulating not only their own desires and sexual conduct but those of their wives and other household dependents as well. As the lesson of the biblical tale of Sodom and Gomorrah taught, sexual transgressions also jeopardized the spiritual state of the entire covenanted community. Manly ideals thus held men responsible not only for their own sexuality and that of their dependents but for maintaining the moral integrity of the Bay Colony. This moral responsibility linked private sexual behavior with public welfare.

Anglo-American discourses of sex and manliness in the first half of the eighteenth century were a distinctive blend of Puritan commentary and secular viewpoints and concerns. Fathering children, for example, obeyed the biblical teaching to go forth and multiply and satisfied a manly ideal of sexual virility. Newspaper notices of arrests for sodomy in Europe drew upon the age-old biblical condemnation of sodomites as irreligious and used the story of Sodom and Gomorrah to castigate the new subcultures of men who gathered in public places for sexual liaisons. Because it linked sexual licentiousness to the city, the Sodom and Gomorrah story also melded especially well with newer eighteenth-century discourses that viewed imperial commerce and modern cities as sources of moral corruption. In one final example, idleness and luxury, sins long railed against in Christian doctrine, became the special hallmark of effeminate men as a way of signifying eighteenth-century concerns over the moral effects of a new culture of consumption and fashionable display.

Colonial discourses of male sexuality popularized an array of male sexual types not because they directly identified a social conflict or pattern of social practices in Massachusetts, but because they distilled concerns that applied to Bay Colonists in general, including the importance of sexual self-regulation, the damaging effects of commerce and urban development on that capacity for self-regulation, and the decline of a Puritan ethos. Discourses of male sexuality, thus, had both universalizing and particularizing effects. Given the relatively homogeneous population of early eighteenth-century Massachusetts, for example, there was no immediate crisis in race relations between blacks and whites. Yet black men were singled out as especially threatening in a way that reinforced racial hierarchies. At the same time, black rapists symbolized the general threat to social order posed by a lack of self-mastery over the passions. A visible subculture of sodomites or effeminate fops did not exist in Massachusetts, yet such types were well delineated for newspaper readers. Depictions of sodomites and fops were warnings against capitulation to appetites directed to all Bay Colonists, but they also fostered an awareness of sexual desire and expression between men. Finally, rape was relatively rare in the courts, yet narratives of rape were ubiquitous. They underscored the importance of manly self-control by carving out the figure of a predatory rake—a man marked by his ability to charm and seduce and against whom women needed to be vigilant. These sexual figures were moral object lessons for all. At the same time, these narratives and figures defined particular types of men according to their sexual proclivities.

The enduring influence of Puritan understandings of general human depravity gave voice to the figures of the black rapist, the sodomite, the foppish bachelor, and others. Although not reflecting an immediate social concern, these stereotypes resonated in colonial Massachusetts, given the broader message of self-control and moderation applicable to all men. Scholars have assumed that such figures emerged only later because many studies have not looked back to the early eighteenth century, beginning instead in the Revolutionary era. Studying the entire eighteenth century shows a surprising and peculiar trajectory that reveals sexualities embodied in specific types—such as the fop, sodomite, and black rapist—earlier in the century, and others—such as the British soldier as rapist and the bachelor—in the Revolutionary and New Republic eras, respectively.

Throughout the eighteenth century, the ability to control one's sexual desires had deep cultural importance; it was at the core of the hegemonic norm of male sexuality. Self-control and moderation were the guiding principles, as was a concomitant loathing of excess. Capitulation to the sexual appetites signaled an inner moral weakness or lack of character that was as important for normative masculinity as it was for femininity. Sexual desire, like other carnal urges, when left unchecked even had detrimental effects on the body. Sexual excess, according to eighteenth-century medical understandings, was enervating and emasculating; men who debauched themselves risked physical depletion. The fop's enervated, effeminate body, for example, indicated his immoderate self-regard and gestured toward his nonreproductive sexuality, including masturbation and sodomy. In contrast, the well-proportioned physique of the normative man underscored his properly modulated virility.

Yet, despite the dominant norm of moderation, norms of masculinity were not univocal. Anglo-American narratives of male sexuality and manliness were riddled with internal tensions and contradictions. Thus, in some narratives of rape and seduction, misogynist portrayals of the threat that female lust posed to vulnerable men countered depictions of women as the submissive and helpless victims of predatory men. These portrayals were a covert repudiation of the norm of moderation and of male responsibility for their own and for women's sexuality. They also made use of counternorms that touted an aggressive ideal of male sexual prowess. Thus, the colloquial language of sex often celebrated male mastery and power, and even the figure of the seductive rake could appear compellingly attractive.

Sexual behavior was identified and labeled criminal when it threatened orderly relations between hierarchically structured communities of men. Rape and sexual assault were, of course, roundly condemned from pulpits and the courts alike. But these crimes were condemned not simply in the name of outraged womanhood or primarily because of the criminal's failure to adhere to the most basic standards of manly self-control. Given that women were social dependents, rarely living independently of male-headed households, these crimes were condemned because men who assaulted women (and children) insulted the patriarchal authority of other men. Gossip and talk about sex among men played an important role in securing networks for trade and reputation. Sex figured in the definition and consolidation of communities of men at both the micro and the macro level.

The dominant scholarly model for conceptualizing early American understandings of sexuality as based on "acts" rather than "orientations" devalues the specific meanings attached to early modern sexual behaviors. That model evaluates early modern sexuality from the vantage point of late nineteenth- and twentieth-century medical and psychological discourses of sexual orientation. My analysis shows that sexual behavior was considered indicative of moral character and the disposition of the passions: in short, of manly personhood or its lack. When the language of sexuality became professionalized in the late nineteenth century, psychologists and sexologists were drawing on a long tradition in America of linking sex and gendered personhood. Connections between sexual behavior and the sexual self in eighteenth-century Massachusetts did not, however, highlight a divide between heterosexuality and homosexuality; a large array of deviant sexualities, together with positive norms of marital sexuality, had as their focal point, instead, the moral problematic of regulation of desires and self-mastery. To view eighteenth-century discourses of sex as centering on a series of "acts" flattens them. When probed, they establish rich connections between sexual proclivity and gendered character.

Although dominant ideals seem static throughout the eighteenth century, continually emphasizing moderation, marriage, and monogamy, there is great dynamism hidden in the shadows. Even though significant changes occurred in loosening the strictures on conduct and moral judgment especially regarding premarital sexual behaviors, the marital norm remained consistent. However, the emphasis on the importance of marriage and family for men prevalent in print culture after the Revolution must be viewed in context. Although it appears to be simply a carryover from earlier Puritan messages, in the late eighteenth century, given the changing sexual standards of and around courtship and marriage, the frightening figure of the morose bachelor and the image of the happily married man must be viewed as aggressive reassertions of dominant ideals in the face of a "sexual revolution," rather than simply as more of the same.[1]

Finally, this book's analysis of print culture and the courts suggests that eighteenth-century Anglo-American sexual culture and print culture developed in tandem. Sexually laden items, such as information on arrests, trials, and criminal behaviors, peppered early newspapers in part to increase sales and circulation. Sex sells: notices of a sexual nature sold not only newspapers but also, we may assume, sermons and other literature. At the same time, Boston's newspapers, published sermons, and other literature popularized the narratives, figures, and discourses described in this book and reflexively worked over and promoted gendered norms and ideals of sexuality. Print also multiplied the possibilities that one could imagine for sexual expression and, thus, had a subversive potential. Notices of molly houses in Europe, for example, created awareness that alternatives to official religious doctrine were possible, at least in urban spaces. Print representations of sex and manliness brought sexuality and gender into the domain of the political, the economic, and the public and produced new cultural understandings about the relationship between sex and the eighteenth-century man.

⤙ *Acknowledgments*

T HIS BOOK BEGAN AS a Ph.D. dissertation. In that incarnation, the project benefited enormously from the guidance of my adviser, Toby L. Ditz, and also the comments and assistance of many, especially Sharon Block, Libby Bouvier, Mary Fissell, Richard Godbeer, Jonathan Goldberg, Philip Morgan, Mary Beth Norton, and Alfred F. Young. As I revised and expanded the book, I was assisted in my research by a postdoctoral fellowship from the Sexuality Research Fellowship program of the Social Science Research Council with funds provided by the Ford Foundation. The help of the staff at the American Antiquarian Society, Boston Public Library, Houghton Library at Harvard University, Kinsey Institute, Library of Congress Manuscript Division, Massachusetts Historical Society, Massachusetts State Archives, New England Historical and Genealogical Society, and the Phillips Library of the Peabody Essex Museum greatly aided my research. I am especially appreciative of help from Sharon Block and the head archivist of the Massachusetts State Archives, Libby Bouvier.

I am grateful to have had inspiring and encouraging teachers and mentors, including Robert K. Andrian, of the Loomis Chaffee School, who first encouraged me to pursue my interest in the history of sexuality via a term paper on the gay rights movement, and Mary Beth Norton, who encouraged me to become a historian and sparked my interest in studying early American gender and sexuality. Beth, Brad, Ben, and Alex Koltz, Mary Foster, and Supriya Mehta graciously provided housing and made my trips to archives and libraries in Massachusetts feel like vacations. Kutraluk Bolton, Jessica Cannon, Lynne Cohen, John D'Emilio, Toby L. Ditz, John Gray, Rusty Hawkins, Marlon Henry, Anne S. Lombard, Mary Beth Norton, Parna Sengupta, and D. Brenton Simons all read and commented on portions of earlier versions of this manuscript.

Various parts of the book were presented before and aided by groups kind enough to invite me to discuss my work. I would like to thank the Colonial Society of Massachusetts and Richard Godbeer and participants in the Gender and Sexuality conference at the University of California at Riverside. I would also like to thank Lisa Moore for inviting me to the University of Texas at Austin to present a portion of chapter 6 and George Chauncey and the Gender and Sexuality Workshop at the University of Chicago for inviting me to present a portion of chapter 7. The history departments at the University of Miami, Rice University, and DePaul University provided institutional support and employment while I wrote the book. Finally, I would like to thank Toby Ditz, who, through extraordinary mentoring, more than anyone made this project possible. I dedicate the book also to her.

⤜ *Notes*

INTRODUCTION

1. Kathleen Brown, *Good Wives, Nasty Wenches, and Anxious Patriarchs: Gender, Race, and Power in Colonial Virginia* (Chapel Hill: University of North Carolina Press for the Omohundro Institute of Early American History and Culture [henceforth UNC-OIEAHC], 1996); Cornelia Dayton, *Women Before the Bar: Gender, Law, and Society in Connecticut, 1639–1789* (Chapel Hill: UNC-OIEAHC, 1995); Kirsten Fischer, *Suspect Relations: Sex, Race, and Resistance in Colonial North Carolina* (Ithaca: Cornell University Press, 2002); Richard Godbeer, *Sexual Revolution in Early America* (Baltimore: Johns Hopkins University Press, 2001); and Mary Beth Norton, *Founding Mothers and Fathers: Gendered Power and the Forming of American Society* (New York: Vintage Books, 1997).

2. On minoritizing and universalizing, see Eve Kosofsky Sedgwick, *Epistemology of the Closet* (Berkeley: University of California Press, 1990), 1–63.

3. Mark E. Kann, *A Republic of Men: The American Founders, Gendered Language, and Patriarchal Politics* (New York: New York University Press, 1998), 52. On early American masculinity, see, for example, Toby L. Ditz, "Shipwrecked; or, Masculinity Imperiled: Mercantile Representations of Failure and the Gendered Self in Eighteenth-Century Philadelphia," *Journal of American History* 81 (1994): 51–80; Jane Kamensky, "Talk Like a Man: Speech, Power, and Masculinity in Early New England," *Gender and History* 8 (1996): 22–47; Ann M. Little, " 'Shee Would Bump His Mouldy Britch': Authority, Masculinity, and the Harried Husbands of New Haven Colony, 1638–1670," in *Lethal Imagination: Violence and Brutality in American History*, ed. Michael A Bellesiles (New York: New York University Press, 1999); Anne S. Lombard, *Making Manhood: Growing Up Male in Colonial New England* (Cambridge, MA: Harvard University Press, 2003);

Lisa Wilson, *Ye Heart of a Man: The Domestic Life of Men in Colonial New England* (New Haven: Yale University Press, 1999).

4. Benedict Anderson, *Imagined Communities: Reflections on the Origin and Spread of Nationalism*, rev. ed. (London: Verso, 1991); Jürgen Habermas, *The Structural Transformation of the Public Sphere: An Inquiry into a Category of Bourgeois Society*, trans. Thomas Burger (Cambridge, MA: MIT Press, 1989); and Michael Warner, *The Republic of Letters: Publication and the Public Sphere in Eighteenth-Century America* (Cambridge, MA: Harvard University Press, 1990).

5. On "acts versus identities," see, for example, Michel Foucault, *The History of Sexuality: An Introduction*, trans. Robert Hurley (New York: Pantheon Books, 1978); and John D'Emilio and Estelle Freedman, *Intimate Matters: A History of Sexuality in America* (New York: Harper & Row, 1988). Scholarship on sexuality in early modern Europe has offered significant challenges to this paradigm, and studies of early America have not. See Kim M. Phillips and Barry Reay, eds., *Sexualities in History: A Reader* (New York: Routledge, 2002). On same-sex sexuality in early America, see *Long Before Stonewall: Histories of Same-Sex Sexuality in Early America*, ed. Thomas A. Foster (New York: New York University Press, forthcoming). Edmund S. Morgan, ed., *Diary of Michael Wigglesworth, 1653–1657: The Conscience of a Puritan* (New York: Harper & Row, 1965).

6. On early modern interiority, see, for example, Jean-Christophe Agnew, *Worlds Apart: The Market and the Theater in Anglo-American Thought, 1550–1750* (Cambridge: Cambridge University Press, 1988), 9–12; Toby L. Ditz, "Secret Selves, Credible Personas: The Problematics of Trust and Public Display in the Writing of Eighteenth-Century Philadelphia Merchants," in *Possible Pasts: Becoming Colonial in Early America*, ed. Robert Blair St. George (Ithaca: Cornell University Press, 2000), 219–42; and Ronald Hoffman, Mechal Sobel, and Frederika J. Teute, eds., *Through a Glass Darkly: Reflections on Personal Identity in Early America* (Chapel Hill: UNC-OIEAHC, 1997).

7. Richard P. Gildrie, *The Profane, the Civil, and the Godly: The Reformation of Manners in Orthodox New England, 1679–1749* (University Park: Pennsylvania State University Press, 1994), 15, 211.

8. Anderson, *Imagined Communities*; Charles E. Clark, *The Public Prints: The Newspaper in Anglo-American Culture, 1665–1740* (New York: Oxford University Press, 1994), 259; Clark, "Early American Journalism: News and Opinion in the Popular Press," in *A History of the Book in America*, vol. 1, *The Colonial Book in the Atlantic World*, ed. Hugh Amory and David D. Hall (Cambridge: Cambridge University Press for the American Antiquarian Society, 2000), 347–66; David A. Copeland, *Debating the Issues in Colonial Newspapers: Primary Documents on Events of the Period* (Westport: Greenwood Press, 2000), viii.

9. Hugh Amory, "Appendix One: A Note on Statistics," in *A History of the Book in America,* ed. Amory and Hall, 511–12. Gildrie, *The Profane, the Civil, and the Godly;* Godbeer, *Sexual Revolution;* David D. Hall, *Worlds of Wonder, Days of Judgment: Popular Religious Belief in Early New England* (Cambridge, MA: Harvard University Press, 1990); Christine Leigh Heyrman, *Commerce and Culture: The Maritime Communities of Colonial Massachusetts, 1690–1750* (New York: W. W. Norton, 1984); Susan Juster, *Disorderly Women: Sexual Politics and Evangelicalism in Revolutionary New England* (Ithaca: Cornell University Press, 1994); Edmund Morgan, *The Puritan Family: Religion and Domestic Relations in Seventeenth-Century New England* (New York: Harper & Row, Harper Torchbook edition, 1966), esp. 29–64; Morgan, "The Puritans and Sex," *New England Quarterly* 15 (1942): 591–607; Erik R. Seeman, *Pious Persuasions: Laity and Clergy in Eighteenth-Century New England* (Baltimore: Johns Hopkins University Press, 1999); Laurel Thatcher Ulrich, *Good Wives: Image and Reality in the Lives of Women in Northern New England, 1650–1750* (New York: Vintage Books, 1991), 106–25.

10. Godbeer, *Sexual Revolution,* ch. 7.

11. Clark, *Public Prints,* 141. On political differences between the *Boston News Letter,* the *Boston Gazette,* and the *New England Courant,* see William David Sloan and Julie Hedgepeth Williams, *The Early American Press, 1690–1783* (Westport: Greenwood Press, 1994), 18–32. For a quantitative analysis of the content of early American newspapers, see David A. Copeland, *Colonial American Newspapers: Character and Content* (Newark: University of Delaware Press, 1997). See also Copeland, *Debating the Issues in Colonial Newspapers.* From 1701 to 1780, New England received nearly 30 percent of all books exported from London to North America and the British West Indies. See Amory, "Appendix One: A Note on Statistics," 514. See also Amory, "The New England Book Trade, 1713–1790," in *A History of the Book,* ed. Amory and Hall, 314–46; James Raven, "The Importation of Books in the Eighteenth Century," in *A History of the Book,* ed. Amory and Hall, 183–98.

On *The Spectator,* see, for example, Lawrence E. Klein, "Property and Politeness in the Early Eighteenth-Century Whig Moralists: The Case of the *Spectator,"* in *Early Modern Conceptions of Property,* ed. John Brewer and Susan Staves (London: Routledge, 1995), 221–33; Erin Mackie, *Market à la Mode: Fashion, Commodity, and Gender in "The Tatler" and "The Spectator"* (Baltimore: Johns Hopkins University Press, 1997). Shawn Lisa Maurer, *Proposing Men: Dialectics of Gender and Class in the Eighteenth-Century English Periodical* (Stanford: Stanford University Press, 1998).

CHAPTER 1: *"He Is Not a Man, That Hath Not a Woman"*

1. Dr. Aaron Wight, Pre-Revolutionary Diaries, roll 11, Library of Congress, Manuscript Division (henceforth LOCMD), original at Massachusetts Historical Society (henceforth MHS); the quotations in the next five paragraphs came from this source. *Vital Records of Medway, Massachusetts to 1850* (Boston: New England Historic Genealogical Society, 1905), 275–76. Francis B. Heitman, *Historical Register of Officers of the Continental Army* (1914; reprint, Baltimore: Genealogical Publishing Co., 1982), 585.

2. Benjamin Bangs, Pre-Revolutionary Diaries, roll 1, LOCMD, original at MHS. For another example, see the entry of December 8, 1785, in Justus Forward's diary (1785), diaries of 1762–1799, American Antiquarian Society (henceforth AAS).

3. Companionate ideals flourished and became more robust in the eighteenth century. See Edmund Morgan, *The Puritan Family: Religion and Domestic Relations in Seventeenth-Century New England* (New York: Harper & Row, Harper Torchbook edition, 1966), esp. 29–64; Morgan, "The Puritans and Sex," *New England Quarterly* 15 (1942): 591–607; Lawrence Stone, *The Family, Sex, and Marriage in England, 1500–1800* (New York: Harper & Row, 1977), chs. 7–8; Randolph Trumbach, *The Rise of the Egalitarian Family: Aristocratic Kinship and Domestic Relations in Eighteenth-Century England* (New York: Academic Press, 1978), 83–87, 97–113; Lisa Wilson, *Ye Heart of a Man: The Domestic Life of Men in Colonial New England* (New Haven: Yale University Press, 1999).

   On sexual intimacy and companionate marriage, see Ruth H. Bloch, "Changing Conceptions of Sexuality and Romance in Eighteenth-century America," *William and Mary Quarterly* (January 2003): 13–42; Richard Godbeer, *Sexual Revolution in Early America* (Baltimore: Johns Hopkins University Press, 2001), chs. 2–3; Laurel Thatcher Ulrich, *Good Wives: Image and Reality in the Lives of Women in Northern New England, 1650–1750* (New York: Vintage Books, 1991), 106–25.

4. Daniel Defoe, *Conjugal Lewdness; or, Matrimonial Whoredom. A Treatise Concerning the Use and Abuse of the Marriage Bed* (London, 1727; Gainesville, FL: Scholars' Facsimiles and Reprints, 1967), 55. The Harvard library catalog of 1735 includes a copy of Defoe's *Conjugal Lewdness*; W. H. Bond and Hugh Amory, eds., *The Printed Catalogues of the Harvard College Library, 1723–1790* (Boston: Colonial Society of Massachusetts, 1996), 126. See also *A Confession of Faith* (Boston, 1680), 53; William Gouge, *Of Domesticall Duties* (London, 1622; reprint, Amsterdam: Walter J. Johnson, 1976), 209–10. On the availability of copies of *Domesticall Duties* in eighteenth-century Massachusetts, see Samuel Gerrish, *Catalogue of Choice and Valuable Books* [Boston, 1723]; Gerrish, *A Cat-*

alogue of Curious and Valuable Books [Boston, 1725]; and the Harvard College Library Catalogue, 1723, in *Printed Catalogues of the Harvard College Library*, ed. Bond and Amory, 52.

5. Thomas Humphreys, *Marriage an Honourable Estate* (Boston, 1752), 10; *Reflections on Courtship and Marriage* (Philadelphia, 1746), v. Reprinted in part in *Continental Journal*, August 18, 1785.

6. *Eunuchism Display'd: Describing all the Different Sorts of Eunuchs* (London, 1718); *A Catalogue of Books* (Boston, 1734).

7. *Eunuchism Display'd*, 8, 143, 205–7.

8. Diaries (Unidentified) Collection, Boston, MA, 1783, AAS. *Boston Weekly News Letter*, May 14, 1752; *Boston Evening Post*, May 11, 1752. See also *Boston Gazette*, March 13, 1744.

9. *Boston Gazette*, July 23–30, 1733; *Boston News Letter*, March 24–31, 1727.

10. *Boston News Letter*, August 5–12, 1742.

11. *American Herald* (Boston), November 27, 1786; *Hampshire Gazette*, June 10, 1789.

12. *American Herald*, March 6, 1786.

13. B. Wadsworth, *Unchast Practices Procure Divine Judgments* (Boston, 1716), 3, 26; William Secker, *A Wedding Ring, Fit for the Finger* (Boston, 1750), 9. See also John Cotton, *A Help Meet* (Boston, 1699), 22.

14. *Marriage an Honourable Estate*, 12.

15. *The Problems of Aristotle* (London, 1684), unpaginated edition.

16. Ibid. See Thomas H. Johnson, "Jonathan Edwards and the 'Young Folks' Bible," *New England Quarterly* 5 (1932): 37–54.

17. *American Herald*, June 19, 1788. Defoe, *Conjugal Lewdness*, 56. *Boston Evening Post*, January 15, 1770. See also, for example, *Berkshire Chronicle*, April 24, 1789.

18. *Boston Evening Post*, January 19, 1741. Oliver Family Papers, undated notebook, reel 1, "historical notes possibly by Andrew Oliver (1731–1799)," LOCMD, original at MHS. *Boston Evening Post*, December 24, 1759.

19. John Cleaveland, "Family Correspondence," box 1, folder 2, Phillips Library, Peabody Essex Museum. Salisbury Family Papers, box 1, folder 5 (1768), AAS.

20. *New England Weekly Journal*, February 5, 1733 (reprinted five years later in *New England Weekly Journal*, June 20, 1738). *Boston Chronicle*, December 21, 1767. Secker, *Wedding Ring* 1:23.

21. *The Gentleman and Lady's Town and Country Magazine* (Boston) (October 1789): 453. *Hampshire Gazette*, August 15, 1787.

22. *The Journals of Ashley Bowen of Marblehead,* Publications of the Colonial Society of Massachusetts, vol. 44 (Boston: Colonial Society of Massachusetts, 1973), 49.

23. *Marriage an Honourable Estate,* 22; See also *The Spectator* 4:371. For an example of circulation in the later eighteenth century, see Betsy Smith to her sister Mary Cranch, February 18, 1774, Elizabeth (Smith) Shaw Peabody Papers, Shaw Family Papers, reel 1, LOCMD, original at MHS.

24. *Boston Chronicle,* May 9–16, 1768.

25. Gouge, *Of Domesticall Duties,* 222. Nicholas Culpeper, *Directory for Midwives* (London, 1681), 69.

26. *Reflections on Courtship and Marriage,* 8; See also [Ned Ward], *Nuptial Dialogues and Debates* (London, 1723), 248–56. *Nuptial Dialogues'* block advertisement in the *Boston Evening Post,* February 19, 1753. See also Thomas Cox, *A Catalogue of Books* (Boston, 1734).

27. *Wedding Ring,* 22. *Boston Evening Post,* July 20, 1752. See also *New England Weekly Journal,* August 2, 1731.

28. *Wedding Ring,* 22. See also Defoe, *Conjugal Lewdness,* 230–31.

29. On mercenary motives, see *Boston Weekly News Letter,* September 9–16, 1731, June 24–July 1, 1731; *Essex Gazette,* August 2, 1768, September 6–13, 1768, and November 29–December 6, 1768. On sexual lust, see *Boston Weekly News Letter,* October 30–November 6, 1729, August 19–26, 1731, and January 1–8, 1730; *New England Weekly Journal,* March 13, 1732; *Weekly Rehearsal,* October 2, 1732.

30. *Boston Gazette,* February 23–March 2, 1741; *Boston News Letter,* April 7–13, November 23–30, 1732. *Postscript to the Boston Gazette,* August 13–20, 1733.

31. Benjamin Gilbert to Lieutenant Park Holland, August 1781; to Isaac Cutler, April 26, 1782; to Captain Jonathan Stone, March 1, 1783; in *Winding Down: The Revolutionary War Letters of Lieutenant Benjamin Gilbert of Massachusetts, 1780–1783,* ed. John Shy (Ann Arbor: University of Michigan Press, 1989), 47, 54, 86–87.

32. *Independent Chronicle,* January 16, 1777 (reprinted on May 22, 1777), June 25, 1778.

33. Major Henry Blake, Diary 1776, AAS. *Boston Gazette,* February 11, 1782. For another example, see the ballad in Benjamin Gilbert's diary, Rebecca D. Symmes, ed., *A Citizen-Soldier in the American Revolution: The Diary of Benjamin Gilbert in Massachusetts and New York* (Cooperstown: New York State Historical Association, 1980), appendix C.

34. *Continental Journal,* July 14, 1785. Newspaper accounts were often copied in diaries and letters. "The Choice of a Wife," in "Boston, Mass. 1783" Diaries (Unidentified) Collection, AAS.

35. *Continental Journal,* March 23, 1787. For other examples, see *Continental Journal,* July 14, 1785, August 18, 1785, December 22, 1785, June 13, 1786; *Boston Gazette,* January 28, 1782, February 18, 1782, March 22, 1784, August 30, 1784; *Hampshire Gazette,* August 13, 1788, September 10, 1788, March 18, 1789, June 3, 1789; *Independent Chronicle* (Boston), February 3, 1785, October 4, 1787; *Plymouth Journal,* June 6, 1786; *Salem Chronicle,* June 29, 1786; *American Herald* (Boston), April 3, 1788; *Massachusetts Gazette,* July 11, 1788; *Massachusetts Magazine,* January 1789, 53; *Berkshire Chronicle,* June 12, 1788.

36. *Boston Gazette,* April 14, 1788; *American Herald* (Worcester, MA), August 21, 1788.

37. *Hampshire Gazette,* August 29, 1787.

38. *Boston Gazette,* April 14, 1788. *Plymouth Journal,* June 6, 1786 (reprinted in *Salem Chronicle,* June 29, 1786). *Hampshire Gazette,* August 29, 1787.

39. *Berkshire Chronicle* (Pittsfield), August 31, 1789.

40. John Wood Sweet, *Bodies Politic: Negotiating Race in the American North, 1730–1830* (Baltimore: Johns Hopkins University Press, 2003), 157–58.

41. William Taylor, Esq., to Joseph Taylor, August 20, 1783, Lovering Taylor Papers, LOCMD.

CHAPTER 2: *Sex and the Shattering of Household Order*

1. Nancy F. Cott, "Divorce and the Changing Status of Women in Eighteenth-Century Massachusetts," *William and Mary Quarterly* (henceforth *WMQ*) (January 1976): 611.

2. Thomas A. Foster, "Deficient Husbands: Manhood, Sexual Incapacity, and Male Marital Sexuality in Seventeenth-Century New England," *WMQ* 56 (October 1999): 723–44. See, for example, Suffolk Files nos. 12977, 129742, Massachusetts State Archives (henceforth MSA).

3. Foster, "Deficient Husbands," 733, 741.

4. Ibid., 727. On the incidence of premarital sex increasing through the eighteenth century, see, for example, Richard Godbeer, *Sexual Revolution in Early America* (Baltimore: Johns Hopkins University Press, 2001), 228–33.

5. *Boston Gazette,* July 18, 1749.

6. *Aristotle's Compleat Masterpiece* (London, 1749), 38. Richard Godbeer, "William Byrd's Flourish: The Sexual Cosmos of a Southern Planter," in *Sex and Sexuality in Early America,* ed. Merril D. Smith (New York: New York University Press, 1998), 135–62; Kenneth Lockridge, *On the Sources of Patriarchal Rage: The Commonplace Books of William Byrd and Thomas Jefferson and the Gendering of*

Power in the Eighteenth Century (New York: New York University Press, 1992). David Thomas Konig, ed., *Plymouth Court Records, 1686–1859,* 16 vols. (Wilmington, DE: Michael Glazier, 1978), 6:144, 7:58, 423. Neal W. Allen, *Province and Court Records of Maine* (Portland: Maine Historical Society, 1958), 4:288–89. Roger Thompson, *Sex in Middlesex: Popular Mores in a Massachusetts County, 1649–1699* (Amherst: University of Massachusetts Press, 1986), 191. Jane Sharp, *The Midwives Book; or, The Whole Art of Midwifery Discovered* (London, 1671), 31.

7. Suffolk Files nos. 129827, 129844, MSA.

8. Suffolk Files no. 129728, MSA.

9. *The Problems of Aristotle* (London, 1684), unpaginated edition.

10. *Aristotle's Compleat Masterpiece,* 53. See also William Gouge, *Of Domesticall Duties* (London, 1622; reprint, Amsterdam: Walter J. Johnson, 1976), 182.

11. Suffolk Files no. 129727, MSA. Cott, "Divorce and the Changing Status of Women." [Cotton Mather], *Thirty Important Cases* (Boston, 1699), 33.

12. Benjamin Walker Junior, June 21, 1740, Pre-Revolutionary Diaries, roll 10, Library of Congress Manuscript Division (henceforth LOCMD), original at Massachusetts Historical Society (henceforth MHS). *Vital Records of Scituate, Massachusetts, to the Year 1850* (Boston: New England Historic Genealogical Society, 1976), 70–71, 303, 369.

13. Suffolk Files no. 129810, MSA.

14. Ibid.

15. Suffolk Files no. 129777, MSA. The quotations in the next five paragraphs are from this source.

16. Jay Fliegelman, *Prodigals and Pilgrims: The American Revolution against Patriarchal Authority, 1750–1800* (Cambridge: Cambridge University Press, 1982).

17. *Boston Gazette,* October 26–November 2, 1730.

18. Suffolk Files no. 129756, MSA.

19. David Hall Diary, 1740–1769, Pre-Revolutionary Diaries, roll 5, LOCMD, original at MHS.

20. Suffolk Files nos. 129797, 129762, MSA.

21. *Superior Court of Judicature* (henceforth *SCJ*), Record Books, vol. 9, p. 383–39, MSA.

22. *Essex Gazette,* March 9–16, 1773. *Plymouth Journal,* March 14, 1786 (reprinted in *Boston Gazette,* February, 21, 1786). See also *American Herald,* August 14, 1786. *Boston Newsletter,* April 4, 1771. On exploitation in seventeenth-century New

England, see Lyle Koehler, *A Search for Power: The "Weaker Sex" in Seventeenth-Century New England* (Urbana: University of Illinois Press, 1980), 92; Thompson, *Sex in Middlesex,* 34–53. On Virginia, see Brown, *Good Wives, Nasty Wenches, and Anxious Patriarchs;* Cornelia Dayton, *Women Before the Bar: Gender, Law, and Society in Connecticut, 1639–1789* (Chapel Hill: University of North Carolina Press for the Omohundro Institute of Early American History and Culture, 1995), 208–10, 365–66.

23. *New England Weekly Journal,* June 26, 1739.

24. *SCJ,* reel 9, 1752–1753, p. 181, MSA. *Boston Evening Post,* October 9, 1752. For another example, see *New England Weekly Journal,* August 2, August 9, 1731.

25. *SCJ,* reel 9, 1752–1753, p. 181, MSA. *Boston Evening Post,* October 9, 1752. For another example, see the *Boston Evening Post,* October 7, 1754.

26. Suffolk Files no. 129821, MSA. The next two paragraphs come from this source. See also *Boston Gazette,* October 11, 1784; *Essex Gazette,* February 14–21, 1769.

27. *Independent Chronicle,* November 12, 1789. For Dublin, see *Boston Evening Post,* July 5, 1783, and *Independent Chronicle,* September 22, 1785; for Greece, see *Berkshire Chronicle,* August 12, 1790; for France, *American Herald,* June 16, 1788; for Georgia (Russia), *American Herald,* December 25, 1788; for Vienna, *American Herald,* August 14, 1786; and for a Russian nobleman, *American Herald,* February 9, 1784.

28. Cott, "Divorce and the Changing Status of Women," 599.

29. Benjamin Bangs's diary transcript, October 18, 1763, MHS.

30. *Boston Evening Post,* October 16, 1752. For another story expressing anxiety over castration (related to urban crime rather than adultery), see *Boston Evening Post,* April 14, 1755. *Boston News Letter,* December 14–21, 1732.

31. John Cleaveland, "Family Correspondence," letter dated March 2, 1751, box 1, folder 2, Phillips Library, Peabody Essex Museum.

32. John Adams's diary 3, 1759 [electronic edition]. *Adams Family Papers: An Electronic Archive.* Boston: Massachusetts Historical Society, 2002. www.masshist .org/digitaladams/

33. Suffolk Files no. 129789, MSA.

34. Suffolk Files no. 129815, MSA.

35. Suffolk Files no. 129782, MSA; see also Suffolk Files nos. 129775 and 129789, MSA.

36. Suffolk Files no. 129782, MSA.

37. Suffolk Files no. 129773, MSA.

38. Suffolk Files no. 129779, MSA.

39. *SCJ,* Record Books, vol. 9, 318–20, 424–28, MSA. Suffolk Files no. 129742, MSA.

40. *SCJ,* Record Books, vol. 9, 211–13, MSA.

41. Suffolk Files no. 129790, MSA.

42. Ibid.

43. *American Herald,* January 22, 1789. See also *American Herald,* April 12, 1784; *Boston Evening Post,* December 15, 1781, December 22, 1781, May 17, 1783; *Continental Journal,* June 7, 1776; *Essex Gazette,* March 19–26, 1771, November 26– December 3, 1771, December 29, 1772–January 5, 1773; *Berkshire Chronicle,* September 23, 1790; *Boston Gazette,* October 4, 1784; *Independent Chronicle,* May 8, 1789; *Independent Chronicle,* December 16, 1785; *Continental Journal,* October 9, 1777; *Boston Gazette,* June 16, 1788; *Berkshire Chronicle,* April 24, 1789.

44. John Demos, *A Little Commonwealth: Family Life in Plymouth Colony* (New York: Oxford University Press, 1970).

45. [Cotton Mather], *The Hatchets, to hew down the Tree of Sin* (Boston, 1705), 7– 10; polygamy was also associated with Oriental despotism. For depictions of polygamy and Muslims, see, for example, *Boston Evening Post,* March 25, 1754. See also Giovanni Marana, *Letters Writ by a Turkish Spy,* 8 vols. (London, 1741); *Arabian Nights Entertainment,* 2 vols. (London, 1725).

46. *New England Weekly Journal,* December 3, 1733. In the nineteenth century, American officials focused on polygamy as a sign of Indian immorality. See Nancy Cott, *Public Vows: A History of Marriage and the Nation* (Cambridge, MA: Harvard University Press, 2000), 25–26.

47. See *Bickerstaff's Boston Almanac* (Boston, 1774), Jeremy Belknap Diary, Pre-Revolutionary Diaries, roll 2, LOCMD, original at MHS.

48. Cott, "Divorce and the Changing Status of Women," 599.

49. *Acts and Laws of Massachusetts Bay* (Boston, 1699), 65–66; *Superior Court of Judicature (SCJ),* Record Books, vol. 9, 248–49, MSA; *SCJ,* Record Books, vol. 9, 218–19, MSA; *SCJ,* Record Books, vol. 9, 383–39, MSA; see, for example, Suffolk Files no. 129741, MSA; Suffolk Files no. 129741, MSA.

50. Konig, *Plymouth Court Records* 6:275. "Negro whore" was a slur used against white women accused of sexual relations with black men. For other examples, see Dayton, *Women Before the Bar,* 315; Philip Morgan, "Interracial Sex in the Chesapeake and the British Atlantic World, c. 1700–1820," in *Sally Hemings and Thomas Jefferson: History, Memory, and Civic Culture,* ed. Jan Ellen Lewis and Peter S. Onuf (Charlottesville: University Press of Virginia, 1999), 61.

51. *Independent Chronicle,* May 10, 1781.

52. *Boston Newsletter,* April 4, 1771.

53. Suffolk Files no. 129811, MSA.

54. Wilson, *Ye Heart of a Man,* 92; *Boston Evening Post,* March 25, 1754; *SCJ,* Record Books, vol. 9, 218–19, MSA. See also Suffolk Files no. 129820, MSA.

55. Isaiah Thomas Papers, box 1, folder 4, 1777–1785; folder 2, undated, American Antiquarian Society, Worcester, Massachusetts.

CHAPTER 3: *Rape and Seduction:*
Masculinity, Misogyny, and Male Sexuality

1. *Boston Chronicle,* December 21, 1767. Richard Godbeer, "'Love Raptures': Marital, Romantic, and Erotic Images of Jesus Christ in Puritan New England, 1670–1730," *New England Quarterly* 68 (September 1995): 355–84. On Christian "sacred eroticism," see also Richard Rambuss, *Closet Devotions* (Durham: Duke University Press, 1998).

2. On rape in colonial America, see Sharon Block, "Rape without Women: Print Culture and the Politicization of Rape, 1765–1815," *Journal of American History* 89 (2002): 849–68; Cornelia Hughes Dayton, *Women Before the Bar: Gender, Law, and Society in Connecticut, 1639–1789* (Chapel Hill: University of North Carolina Press for the Institute of Early American History and Culture, 1995), 231–84; Barbara S. Lindemann, "'To Ravish and Carnally Know': Rape in Eighteenth-Century Massachusetts," *Signs* 10 (1984): 63–82.

On seduction literature, see Jocelyn Catty, *Writing Rape, Writing Women in Early Modern England: Unbridled Speech* (New York: St. Martin's Press, 1999); Jean H. Hagstrum, *Sex and Sensibility: Ideal and Erotic Love from Milton to Mozart* (Chicago: University of Chicago Press, 1980); Laura Mandell, *Misogynous Economies: The Business of Literature in Eighteenth-Century Britain* (Lexington: University of Kentucky Press, 1999); Janet Todd, *Sensibility: An Introduction* (London: Methuen, 1986).

3. *Acts and Laws of His Majesties Province of the Massachusetts Bay, in New England* (Boston, 1699), 98; Thomas Gouge, *The Young Man's Guide, Through the Wilderness of this World, to the Heavenly Canaan* (Boston, 1742), 103.

4. I have reexamined the cases heard by the Superior Court of Judicature discussed by Lindemann, "'To Ravish and Carnally Know,'" 69, 72–75. I thank Elizabeth Bouvier, head archivist at the Massachusetts State Archives, for locating cases tried in 1755–1790. I am also grateful to Sharon Block for additional information on rape cases.

5. *Boston Evening Post,* June 12, 1758.

6. Suffolk Files no. 129747, Massachusetts State Archives (henceforth MSA).

7. *Superior Court of Judicature* (henceforth *SCJ*), Record Books, 1699, p. 291, MSA. Lindemann, "'To Ravish and Carnally Know,'" 66.

8. Ibid.

9. Suffolk Files no. 23157, MSA.

10. David Thomas Konig, ed., *Plymouth Court Records, 1686–1859,* 16 vols. (Wilmington, DE: Michael Glazier, 1978), 3:58.

11. *SCJ*, reel 6, 1739–1740, p. 106, MSA; Suffolk Files no. 49822, MSA.

12. Neal W. Allen, *Province and Court Records of Maine* (Portland: Maine Historical Society, 1958), 4:288–89. For another example, see Suffolk Files no. 17129, MSA.

13. Konig, *Plymouth Court Records* 2:243.

14. Benjamin Walker Diary, October 23, 1734, Pre-Revolutionary Diaries, roll 10, Library of Congress Manuscript Division (henceforth LOCMD), original at Massachusetts Historical Society (henceforth MHS). Suffolk Files nos. 38267, 37890, MSA. *Weekly Review,* October 28, November 18, 1734; *New England Weekly Journal,* November 18, 1734.

15. *Essex Gazette,* October 12–19, 1773. See also, for example, *Boston Gazette,* March 15, 1784; *Berkshire Chronicle,* December 19, 1788; and *Essex Gazette,* June 1–8, 1773.

16. *Boston Evening Post,* August 23, 1736.

17. Ibid., November 12, 1750.

18. *Boston Gazette,* August 6–13, 1733. The next two paragraphs come from this source.

19. On the restoration of social order, see also *Boston News Letter,* February 24–March 3, 1718; *New England Weekly Journal,* February 18, 1734; *Boston Evening Post,* June 12, 1758, December 5, 1763. For rape by strangers, see *Boston News Letter,* February 24–March 3, 1718; *New England Weekly Journal,* February 18, 1734; *Boston Gazette,* December 8–15, 1735; *Boston Evening Post,* January 3, 1743, November 26, 1750; *Supplement to the Boston Evening Post,* March 15, 1756.

20. See Dayton, *Women Before the Bar,* 231 and n. 2. See, for example, *New England Weekly Journal,* January 6, 1729, July 13, 1730; *Boston Gazette,* August 6–13, 1733, June 28, 1743; *Boston News Letter,* October 14–28, 1736; *Boston Evening Post,* August 23, 1736, October 25, 1736, June 27, 1743, November 12, 1750, and November 26, 1750.

21. Of the 29 accounts, 23 involved soldiers (14 British, 9 American) and 6 civilian

perpetrators. *Essex Gazette,* June 27 and July 4–11, 1769. On British soldiers as rapists, see also Block, "Rape without Women."

22. *Continental Journal,* January 23, 1777. See also two notices in the *Continental Journal,* January 2, 1777, also printed in *Independent Chronicle,* January 2, 1777. For another example, see *Independent Chronicle,* September 25, 1777.

23. *Continental Journal,* January 2, February 6, 1777.

24. *Independent Chronicle,* January 30, February 20, 1777, and February 3, 1780. Paul Revere to John Rivoire in Guernsey, July 1, 1782, Revere Family Papers, roll 1, LOCMD, original at MHS.

25. Gouge, *Young Man's Guide,* 103. *Boston News Letter,* November 29, 1750.

26. Frank Luther Mott, *Golden Multitudes: The Story of Best Sellers in the United States* (New York: Macmillan, 1947), 37–38. Ten thousand copies were sold in the colonies in the 1740s; see Mott, *Golden Multitudes,* appendix A.

27. On *Pamela* and *Clarissa,* see, for example, Cathy N. Davidson, *Revolution and the Word: The Rise of the Novel in America* (New York: Oxford University Press, 1986); Jay Fliegelman, *Prodigals and Pilgrims: The American Revolution against Patriarchal Authority, 1750–1800* (Cambridge: Cambridge University Press, 1982), 88; Christina Roulston, *Virtue, Gender, and the Authentic Self in Eighteenth-Century Fiction: Richardson, Rousseau, and Laclos* (Gainesville: University of Florida Press, 1998); Ian Watt, *The Rise of the Novel* (Berkeley: University of California Press, 1971), 135–73; Richard Godbeer, *Sexual Revolution in Early America* (Baltimore: Johns Hopkins University Press, 2001), 255–63, 264–98. *Independent Chronicle,* May 17, 1787, January 1, 1789; *Hampshire Gazette,* May 23, 1787, August 4, 1790, October 29, 1788; *Salem Chronicle,* May 25, 1786; *Plymouth Journal,* March 19, 1785; *Salem Mercury,* July 29, 1788. Cathy N. Davidson, ed., *The Coquette* (Oxford: Oxford University Press, 1987), vii, 163.

28. Samuel Richardson, *Clarissa; or, The History of a Young Lady,* ed. Angus Ross, reprint of complete text of first edition, 1747–1748 (London: Penguin Books, 1985), 1182, 868, 742. See *Valentinian. A Tragedy as 'tis altered by the late Earl of Rochester* (1685), iv, ii. See *Clarissa,* n. 2, letter 228, p. 1519. Samuel Richardson, *Pamela; or, Virtue Rewarded,* reprint of 8th ed., 1762 (New York: New American Library, 1980), 242.

29. Suffolk Files no. 4022, MSA.

30. Konig, *Plymouth Court Records* 6:144, 8:129–30.

31. *Essex Gazette,* March 28–April 4, 1769. Reprinted in *Massachusetts Gazette,* March 30, 1769. *Essex Gazette,* October 12–19, 1773. For another example, see *Hampshire Gazette,* September 13, 1786.

32. *Clarissa,* 742, 670.

33. Konig, *Plymouth Court Records* 2:243.

34. Carol F. Karlsen, *The Devil in the Shape of a Woman: Witchcraft in Colonial New England* (New York: W. W. Norton, 1987; Vintage Books, 1989), 174–77; Laurel Thatcher Ulrich, *Good Wives: Image and Reality in the Lives of Women in Northern New England, 1650–1750* (New York: Alfred Knopf, 1982; New York: Vintage Books, 1991), 103–5, 113–17; Kenneth Lockridge, *On the Sources of Patriarchal Rage: The Commonplace Books of William Byrd and Thomas Jefferson and the Gendering of Power in the Eighteenth Century* (New York: New York University Press, 1992), 16.

35. *Pamela,* 82, 256. *Clarissa,* 801.

36. Otho T. Beall, Jr., *"Aristotle's Master Piece* in America: A Landmark in the Folklore of Medicine," *William and Mary Quarterly* 20 (April 1963): 214.

37. *New England Weekly Journal,* March 6, 1732.

38. Ibid., February 28, 1732.

39. Konig, *Plymouth Court Records* 3:128, 183. For another example, see *Boston Evening Post,* May 14, 1753.

40. *Look e're you Leap; or, A History of Lewd Women* (Boston, 1762), 61–65, 78–79. For another example, see *New England Courant,* September 18–25, 1721.

41. *Weekly Rehearsal,* October 2, 1732.

42. *Boston Gazette,* February 26–March 5, 1733.

43. *American Herald,* June 2, 1788.

44. Dukes County Court Records, Peter Force Collection, reels 37–38, LOCMD, originals at MSA.

45. Suffolk Files no. 37793. See also *SCJ,* 1733–1736, reel 5, pp. 119–20, MSA.

CHAPTER 4: *Sex and the Community of Men*

1. Benjamin Walker Diary, August 11, 1744. See also July 24, 29, 1744, Pre-Revolutionary Diaries, roll 10, Library of Congress Manuscript Division (henceforth LOCMD), originals at Massachusetts Historical Society (henceforth MHS). For another example, see a diary entry about a "vagrant Precher" who left town disgraced as "a Liar, Cheat, & Whoremaster." Jeremy Belknap's *Bickerstaff Almanac,* August 1772, Pre-Revolutionary Diaries, roll 2, LOCMD, original at MHS.

2. Patricia Bonomi, *The Lord Cornbury Scandal: The Politics of Reputation in British America* (Chapel Hill: University of North Carolina Press for the Omohundro

Institute of Early American History and Culture, henceforth UNC-OIEAHC, 1998); Kathleen M. Brown, *Good Wives, Nasty Wenches, and Anxious Patriarchs: Gender, Race, and Power in Colonial Virginia* (Chapel Hill: UNC-OIEAHC, 1996); Cornelia Hughes Dayton, *Women Before the Bar: Gender, Law, and Society in Connecticut, 1639–1789* (Chapel Hill: UNC-OIEAHC, 1995), 285–328; Edith B. Gelles, "Gossip an Eighteenth-Century Case," *Journal of Social History* 22 (1989): 667–84; Mary Beth Norton, "Gender and Defamation in Seventeenth-Century Maryland," *William and Mary Quarterly* 44 (1987): 3–39. On slander and race, see Kirsten Fischer, *Suspect Relations: Sex, Race, and Resistance in Colonial North Carolina* (Ithaca: Cornell University Press, 2002), 131–58. On speech, see Jane Kamensky, *Governing the Tongue: The Politics of Speech in Early New England* (Oxford: Oxford University Press, 1997). On reputation and masculinity, see Toby L. Ditz, "Shipwrecked; or, Masculinity Imperiled: Mercantile Representations of Failure and the Gendered Self in Eighteenth-Century Philadelphia," *Journal of American History* (June 1994): 51–80.

3. Salisbury Family Papers, box 2, folder 3 (1771), American Antiquarian Society, Worcester, Massachusetts.

4. Benjamin Gilbert to Isaac Cutler, November 5, 1780, in *Winding Down: The Revolutionary War Letters of Lieutenant Benjamin Gilbert of Massachusetts, 1780–1783*, ed. John Shy (Ann Arbor: University of Michigan Press, 1989), 28.

5. Benjamin Bangs, diary transcript, July 23, 1759, October 29, 1763, MHS.

6. Ibid., February 16, 1754, MHS. Benjamin Walker Diary, March 4, 1731, Pre-Revolutionary Diaries, roll 10, LOCMD, original at MHS. For another example, see Monday, October 4, 1762.

7. Benjamin Walker Diary, June 21, 1740, June 19, 1742.

8. Benjamin Gilbert to Azubah Bartlett, December 1780, in *Winding Down*, by Shy, 30–31.

9. Benjamin Walker Diary, Friday, April 21 1749.

10. Suffolk Court of General Sessions, April 1719, Massachusetts State Archives (henceforth MSA).

11. Benjamin Walker Diary, August 11, 1744, August 19 or 20, 1748. For another example, see Benjamin Walker Diary, November 11, 1728.

12. Benjamin Walker Diary, May 9, 1746. On Brattle Street Church, see Harry S. Stout, *The New England Soul: Preaching and Religious Culture in Colonial New England* (New York: Oxford University Press, 1986), 130–31.

13. Benjamin Bangs, diary transcript, January 2, 1760, MHS. William Pynchon to his mother, May 14, 1774, Oliver Family Papers, reel 1, LOCMD, original at MHS.

14. On secrecy and credibility, see Toby L. Ditz, "Secret Selves, Credible Personas: The Problematics of Trust and Public Display in the Writing of Eighteenth-Century Philadelphia Merchants," in *Possible Pasts: Becoming Colonial in Early America,* ed. Robert Blair St. George (Ithaca: Cornell University Press, 2000), 219–42. Benjamin Walker Diary, February 4, 1747.

15. Suffolk Files no. 129726, MSA.

16. Suffolk Files no. 129745, MSA.

17. Benjamin Bangs, diary transcript, July 23, 1759, November 16, 1762, MHS. Benjamin Walker Diary, July 24, 1744, August 14, 1748.

18. Shy, *Winding Down,* 69, 77. I am grateful to Al Young for pointing me to this source.

19. Benjamin Gilbert to his father, January 30, 1783, 80–81; Gilbert to Charles Bruce, March 6, 1783, 88; March 25, 1783, 92–93; n. 194, 92–93, in *Winding Down,* by Shy. For other examples of young men trying to save their reputation after sexual transgressions with single women, see Anne S. Lombard, *Making Manhood: Growing Up Male in Colonial New England* (Cambridge, MA: Harvard University Press, 2003), 67, 85–86, 211 n. 51.

20. Suffolk Files no. 129824, MSA. The next seven paragraphs are taken from this source.

21. Suffolk Files nos. 129752, 129766, MSA.

22. David Holden Diary, October 30, 1760, Pre-Revolutionary Diaries, roll 5, LOCMD, original at MHS.

23. Revere Family Papers, roll 1, LOCMD, original at MHS. The next five paragraphs come from this source.

24. Suffolk Files no. 129839, MSA.

25. Godbeer, *Sexual Revolution in Early America,* 255–57; Laurel Thatcher Ulrich, *A Midwife's Tale: The Life of Martha Ballard, Based on Her Diary, 1785–1812* (New York: Vintage, reprint edition, 1991), 148; Dayton, *Women Before the Bar,* 194–97.

26. Suffolk Files no. 129726, MSA.

27. *American Herald,* October 18, 1784; reprinted in the *Boston Gazette,* October 18, 1784.

28. See, for example, *Plymouth Journal,* March 19, 1785; *Hampshire Gazette,* August 19, 1789; *Berkshire Chronicle,* March 4, August 26, 1790.

29. *Independent Chronicle,* July 2, 1789.

30. *Boston Evening Post,* July 22, 1765.

31. *New England Weekly Journal,* August 31, 1730; *Boston Evening Post,* April 23, 1750.

32. *Boston Evening Post,* August 24, 1752.

33. On caricature and satire, see Richard L. Bushman, "Caricature and Satire in Old and New England before the American Revolution," *Proceedings of the Massachusetts Historical Society,* vol. 88 (Boston: Massachusetts Historical Society, 1977), 19–34; David Waldstreicher, "Federalism, the Styles of Politics, and the Politics of Style," in *Federalists Reconsidered,* ed. Doron Ben-Atar and Barbara B. Oberg (Charlottesville: University of Virginia, 1998), 99–117.

34. David S. Shields, "Clio Mocks the Masons: Joseph Green's Anti-Masonic Satires," in *Deism, Masonry, and the Enlightenment,* ed. J. A. Leo Lemay (Newark: University of Delaware Press, 1987), 109–26. *Boston Evening Post,* January 21, 1751.

35. Ibid.

CHAPTER 5: *"Half-men": Bachelors,*
Effeminacy, and Sociability

1. Stephen T. Riley and Edward W. Hanson, eds., *The Papers of Robert Treat Paine,* 2 vols. (Boston: Massachusetts Historical Society, 1992), 1:78–79, 149, 245–48. Revere Family Papers, roll 1, Library of Congress Manuscript Division (henceforth LOCMD), original at Massachusetts Historical Society (henceforth MHS). See Michael R. Haines and Richard H. Steckel, eds., *A Population History of North America* (Cambridge: Cambridge University Press, 2000), 153. See also, for example, Philip J. Greven, Jr., *Four Generations: Population, Land, and Family in Colonial Andover, Massachusetts* (Ithaca: Cornell Paperbacks, 1972), 206–7; Daniel Vickers, *Farmers and Fisherman: Two Centuries of Work in Essex County, Massachusetts, 1630–1850* (Chapel Hill: University of North Carolina Press for the Institute of Early American History and Culture, 1994), 222; Lisa Wilson, *Ye Heart of a Man: The Domestic Life of Men in Colonial New England* (New Haven: Yale University Press, 1999), 46.

2. Mark E. Kann, *A Republic of Men: The American Founders, Gendered Language, and Patriarchal Politics* (New York: New York University Press, 1998), 53. See also David S. Shields, *Civil Tongues and Polite Letters in British America* (Chapel Hill: University of North Carolina Press for the Institute of Early American History and Culture, 1997), 40.

3. William Secker, *A Wedding Ring, Fit for the Finger* (Boston, 1750), 9; *Independent Chronicle,* July 29, 1785. Richard Godbeer, *Sexual Revolution in Early America* (Baltimore: Johns Hopkins University Press, 2001).

4. Secker, *A Wedding Ring,* 9, 15. Donald F. Bond, ed., *The Spectator,* 5 vols. (Oxford: Clarendon Press, 1965), 4:15. *The Spectator* was available for sale in Massachusetts through the eighteenth century. See, for example, James Murray's book inventory, January 25, 1766, film P-141, reel 2, MHS; Boston Merchant Inventories in Henry Knox Papers, 1771, 1773, P-17, reel 48, MHS. *Continental Journal,* July 14, 1785.

5. *Boston Evening Post,* April 17, 1742.

6. Ibid.

7. Ibid., August 4, 1746.

8. Donald F. Bond, ed., *The Tatler,* 3 vols. (Oxford: Clarendon Press, 1987), 3:323–24. *Boston News Letter,* October 26, 1752; *Reflections on Courtship and Marriage* (Philadelphia, 1746), vi. *Boston Gazette,* March 25–April 1, 1734.

9. See, for example, Christopher M. Jedrey, *The World of John Cleaveland: Family and Community in Eighteenth-Century New England* (New York: W. W. Norton, 1979), 88, 149–50; Douglas Lamar Jones, *Village and Seaport: Migration and Society in Eighteenth-Century Massachusetts* (Hanover, NH: Published for Tufts University by University Press of New England, 1981), 79–80. John Cotton, *A Help Meet* (Boston, 1699), 17.

10. Salisbury Family Papers, box 2, folder 1 (1769), American Antiquarian Society.

11. Rev. David Hall Diary, March 19, 1769, vol. 2, 1769–1789, Pre-Revolutionary Diaries, roll 5, LOCMD, original at MHS.

12. *New England Weekly Journal,* November 26, 1733.

13. *Boston Gazette,* August 27–September 3, 1733; *New England Weekly Journal,* August 7, 1739. *Boston News Letter,* May 10–17, 1733; *New England Weekly Journal,* May 14, 1733. For another example, see *New England Weekly Journal,* October 20, 1729. Wilson, *Ye Heart of a Man,* 37–71. On the importance of career and property ownership, see Anne S. Lombard, *Making Manhood: Growing Up Male in Colonial New England* (Cambridge, MA: Harvard University Press, 2003). On the late eighteenth century, see Kann, *Republic of Men,* esp. 52–78.

14. *New England Weekly Journal,* November 24, 1729, May 10, 1731.

15. *Independent Chronicle* (Boston), October 4, 1787.

16. *Massachusetts Spy,* March 14, 21, 1771.

17. Oliver Family Papers, Pre-Revolutionary Diaries, reel 1, LOCMD, original at MHS.

18. Eliza Shaw to Mary Cranch, March 28, 1780, April 26, 1784, Shaw Family Papers, reel 1, LOCMD, original at MHS.

19. See, for example, *Berkshire Chronicle,* March 18, 1790. *Boston Gazette,* February 23, 1784. See also *Hampshire Gazette,* November 12, 1788.

20. *Continental Journal,* July 14, 1785. *American Herald,* March 6, 1786. *Boston Gazette,* April 10, 1786.

21. *Independent Chronicle,* July 29, 1785. On essays in favor of bachelors, see *Boston Gazette,* September 9, 1782, September 20, 1790. On essays ridiculing bachelors, see *Independent Chronicle,* August 25, 1785; *Continental Journal,* July 21, 1785; *Massachusetts Gazette,* July 11, 1788; *Boston Gazette,* April 14, 1788.

22. *New England Weekly Journal,* August 4, 11, 18, 1729.

23. On the fop in Britain, see Philip Carter, "Men About Town: Representations of Foppery and Masculinity in Early Eighteenth-Century Urban Society," in *Gender in Eighteenth-Century England: Roles, Representations and Responsibilities,* ed. Hannah Barker and Elaine Chalus (London: Longman, 1997); George Haggerty, *Men in Love: Masculinity and Sexuality in the Eighteenth Century* (New York: Columbia University Press, 1999), 44–80; Susan Staves, "A Few Kind Words for the Fop," *Studies in English Literature* 22 (1982); Randolph Trumbach, "The Birth of the Queen: Sodomy and the Emergence of Gender Equality in Modern Culture, 1660–1750," in *Hidden from History: Reclaiming the Gay and Lesbian Past,* ed. Martin Bauml Duberman, Martha Vicinus, and George Chauncey, Jr. (New York: NAL Books, 1989).

24. On molly houses, see Alan Bray, *Homosexuality in Renaissance England* (New York: Columbia University Press, 1995), 89–104; Randolph Trumbach, *Sex and the Gender Revolution,* vol. 1, *Heterosexuality and the Third Gender in Enlightenment London* (Chicago: University of Chicago Press, 1998); Stephen Shapiro, "Of Mollies: Class and Same-Sex Sexualities in the Eighteenth-Century," in *In a Queer Place: Sexuality and Belonging in British and European Contexts,* ed. Kate Chedgzoy, Emma Francis, and Murray Pratt (Burlington, VT: Ashgate, 2002), 154–76.

25. T. H. Breen, *The Marketplace of Revolution: How Consumer Politics Shaped American Independence* (Oxford: Oxford University Press, 2005); Richard P. Gildrie, *The Profane, the Civil, and the Godly: The Reformation of Manners in Orthodox New England, 1679–1749* (University Park: Pennsylvania State University Press, 1994), 211.

26. G. J. Barker-Benfield, *The Culture of Sensibility: Sex and Society in Eighteenth-Century Britain* (Chicago: University of Chicago Press, 1992), 113. Michèle Cohen, *Fashioning Masculinity: National Identity and Language in the Eighteenth Century* (London: Routledge, 1996), 5. According to the *Oxford English Dictionary,* effeminacy could also mean "unmanly weakness, softness, or delicacy" and "womanish, unmanly, enervated, feeble; self-indulgent, voluptuous; unbecom-

ingly delicate or over-refined"; "delicacy," "feeble," "over-refined," and "enervated." *OED*, s.v. "effeminacy," "effeminate."

27. Barker-Benfield, *Culture of Sensibility*, 105–53; J. G. A. Pocock, *Virtue, Commerce, and History: Essays on Political Thought and History, Chiefly in the Eighteenth Century* (Cambridge: Cambridge University Press, 1985), 114.

28. Thomas Foxcroft, *Lessons of Caution to Young Sinners* (Boston, 1733), 42. One
meaning of *effeminate persons*, or "Effeminates," was "Sodomites." *OED*, s.v.
"effeminate." Cotton Mather, *Addresses to Old Men, and Young Men, and Little
Children* (Boston, 1690), 73.

29. Donald F. Bond, ed., *The Spectator*, 5 vols. (Oxford: Clarendon Press, 1965), no.
150. On the importance of dress, see Anne Buck, *Dress in Eighteenth-Century
England* (New York: Holmes & Meier Publishers, 1979), 57–59, 100–102; Karin
Calvert, "The Function of Fashion in Eighteenth-Century America," in *Of Con-
suming Interests: The Style of Life in the Eighteenth Century*, ed. Cary Carson,
Ronald Hoffman, and Peter J. Albert (Charlottesville: University Press of Virginia, 1994), 252–83; Elisabeth McClellan, *History of American Costume, 1607–
1870* (New York: Tudor Publishing Company, 1937), 179–81; Aileen Ribeiro,
The Art of Dress: Fashion in England and France, 1750 to 1820 (New Haven: Yale
University Press, 1995), 45, 94, 101, 211. *New England Magazine*, September
1758.

30. *New England Weekly Journal*, August 4, 18, 1729.

31. *Boston Evening Post*, December 12, 1757. Increase Mather, *Burnings Bewailed in
a Sermon* (Boston, 1712), 23.

32. *The Spectator*, no. 404, June 13, 1712. *Essex Gazette*, February 21–28, 1769. *New
England Weekly Journal*, August 18, 1729.

33. Cohen, *Fashioning Masculinity*, 4. On conversation and foppishness, see Shields,
Civil Tongues and Polite Letters, 99–104, 168–74. On manners, see C. Dallett
Hemphill, *Bowing to Necessities: A History of Manners in America, 1620–1860*
(New York: Oxford University Press, 1999). *New England Weekly Journal*, Jan-
uary 29, 1728, August 4, 1729.

34. *Tatler*, no. 219, September 2, 1710.

35. *New England Weekly Journal*, August 18, 1729.

36. *Spectator*, no. 288, January 30, 1712.

37. Bruce C. Daniels, *Puritans at Play: Leisure and Recreation in Colonial New En-
gland* (New York: St. Martin's Griffin, 1995), 125–40; Anthony Fletcher, *Gender,
Sex and Subordination in England, 1500–1800* (New Haven: Yale University
Press, 1995); and Wilson, *Ye Heart of a Man*, esp. 37–74. John Calhoun Stephens,

ed., *The Guardian* (Lexington: University of Kentucky Press, 1982), no. 26, April 10, 1713.

38. *Boston Gazette*, February 8–15, 1731.

39. *Spectator*, no. 142, August 13, 1711.

40. Increase Mather, *Burnings Bewailed*, 22. *New England Weekly Courant*, April 1–8, 1723. Josiah Smith, *Burning of Sodom* (Boston, 1741), 11, 14.

41. *Guardian*, no. 20, April 3, 1713. Thomas Gouge, *The Young Man's Guide, Through the Wilderness of this World, to the Heavenly Canaan* (Boston, 1742), 111.

42. On concerns with youth culture, see Roger Thompson, "Adolescent Culture in Colonial Massachusetts," *Journal of Family History* 9 (1984): 127–44; Lombard, *Making Manhood*. Daniel Lewes, *The Sins of Youth* (Boston, 1725), 8. Also see Benjamin Colman, *Warnings of God Unto Young People, Not to Consent When Enticed to Sin* (Boston, 1716), 30. Samuel Phillips, *Advice to a Child; or, Young People Solemnly Warn'd* (Boston, 1729), 25–26. Thomas Foxcroft, *Lessons of Caution to Young Sinners* (Boston, 1733), 46.

43. Terry Castle, "The Culture of Travesty: Sexuality and Masquerade in Eighteenth-Century England," in *Sexual Underworlds of the Enlightenment*, ed. G. S. Rousseau and Roy Porter (Chapel Hill: University of North Carolina Press, 1988), 156–80. Daniels, *Puritans at Play*, 109–24; Cynthia Adams Hoover, "Epilogue to Secular Music in Early Massachusetts," in *Music in Colonial Massachusetts, 1630–1820*, ed. Barbara Lambert, 2 vols. (Boston: Colonial Society of Massachusetts, 1980–1985), 2:732–42.

44. William Palfrey, Memorandum Book, March 17, 1771, Pre-Revolutionary Diaries, roll 7, LOCMD, original at MHS. Benjamin Guild Diary, 1774, Pre-Revolutionary Diaries, roll 4, LOCMD, original at MHS.

45. *Boston Weekly News Letter*, November 16–23, 1732.

46. *An Arrow Against Profane and Promiscuous Dancing* (Boston, 1684), 18; see also [Cotton Mather], *A Cloud of Witnesses* [Boston, 1700]. "Description of a Ball, September, 20th, 1756," in *The Papers of Robert Treat Paine*, ed. Stephen T. Riley and Edward W. Hanson, 2 vols. (Boston: Massachusetts Historical Society, 1992), 1:364.

47. Daniel Lewes, *The Sins of Youth* (Boston, 1725), 4; see also William Cooper, *Serious Exhortations Address'd to Young Men* (Boston, 1732); Joseph Emerson, *An Offering of Memorial* (Boston, 1732); I. Watts, *A Preservative from the Sins and Follies of Childhood and Youth* (Boston, 1748), 26. *Boston Gazette*, December 25–January 1, 1730.

48. Thomas A. Foster, "Deficient Husbands: Manhood, Sexual Incapacity, and Male

Marital Sexuality in Seventeenth-Century New England," *William and Mary Quarterly* 56 (October 1999): 730–31. *Tatler*, no. 32, June 23, 1709. *New England Weekly Journal*, March 24, 1729.

49. Bernard Mandeville, *The Virgin Unmask'd* (London, 1709; Delmar, NY: Scholars' Facsimiles and Reprints, 1975), 200, 39.

50. Josiah Cotton Memoirs, 1726–1756, Massachusetts Historical Society, P-398, pp. 76, 98. On associations between physique and moral states, see Haggerty, *Men in Love*, 84–85; Foster, "Deficient Husbands," 730–33; Sander L. Gilman, *Making the Body Beautiful: A Cultural History of Aesthetic Surgery* (Princeton: Princeton University Press, 1999), 119–56. On the late nineteenth-century association of physical strength with strength of character, see E. Anthony Rotundo, *American Manhood: Transformations in Masculinity from the Revolution to the Modern Era* (New York: Basic Books, 1993), 222–25.

51. Abigail Adams to Mary Cranch, February 19, 1786, Shaw Family Papers, reel 1, LOCMD, original at MHS. *Thomas's Massachusetts, New Hampshire, and Connecticut Almanack* (Worcester, 1781), in Jacob Cushing Diaries, Peter Force Papers, series 8D, reel 36, LOCMD. Tobias Smollett, *The Adventures of Roderick Random*, ed. P. G. Boucé (London, 1748; reprint, Oxford: Oxford University Press, 1979), 119.

52. *New England Weekly Journal*, August 7, 1727. "Letter to George Leonard, Boston, June 10, 1755," *Papers of Robert Treat Paine* 1:273. James Kirby Martin, ed., *Ordinary Courage: The Revolutionary War Adventures of Joseph Plumb Martin*, 2nd ed. (New York: Brandywine Press, 1999), 112. *Hampshire Gazette*, April 7, 1790.

53. *Boston Evening Post*, December 5, 1748. *Independent Chronicle*, September 1, 1783.

54. *Boston Evening Post*, July 27, 1752, February 11, 1754. *Guardian*, no. 97, July 2, 1713. Calvert, "The Function of Fashion in Eighteenth-Century America," 274.

55. *Boston News Letter*, July 18–25, 1734. *Boston Evening Post*, June 8, 1752. *Spectator*, no. 154, August 27, 1711.

56. On masturbation concerns in the diary of Joseph Moody, see Brian D. Carroll, "'I Indulge My Desire Too Freely': Sexuality, Spirituality, and the Sin of Self-Pollution in the Diary of Joseph Moody, 1720–1724," *William and Mary Quarterly* (January 2003): 155–70. See also Thomas W. Laqueur, *Solitary Sex: A Cultural History of Masturbation* (New York: Zone Books, 2003). On English literature and masturbation, see Roy Porter and Leslie Hall, *The Facts of Life: The Creation of Sexual Knowledge in Britain, 1650–1950* (New Haven: Yale University Press, 1995), 91–105. *Onania; or, The Heinous Sin of Self-Pollution* (London,

1723; reprint, New York: Garland Publishing, 1986), 17–19. Cotton Mather, *The Pure Nazarite: Advice to a Young Man* (Boston, 1723), 7.

57. *Onania*, 18–19.

58. *Boston Evening Post*, August 30, 1736, February 11, 1754; *New England Weekly Journal*, September 9–October 1, 1722, July 17, 1727; *Tatler*, no. 57, August 20, 1709.

59. *New England Weekly Journal*, August 18, 1729; *Boston Evening Post*, February 11, 1754; *Weekly Rehearsal*, December 23, 1734

60. *Boston Evening Post*, February 11, 1754; *New England Weekly Journal*, August 18, 1729. By contrast, the normative man of the eighteenth century was to a certain degree modest. See, for example, essays in the *Boston Evening Post*, March 26, 1750; *New England Weekly Journal*, August 4, 1729; and obituaries in the *Boston News Letter*, May 5–18, 1721; *New England Weekly Journal*, October 20, 1729.

61. *American Herald*, March 12, 1789. *Boston Gazette*, August 26, 1782; *Massachusetts Magazine*, August 1799, 323–26.

CHAPTER 6: *"When Day and Night Together Move":* Men and Cross-Cultural Sex

1. Carl N. Degler, "Slavery and the Genesis of American Race Prejudice," *Comparative Studies in Society and History* 2 (October 1959): 65. *Acts and Resolves of the Massachusetts Bay* (Boston: Wright & Potter, 1869), 1:578–80. The next three paragraphs come from the latter source.

2. In 1715 there were approximately 158,000 whites and 4,150 blacks in Massachusetts. It was not until 1790 that a census distinguished between slaves and free blacks. Lorenzo Johnston Greene, *The Negro in Colonial New England, 1620–1776* (New York: Columbia University Press, 1942), 73–74, 84. Robert V. Wells, *The Population of the British Colonies in America before 1776: A Survey of Census Data* (Princeton: Princeton University Press, 1975), 80–83. Figures for the Native American population were not taken by the U.S. Census that year. See www.census.gov/population/documentation/twps0056/tab36.pdf.

3. See Lisa Wilson, *Ye Heart of a Man: The Domestic Life of Men in Colonial New England* (New Haven: Yale University Press, 1999), and Anne S. Lombard, *Making Manhood: Growing Up Male in Colonial New England* (Cambridge, MA: Harvard University Press, 2003). In her study of eighteenth-century sexuality in Philadelphia, Clare Lyons argues that Philadelphians did not find African American sexuality or the issue of interracial sex a source of anxiety until after the Revolution. See Clare A. Lyons, "Sex among the 'Rabble': Gender Transforma-

tion in the Age of Revolution, Philadelphia, 1750–1830" (Ph.D. diss., Yale University, 1996), 146. On the salience of race in Massachusetts, see Jill Lepore, *The Name of War: King Philip's War and the Origins of American Identity* (New York: Vintage Books, 1998); John Wood Sweet, *Bodies Politic: Negotiating Race in the American North, 1730–1830* (Baltimore: Johns Hopkins University Press, 2003).

4. See Lepore, *The Name of War*, 32–33. On scholarship on praying towns and the adoption of Christian values, including sexual mores, see Thomas A. Foster, "Sex and the Eighteenth-Century Man: Anglo-American Discourses of Sex and Manliness in Massachusetts, 1690–1765" (Ph.D. diss., Johns Hopkins University, 2002), 112 n. 6. Benjamin Walker Junior,Pre-Revolutionary Diaries, roll 10, Library of Congress Manuscript Division (henceforth LOCMD), original at Massachusetts Historical Society (henceforth MHS). See, for example, Peter Hulme, *Colonial Encounters: Europe and the Native Caribbean, 1492–1797* (London: Routledge, 1992); James H. Merrell, "'The Customes of Our Countrey': Indians and Colonists in Early America," in *Strangers within the Realm: Cultural Margins of the First British Empire*, ed. Bernard Bailyn and Philip D. Morgan (Chapel Hill: University of North Carolina Press for the Institute of Early American History and Culture, 1991), 146–52.

5. On the mutability of race and identity in colonial America, see, for example, William B. Hart, "Black 'Go-Betweens' and the Mutability of 'Race,' Status, and Identity on New York's Pre-Revolutionary Frontier," in *Contact Points: American Frontiers from the Mohawk Valley to the Mississippi, 1750–1830*, ed. Andrew R. L. Cayton and Fredrika J. Teute (Chapel Hill: University of North Carolina Press for the Omohundro Institute of Early American History and Culture, 1998), 88–113; Nicholas Hudson, "From 'Nation' to 'Race': The Origin of Racial Classification in Eighteenth-Century Thought," *Eighteenth-Century Studies* 29 (1996): 247–64. On early modern British Atlantic culture, see, for example, Roxan Wheeler, *The Complexion of Race: Categories of Difference in Eighteenth-Century British Culture* (Philadelphia: University of Pennsylvania Press, 2000).

6. Richard P. Gildrie, *The Profane, the Civil, and the Godly: The Reformation of Manners in Orthodox New England, 1679–1749* (University Park: Pennsylvania State University Press, 1994), 132–44.

7. Cotton Mather, *A Pillar of Gratitude* (Boston, 1700), 8–9. For another example of ministerial literature using similar reasoning, see Experience Mayhew, *All Mankind, by Nature, Equally under Sin* (Boston, 1724).

8. *New England Weekly Journal*, December 3, 1733.

9. Mary Rowlandson, *The Sovereignty and Goodness of God*, in *Puritans among the Indians: Accounts of Captivity and Redemption, 1676–1724*, ed. Alden T. Vaughan and Edward W. Clark (Cambridge, MA: Belknap Press, 1981), 34–36, 61, 63.

On the conflicting popular depictions of "good" and "bad" Indians, see, for example, Kathryn Zabelle Derounian-Stodola and James Arthur Levernier, *The Indian Captivity Narrative, 1550–1900* (New York: Twayne Publishers, 1993), 51–93.

10. Rowlandson, *The Soveraignty and Goodness of God,* 71; John Gyles, *Memoirs of Odd Adventures,* in *Puritans among the Indians,* 121, 111; Elizabeth Hanson, *God's Mercy Surmounting Man's Cruelty,* in *Puritans among the Indians,* 242. *Boston Evening Post,* June 27, November 28, 1763. Kathleen Joan Bragdon, "Crime and Punishment among the Indians of Massachusetts, 1675–1750," *Ethnohistory* 28 (Winter 1981): 23–32.

    There is, however, a long history of associating sodomy with Native Americans. See Jonathan Goldberg, *Sodometries: Renaissance Texts, Modern Sexualities* (Stanford: Stanford University Press, 1992), 179–222; Jonathan Katz, *Gay American History: Lesbians and Gay Men in the U.S.A.* (New York: Thomas Y. Crowell, 1976), 281–91.

11. See, for example, Israel Loring, *Two Sermons Preached at Rutland* (Boston, 1724). Matthew Mayhew, *A Brief Narrative of the Success which the Gospel hath had, among the INDIANS of Martha's Vineyard* (Boston, 1694), 50–51.

12. Ives Goddard and Kathleen J. Bragdon, eds., *Native Writings in Massachusetts,* 2 vols. (Philadelphia: American Philosophical Society, 1988), 1:377. On language and colonization in Massachusetts, see, for example, Kathleen J. Bragdon, "Native Languages as Spoken and Written: Views from Southern New England," in *The Language Encounter in the Americas, 1492–1800,* ed. Edward G. Gray and Norman Fiering (New York: Berghahn Books, 2000), 173–88.

13. Goddard and Bragdon, *Native Writings in Massachusetts* 1:377, 451.

14. [Cotton Mather], *The Hatchets, to hew down the Tree of Sin* (Boston, 1705), 7–10.

15. *The Indian Primer; or, The First Book by which Children May Know truly To read the Indian Language* (Boston, 1720), 35, 60–61.

16. Ibid.

17. Philip D. Morgan, "British Encounters with Africans and African-Americans, circa 1600–1780," in *Strangers within the Realm: Cultural Margins of the First British Empire,* ed. Bernard Bailyn and Philip D. Morgan (Chapel Hill: University of Chapel Hill Press for the Institute of Early American History and Culture, 1991), 163.

18. Cotton Mather, *Rules for the Society of Negroes* [Boston, 1714?]. Winthrop D. Jordan, *White over Black: American Attitudes toward the Negro, 1550–1812* (Chapel Hill: University of North Carolina Press for the Omohundro Institute of Early American History and Culture, 1968), 200–201; Richard Slotkin, "Narratives of

Negro Crime in New England, 1675–1800," *American Quarterly* (1973): 9. On Christianity and slavery in New England, see, for example, William D. Piersen, *Black Yankees: The Development of an Afro-American Subculture in Eighteenth-Century New England* (Amherst: University of Massachusetts Press, 1988), 49–73.

19. [Cotton Mather], *The Negro Christianized* (Boston, 1706), 2–3, 19, 39, 42. On *The Negro Christianized*, see Dana D. Nelson, *The Word in Black and White: Reading 'Race' in American Literature, 1638–1867* (New York: Oxford University Press, 1992), 24–29.

20. Elihu Coleman, *Testimony Against that Antichristian Practice of Making Slaves of Men* (Boston, 1733), 5, 6, 16.

21. Mass. Archives, vol. 9, 248–50, Massachusetts State Archives (henceforth MSA).

22. Sylvanus Conant, *The Blood of Abel* (Boston, 1764), 20–21, 33–35. T. H. Breen, "Making History: The Force of Public Opinion and the Last Years of Slavery in Revolutionary Massachusetts," in *Through a Glass Darkly: Reflections on Personal Identity in Early America,* ed. Ronald Hoffman, Mechal Sobel, and Frederika J. Teute (Chapel Hill: University of North Carolina Press for the Omohundro Institute of Early American History and Culture, 1997), 74–77; Daniel A. Cohen, "Social Injustice, Sexual Violence, Spiritual Transcendence: Constructions of Interracial Rape in Early American Crime Literature, 1767–1817," *William and Mary Quarterly* 56 (July 1999): 491–93.

23. Many scholars have examined sex between white men and black women in slave societies. See Kathleen M. Brown, *Good Wives, Nasty Wenches, and Anxious Patriarchs: Gender, Race, and Power in Colonial Virginia* (Chapel Hill: University of North Carolina Press for the Omohundro Institute of Early American History and Culture, 1996), esp. 128–35, 187–211; Trevor Burnard, "The Sexual Life of an Eighteenth-Century Jamaican Slave Overseer," in *Sex and Sexuality in Early America,* ed. Merril D. Smith (New York: New York University Press, 1998), 163–89; and Natalie A. Zacek, "Sex, Sexuality, and Social Control in the Eighteenth-Century Leeward Islands," in *Sex and Sexuality,* 190–214.

   For an important and provocative critique of the idea that consensual interracial sexual relationships are possible in a slave-owning context, see Ann Ducille, " 'Othered' Matters: Reconceptualizing Dominance and Difference in the History of Sexuality in America," *Journal of the History of Sexuality* 1 (1990), esp. 116–21.

24. Daniel R. Mandell, "The Saga of Sarah Muckamugg: Indian and African American Intermarriage in Colonial New England," in *Sex, Love, Race: Crossing Boundaries in North American History,* ed. Martha Hodes (New York: New York

University Press, 1999), 75; Mandell, "Shifting Boundaries of Race and Ethnicity: Indian-Black Intermarriage in Southern New England, 1760–1880," *The Journal of American History* 85, no. 2:466–501. The quote is from p. 468. See also Piersen, *Black Yankees*, 19–20; Peter H. Wood, *Black Majority: Negroes in Colonial South Carolina from 1670 through the Stono Rebellion* (New York: W. W. Norton, 1974), 97–100. Jack D. Forbes, "Mulattoes and People of Color in Anglo-North America: Implications for Black-Indian Relations," *The Journal of Ethnic Studies* 12 (1984): 17–62.

25. Stephen Salisbury to "Brother Samuel," Worcester, July 8, 1768, Salisbury Family Papers, box 1, folder 5, American Antiquarian Society (henceforth AAS). Suffolk Files no. 129828, MSA.

26. Greene, *Negro in Colonial New England,* appendix B, 338. Suffolk County Court of General Sessions, MSA.

27. See David Thomas Konig, ed., *Plymouth Court Records, 1686–1859,* 16 vols. (Wilmington, DE: Michael Glazier, 1978), 6:92–93, 189, 275, 7:306. Greene, *Negro in Colonial New England,* appendix C.

28. Konig, *Plymouth Court Records,* 7:306.

29. Ibid., 6:92–93, 189.

30. Mr. Hutchinson, *The History of the Province of Massachusetts-Bay, From the Charter of King William and Queen Mary, in 1691, Until the Year 1750* (Boston, 1768), 48, 52. Mary Beth Norton, *In the Devil's Snare: The Salem Witchcraft Crisis of 1692* (New York: Knopf, 2002), 186–91.

31. *Boston Gazette,* February 3–10, 1735.

32. William G. McLoughlin, *New England Dissent: The Baptists and the Separation of Church and State* (Cambridge, MA: Harvard University Press, 1971), 2:764.

33. Joseph Kirby Martin, ed., *Ordinary Courage: The Revolutionary War Adventures of Joseph Plumb Martin,* 2nd ed. (New York: Brandywine Press, 1999), 144.

34. *Boston Gazette,* May 28, 1770.

35. *Massachusetts Spy,* May 24, 1776.

36. *A Vaudevil* (Boston, 1776). See also Kenneth Silverman, *A Cultural History of the American Revolution* (New York: Thomas Y. Crowell, 1976), 292–93; Sweet, *Bodies Politic,* 149.

37. Jordan, *White over Black,* 37–38. Abigail Adams to Eliza Shaw, March 4, 1786, Shaw Family Papers, reel 1, LOCMD, original at MHS.

38. Sweet, *Bodies Politic,* 177.

39. Suffolk County Court General Sessions, 1705, MSA.

40. Ibid.

41. Sweet, *Bodies Politic*, 147–48.

42. Daniel P. Black, *Dismantling Black Manhood: An Historical and Literary Analysis of the Legacy of Slavery* (New York: Garland, 1997); Pierson, *Black Yankees*. On black masculinity, see also Darlene Clark Hine and Earnstine Jenkins, eds., *A Question of Manhood: A Reader in U.S. Black Men's History of Masculinity*, vol. 1, *"Manhood Rights?": The Construction of Black Male History and Manhood, 1750–1870* (Bloomington: Indiana University Press, 1999).

43. Aaron Hutchinson, *Iniquity Purged by Mercy and Truth* (Boston, 1769), 22. On Arthur, see T. H. Breen, "Making History: The Force of Public Opinion and the Last Years of Slavery in Revolutionary Massachusetts," in *Through a Glass Darkly: Reflections on Personal Identity in Early America,* ed. Ronald Hoffman, Mechal Sobel, and Fredrika J. Teute (Chapel Hill: University of North Carolina Press for the Omohundro Institute of Early American History and Culture, 1997), 77–95.

44. Church Record Book, 1745–1790, box 1, folder 1, Old South Church Records, Worcester, Mass., AAS. Reverend Thaddeus Maccarty to brother Sam, Worcester, October 25, 1768, Salisbury Family Papers, box 1, folder 5, 1768, AAS.

45. *Superior Court of Judicature* (henceforth *SCJ*), reel 5, 1733–1736, p. 142, and Suffolk Files nos. 38267, 37890; *SCJ*, reel 6, 1739–1740, p. 225, and Suffolk Files no. 49240, MSA; Hampshire County Superior Court Docket, September 1732, microfilm no. 9, item 19, MHS. All six men sentenced to death in the neighboring colony of Connecticut in the eighteenth century were "blacks, Indians, foreigners, or transients." Cornelia Hughes Dayton, *Women Before the Bar: Gender, Law, and Society in Connecticut, 1639–1789* (Chapel Hill: University of North Carolina Press for the Institute of Early American History and Culture, 1995), 233.

46. Sweet, *Bodies Politic*, 164.

47. Greene, *Negro in Colonial New England*, 93. The scholarship on race and sexuality has long emphasized the stereotype of the black male as a sexual predator. See, for example, Brown, *Good Wives, Nasty Wenches*, 187–211; Daniel A. Cohen, "Social Injustice, Sexual Violence, Spiritual Transcendence: Constructions of Interracial Rape in Early American Crime Literature, 1767–1817," *William and Mary Quarterly* 56 (July 1999): 491–93; John D'Emilio and Estelle Freedman, *Intimate Matters: A History of Sexuality in America* (New York: Harper & Row, 1988), 34–36; Jordan, *White over Black*, 150–54; Mark Kann, *A Republic of Men: The American Founders, Gendered Language, and Patriarchal Politics* (New York: New York University Press, 1998), 66–69; Edmund Morgan, *American Slavery, American Freedom: The Ordeal of Colonial Virginia* (New York: W. W. Norton, 1995), 333–36.

Other scholars have challenged the early dating of this seemingly monolithic image. See, for example, Sharon Block, "Rape without Women: Print Culture and the Politicization of Rape, 1765–1815," *Journal of American History* 89 (2002): 849–68; Martha Hodes, *White Women, Black Men: Illicit Sex in the Nineteenth-Century South* (New Haven: Yale University Press, 1997), esp. 1–6; Richard Slotkin, "Narratives of Negro Crime in New England, 1675–1800," *American Quarterly* (1973): 3–31; Diane Miller Somerville, "Rape, Race, and Castration in Slave Law in the Colonial and Early South," in *The Devil's Lane: Sex and Race in the Early South,* ed. Catherine Clinton and Michele Gillespie (New York: Oxford University Press, 1997), 74–89.

48. Clare A. Lyons, "Sex among the 'Rabble': Gender Transformation in the Age of Revolution, Philadelphia, 1750–1830" (Ph.D. diss., Yale University, 1996), 146. Leslie Harris, "From Abolitionist Amalgamators to 'Rulers of the Five Points': The Discourse of Interracial Sex and Reform in Antebellum New York City," in *Sex, Love, Race,* ed. Hodes, 191–212.

49. *The Life and Dying Speech of Arthur, a Negro Man*...(Boston, 1768). Slotkin, "Narratives of Negro Crime," 3–31.

50. *New England Weekly Journal,* July 17, 1727; *Boston Evening Post,* December 19, 1743.

51. *New England Weekly Journal,* July 13, 1730, July 26, 1737.

52. Ibid., February 18, 1734; *Boston Evening Post,* November 26, 1750.

53. *Weekly Review,* October 28, 1734; *New England Weekly Journal,* February 18, November 18, 1734.

54. *Boston News Letter,* February 24–March 3, 1718.

CHAPTER 7: *"The Paths of Monstrous Joy"*

1. John Cleaveland Papers, folder 5, diary, January 15, 1742, Phillips Library, Peabody Essex Museum. On "brides of Christ," see Richard Godbeer, "'Loves Raptures': Marital, Romantic, and Erotic Images of Jesus Christ in Puritan New England, 1670–1730," *New England Quarterly* 68 (1995): 355–84. Suffolk Files no. 129796, Massachusetts State Archives (henceforth MSA).

2. Michel Foucault, *The History of Sexuality: An Introduction,* trans. Robert Hurley (New York: Pantheon Books, 1978).

3. See, for example, essays by Ruth Mazo Karras, Theo Van der Meer, and Carla Freccero in *Journal of Women's History* 11 (1999): 159–98. See also David Halperin, *How to Do the History of Homosexuality* (Chicago: University of Chicago Press, 2002). My analysis also builds on Godbeer's observations about Nicholas

Sension. Richard Godbeer, "'The Cry of Sodom': Discourse, Intercourse, and Desire in Colonial New England," in *Long Before Stonewall: Histories of Same-Sex Sexuality in Early America,* ed. Thomas A. Foster (New York: New York University Press, forthcoming). See also the essay "In a French Position: Radical Pornography and Homoerotic Society in Charles Brockden Brown's *Ormund or The Secret Witness,*" by Stephen Shapiro in *Long Before Stonewall.*

4. *Acts and Laws, of His Majesties Province of the Massachusetts Bay, in New-England* (Boston, 1699), 98. Sodomy remained punishable by death until 1805. Jonathan Katz, *Gay/Lesbian Almanac: A New Documentary* (New York: Harper & Row, 1983); John M. Murrin, "'Things Fearful to Name': Bestiality in Colonial America," *Pennsylvania History* 65 (1998): 8–43. I thank Clare Lyons for information on the Pennsylvania case. See also Clare Lyons, "Mapping an Atlantic Sexual Culture: Homoeroticism in Eighteenth-Century Philadelphia," in *Long Before Stonewall,* ed. Foster.

5. Louis Crompton, "Homosexuals and the Death Penalty in Colonial America," *Journal of Homosexuality* 1 (1976): 277–93; David H. Flaherty, "Law and Enforcement of Morals in Early America," in *Perspectives in American History,* 12 vols., ed. Donald Fleming and Bernard Baylin (Cambridge, MA: Harvard University Press, 1967), 5:203–53; Hendrik Hartog, "The Public Law of a County Court: Judicial Government in Eighteenth-Century Massachusetts," *American Journal of Legal History* 20 (1976): 282–329; Paul D. Marsella, *Crime and Community in Early Massachusetts: Essex County, 1700–1785* (Acton, MA: Tapestry Press, 1990); Henry B. Parkes, "Morals and Law Enforcement in Colonial New England," *New England Quarterly* 5 (1932): 431–52. As Godbeer and others have argued, eighteenth-century courts gradually "took less and less interest in the enforcement of moral values." Informal enforcement by community and family, leaving little or no written record, took the place of courts. "'Cry of Sodom,'" in *Long Before Stonewall,* ed. Foster. See also Cornelia Dayton, "Turning Points and the Relevance of Colonial Legal History," *William and Mary Quarterly* 50 (1993): 12–13.

6. I am grateful to Elizabeth Bouvier, head archivist of the Massachusetts Archives, for pointing me to the Superior Court record. *Superior Court of Judicature* (henceforth *SCJ*), Record Books, reel 2, 1700–1714, p. 269, MSA.

7. *SCJ*, Record Books, reel 2, 1700–1714, p. 308, MSA. The term "Infant" may have designated a young boy, but it may also have designated a legal minor.

8. *SCJ*, Record Books, reel 7, 1740–1745, p. 86, MSA. Like Ropier, Fessendon pleaded not guilty and was cleared of the charges by the jury. He was consequently discharged and ordered to pay court costs and thereafter disappeared from extant records.

9. See Francis G. Walett, ed., *The Diary of Ebenezer Parkman, 1703–1782* (Worcester, MA: American Antiquarian Society, 1974); Clifford K. Shipton, *Sibley's Harvard Graduates* (Boston: Massachusetts Historical Society, 1958), 10:169; Worcester Probate Records, 20, 591.

10. Jonathan Goldberg, ed., *Reclaiming Sodom* (New York: Routledge, 1994), 5. See also Alan Bray, *Homosexuality in Renaissance England* (New York: Columbia University Press, 1995), ch. 3. See Murrin, " 'Things Fearful to Name,' " 38 n. 35.

11. Christine Leigh Heyrman, *Commerce and Culture: The Maritime Communities of Colonial Massachusetts, 1690–1750* (New York: W. W. Norton, 1984), 286. See Godbeer, " 'Cry of Sodom,' " 277–79. Murrin concludes from both cases that "sodomy was a forgivable offense." Murrin, " 'Things Fearful to Name,' " 22.

12. John Adams Diary 6, December 2, 1760–March 3, 1761 [electronic edition]. *Adams Family Papers: An Electronic Archive.* Boston: Massachusetts Historical Society, 2002; www.masshist.org/digitaladams/.

    I thank Brenton Simons and Mary Beth Norton for their help in identifying Deacon Savil.

13. See, for example, Daniel Boyarin, "Are There Any Jews in 'The History of Sexuality?' " *Journal of the History of Sexuality* 5 (1995), esp. 348–55. See Michael Warner, "New English Sodom," *American Literature* 64 (March 1992): 19–47; Mark D. Jordan, *The Silence of Sodom: Homosexuality in Modern Catholicism* (Chicago: University of Chicago Press, 2000), 16.

14. Eva Cantarella, *Bisexuality in the Ancient World* (New Haven: Yale University Press, 1992), 195; Robin Scroggs, *The New Testament and Homosexuality: Contextual Background for a Contemporary Debate* (Philadelphia: Fortress Press, 1983), 73–74. John Boswell, *Christianity, Social Tolerance, and Homosexuality: Gay People in Western Europe from the Beginning of the Christian Era to the Fourth Century* (Chicago: University of Chicago Press, 1980), 94.

15. Even "uncleanness" in its general sense included sodomy. See, for example, Samuel Willard, *A Compleat Body of Divinity* (Boston, 1726), sermon 196. Samuel Danforth, *The Cry of Sodom* (Boston, 1674), 3–5.

16. Josiah Smith, *Burning of Sodom* (Boston, 1741), preface, 10.

17. Increase Mather, *Burnings Bewailed in a Sermon Occasioned by the Lamentable Fire which was in Boston, October 2nd 1711* (Boston, 1712), 20. [Cotton Mather], *The Terror of the Lord* (Boston, 1727), 17. Thomas Foxcroft, *The Voice of the Lord* (Boston, 1727), 41. Foxcroft, *The Earthquake, a Divine Visitation* (Boston, 1756), 36. Michael Wigglesworth, *The Day of Doom* (Boston, 1751), 21–22. It was *the*

point of reference, *the* lesson to learn about the dangers of sin. See, for example, Benjamin Colman, *Warnings of God Unto Young People, Not to Consent When Enticed to Sin* (Boston, 1716), 3; Andrew Eliot, *An Evil and Adulterous Generation* (Boston, 1753); Increase Mather, *The Folly of Sinning* (Boston, 1699); Thomas Foxcroft, *Lessons of Caution to Young Sinners* (Boston, 1733).

18. Godbeer, "'Cry of Sodom.'"

19. Benjamin Keach, *The Progress of Sin* (Boston, 1744), 39. *The Oeconomy of Love* (London, 1736), 42–43.

20. *Burning of Sodom*, 10; *Boston News Letter*, September 8–15, 1726.

21. See Bray, *Homosexuality in Renaissance England*, 89–104; Randolph Trumbach, *Sex and the Gender Revolution*, vol. 1, *Heterosexuality and the Third Gender in Enlightenment London* (Chicago: University of Chicago Press, 1998); Stephen Shapiro, "Of Mollies: Class and Same-Sex Sexualities in the Eighteenth-Century," in *In a Queer Place: Sexuality and Belonging in British and European Contexts*, ed. Kate Chedgzoy, Emma Francis, and Murray Pratt (Burlington, VT: Ashgate, 2002), 154–76. Craig Patterson disputes Trumbach's literal reading of the sources ("shifting, unreliable text[s]") as evidence of the existence of "new identities." See Craig Patterson, "The Rage of Caliban: Eighteenth-Century Molly Houses and the Twentieth-Century Search for Sexual Identity," in *Illicit Sex: Identity Politics in Early Modern Culture*, ed. Thomas DiPiero and Pat Gills (Athens: University of Georgia Press, 1997), 256–69. Reports also came in from the Dutch Republic, from Lisbon, and from Paris. *Boston Weekly News Letter*, January 4, 1753. *Boston Evening Post*, January 22, 1753. *New England Weekly Journal*, August 3, 1730.

22. Gert Hekma, "Amsterdam," in *Queer Sites: Gay Urban Histories since 1600*, ed. David Higgs (London: Routledge, 1999), 65; Theo Van der Meer, "The Persecutions of Sodomites in Eighteenth-Century Amsterdam: Changing Perceptions of Sodomy," in *The Pursuit of Sodomy: Male Homosexuality in Renaissance and Enlightenment Europe*, ed. K. Gerard and G. Hekma (New York: Haworth Press, 1989), 263–307. A keyword search for "molly," "sodomy," and "sodom*" in the *Pennsylvania Gazette*, 1728–1800, turned up none of the cases printed in Massachusetts papers. Electronic resource, LOC.

23. *Boston News Letter*, August 25–September 1, September 8–15, 1726.

24. *New England Weekly Journal*, June 19, 1732. *New England Courant*, March 18–25, 1723.

25. *Boston Weekly News Letter*, January 4, 1753; *Boston News Letter*, August 25–September 1 and September 8–15, 1726. *Boston Gazette*, January 2–9, 1727.

26. On the Philadelphia circulation, see Lyons, "Mapping an Atlantic Sexual Culture," in *Long Before Stonewall,* ed. Foster.

27. *Select Trials for Murder, Robbery, Burglary, Rapes, Sodomy, Coining, Forgery, Pyracy, and Other Offences and Misdemeanours, at the Sessions-House in the Old-Bailey,* vol. 1 (London, 1734) [includes trials from 1720–1724], 239, October 1722. This book was advertised in the *Boston Evening Post,* November 14, 1757.

28. *Select Trials,* vol. 4 (London, 1764) [includes 1741–1764], 130, 132; vol. 2 (London, 1735), 210–11.

29. *New England Weekly Journal,* September 7, 1730.

30. John Cleland, *Memoirs of a Woman of Pleasure* (London, 1748; New York, 1985), 194. Boston merchant invoices include *Roderick Random* in 1771 and 1773. See Henry Knox Papers, reel 48, P-17, 1769–1785, MHS. For advertisements, see, for example, *A Catalogue of Mein's Circulating Library* (Boston, 1765); books from Edes' Printing Office listed in *Boston Gazette,* March 29, 1784; list of books from James Foster Condy in *American Herald,* May 3, 1784; Benjamin Larkin's Shop in *Continental Journal,* April 28, 1785; James White's Book and Stationary Store in *Independent Chronicle,* April 21 and September 29, 1785, January 18, 1787, and January 8, 1789; and Benjamin Guild's Boston Book-Store in *American Herald,* August 7, 1786.

31. *Roderick Random,* 5.

32. Ibid., 6–8.

33. The following discussion comes from Thomas A. Foster, "Antimasonic Satire, Sodomy and Eighteenth-Century Masculinity in *The Boston Evening-Post,*" *The William and Mary Quarterly* 60 (January 2003): 171–84. See also Stephen L. Bullock, *Revolutionary Brotherhood: Freemasonry and the Transformation of the American Social Order, 1730–1840* (Chapel Hill: University of North Carolina Press for the Institute of Early American History and Culture, 1996), 80; David S. Shields, "Clio Mocks the Masons: Joseph Green's Anti-Masonic Satires," in *Deism, Masonry, and the Enlightenment,* ed. J. A. Leo Lemay (Newark: University of Delaware Press, 1987), 110.

34. Patricia Bonomi, *The Lord Cornbury Scandal: The Politics of Reputation in British America* (Chapel Hill: University of North Carolina for the Omohundro Institute of Early American History and Culture, 1998). As Mary Beth Norton and others have shown, sexual slander and malicious gossip also characterized seventeenth- and eighteenth-century America. See, for example, Cornelia Hughes Dayton, *Women Before the Bar: Gender, Law, and Society in Connecticut, 1639–1789* (Chapel Hill: University of North Carolina Press for the Institute of

Early American History and Culture, 1995); Norton, "Gender and Defamation in Seventeenth-Century Maryland," *William and Mary Quarterly* 44 (1987): 3–39; Norton, *Founding Mothers and Fathers: Gendered Power and the Forming of American Society* (New York: Vintage Books, 1997); Roger Thompson, *Sex in Middlesex: Popular Mores in a Massachusetts County, 1649–1699* (Amherst: University of Massachusetts Press, 1986). Historian Erik Seeman identifies a case in neighboring Connecticut, where the scandal of "indecency" surrounding two men who "embraced" was part of a controversy between Old Lights and New Lights. See Erik R. Seeman, *Pious Persuasions: Laity and Clergy in Eighteenth-Century New England* (Baltimore: Johns Hopkins University Press, 1999), 172–73.

35. Benjamin Walker Junior, June 24, 1737, Pre-Revolutionary Diaries, roll 10, LOCMD, original at MHS. Bullock, *Revolutionary Brotherhood*, 51–53.

36. Marcus Rediker, "A Motley Crew of Rebels: Sailors, Slaves, and the Coming of the American Revolution," in *The Transforming Hand of Revolution: Reconsidering the American Revolution as a Social Movement,* ed. Ronald Hoffman and Peter J. Albert (Charlottesville: University Press of Virginia, 1996), 159–65, 191. Gary B. Nash, *The Urban Crucible: The Northern Seaports and the Origins of the American Revolution,* abridged ed. (Cambridge, MA: Harvard University Press, 1979), 80–87, 114–22.

37. See, for example, Richard L. Bushman, "Caricature and Satire in Old and New England before the American Revolution," *Proceedings of the Massachusetts Historical Society,* vol. 88 (Boston: Massachusetts Historical Society, 1977), 19–34; David Waldstreicher, "Federalism, the Styles of Politics, and the Politics of Style," in *Federalists Reconsidered,* ed. Doron Ben-Atar and Barbara B. Oberg (Charlottesville: University of Virginia, 1998), 99–117.

38. *Boston Evening Post,* January 7, 1751.

39. Shields, "Clio Mocks the Masons," 109–26; *Boston Evening Post,* January 21, 1751. Green's published satires anticipated a full-blown anti-Freemason critique that would develop during the Revolutionary era. At that time, however, the criticism would center on the issue of national loyalty and suspect foreign influences. See Bullock, *Revolutionary Brotherhood,* 80.

40. [Joseph Green], *The Grand Arcanum Detected* (Boston, 1755), 9.

41. On Green's other satires, see David Shields, *Oracles of Empire: Poetry, Politics, and Commerce in British America, 1690–1750* (Chicago: University of Chicago Press, 1990), esp. 131–37. Using overtones of homosexual rape, a story from Philadelphia about a mock initiation involving two rogue Freemasons also highlighted an association between posterior-centered activities and corruption. See Bullock, *Revolutionary Brotherhood,* 50–52.

42. Joseph Green, *An Entertainment for a Winter's Evening* (Boston, 1750), 14.

43. Ibid.

44. *Boston Gazette,* December 29, 1777. See also *Independent Chronicle,* January 8, 1778, and *Boston Gazette,* January 12, 1778. Diaries (unidentified) Collection, 1760–1832, AAS.

CONCLUSION

1. Richard Godbeer, *Sexual Revolution in Early America* (Baltimore: Johns Hopkins University Press, 2001).

⤞ Index